PLEASE
★ ★ ★ EVERY ★ ★ ★
CUSTOMER

PLEASE

★ ★ ★ EVERY ★ ★ ★

CUSTOMER

Delivering Stellar Customer Service Across Cultures

ROBERT W. LUCAS

New York   Chicago   San Francisco
Lisbon   London   Madrid   Mexico City   Milan
New Delhi   San Juan   Seoul   Singapore
Sydney   Toronto

The *McGraw-Hill* Companies

1 2 3 4 5 6 7 8 9 10 DOC/DOC 1 6 5 4 3 2 1

ISBN 978-0-07-174836-0 (print book)
MHID 0-07-174836-9

ISBN 978-0-07-174854-4 (e-book book)
MHID 0-07-174854-7

This publication is designed to provide accurate and authoritative information in regard to the subject matter covered. It is sold with the understanding that neither the author nor the publisher is engaged in rendering legal, accounting, securities trading, or other professional services. If legal advice or other expert assistance is required, the services of a competent professional person should be sought.

> —*From a Declaration of Principles Jointly Adopted by a Committee of the American Bar Association and a Committee of Publishers and Associations*

McGraw-Hill books are available at special quantity discounts to use as premiums and sales promotions or for use in corporate training programs. To contact a representative, please e-mail us at bulksales@mcgraw-hill.com.

This book is printed on acid-free paper.

To my step-son, Todd, who is one of the most focused, conscientious people I know and a true advocate of positive global customer service. To my son Mike, who is defending our country in the global war on terrorism in the U.S. Army. To my three grandsons—Wesley, Nathaniel, and Evan, who are part of the future generation of service providers.

Also to my supportive wife, M. J., and to my mother, Rosie, who both help keep me focused as I work on projects such as this.

Contents

Preface

As the character Dorothy said to her dog Toto following the fantastic, rapid transfer from her world to one totally foreign to her in the classic film *The Wizard of Oz*, "I've a feeling that we're not in Kansas anymore." That is the way that most customer service and business professionals who have been in the workforce for any period of time are likely to feel these days. Things are changing so fast that before these professionals can adapt to any type of status quo, the world around them has morphed into something different again. Demographics, work processes, technology, social values, customer needs and wants, career opportunities, and just about everything with which they come into contact all look different today than they did only a short time ago. And every one of these shifting factors has a direct impact on service providers, their employers, and the customers whom they serve.

Research shows that minority buying power continues to increase dramatically. As examples, between 1990 and 2011 the growth in projected spending by Hispanics is estimated to be about 457 percent, Asians 434 percent, and Native Americans 270 percent. African Americans rank just slightly below Hispanics in spending. Additionally, Generation Y consumers are estimated to spend close to $150 billion a year. With numbers like these, it all comes down to sound financial sense for service providers to prepare to effectively work with a diverse customer base. Organizations and service providers must ramp up their skills and knowledge in dealing with people from diverse backgrounds if they want to be successful and remain competitive in a global marketplace.

Not only do today's service providers have to be concerned with job knowledge, skills, and professional standards, but they also have to be cognizant of the values, beliefs, social mores, expectations, needs, and preferences of customers. All of this lends itself to a need for a higher level of training and self-development. Even so, many organizations do not invest large sums of money in customer service training and often view such training as "fluff"—nice to have but not necessary. In many instances managers see customer service training as not contributing to the bottom line and therefore relegate it to a lower priority, especially in an economy where training dollars are tight.

Frontline employees and their direct supervisors are the backbone of any organization and the people with whom customers have contact. They are the "face" of the organization. These professionals can make or break a company and need all the knowledge and skills they can get in order to provide stellar customer service. Ultimately, the responsibility for gaining new and necessary knowledge and skills that allow for effective service delivery rests on the individual service provider. That is why I have written *Please Every Customer: Delivering Stellar Customer Service Across Cultures*. By using the information provided in this book, you can effectively prevent your customers from defecting to your competition.

Whether you are new to customer service or already have experience, this book will be a valuable resource for you. In it, you will find a variety of helpful information and hundreds of tips, ideas, and suggestions related to how people from different cultures communicate, how they view relationships and time, and what they value and believe. You will also explore strategies for dealing with people who speak other languages, have diverse abilities, differ in age and gender, or have various behavioral preferences. Additionally, you will identify proven strategies that can assist you in better communicating with customers and in modifying your behavior to meet a given situation when dealing with other people. To help you deal with others, you will have an opportunity through activities called "Focus on Positive Global Service" to think about ways that you can apply concepts that you learn in the book. You will also read specific service implementation suggestions called "Positive Global Service Action Tips" that can be applied immediately to enhance your success when engaging customers.

Once you finish reading this book of proven service strategies, I am sure that you will have the basic tools you need to provide positive global service to all your customers.

PLEASE
★ ★ ★ EVERY ★ ★ ★
CUSTOMER

CHAPTER

1

Delivering Positive Global Service in a Diverse World

*The key to positive global service success is to treat customers
as if they are the only people in the world at that moment.*

KEY CONCEPTS

After reading this chapter and when applying concepts learned, you will
be able to:

1. Define diversity from a broader perspective than just race and
   color.
2. Describe some of the societal and world events that are affecting
   the scope of diversity.
3. Recognize the impact that diversity is having on various societies
   from a business, legal, and financial standpoint.
4. Determine strategies for delivering positive global customer
   service that will attract and retain customers.
5. Apply proven strategies to gain or regain customer trust.

6. Identify potential cultural values that are influencing a given customer situation and act accordingly.
7. Avoid stereotyping by taking decisive actions to prevent letting personal beliefs or predispositions interfere with positive global customer service.

In the 1960s popular singer, songwriter, and poet Bob Dylan lamented in one of his best-known songs that "The times they are a changing." Actually, every generation ponders how it will be able to keep up with all the progress and evolution. While some people wish for the good old days, the reality is that today will be tomorrow's "good old days" that the next generation looks back upon.

It makes no difference whether you work in a retail service environment (e.g., vehicle dealership, department store, or restaurant) or a non-retail one (e.g., doctor's office, car wash, association, personal services, or courthouse), your primary role is to prepare for and professionally serve every customer equally and in a timely and effective manner. This will require your full attention. It takes effort to create an atmosphere that says to your customers, "We were expecting you and are ready and happy to serve you." You can never let personal feelings, emotions, or issues interfere in this effort.

As times continue to change, the way that you and other professionals deliver products and services will continue to evolve as you strive to meet the needs of a drastically altered landscape of customers representing different colors, religions, races, ethnicities, socioeconomic classes, personal backgrounds, and many other diverse factors.

 POSITIVE GLOBAL SERVICE ACTION TIP

To prepare for positive global service delivery to every customer with whom you come into contact, continually analyze your workplace to ensure that everything is in its place, you have the materials and tools at hand to perform your job requirements, and you have the knowledge about various diverse customer types so that you can make appropriate decisions about how to best serve each customer.

WHAT IS DIVERSITY?

The word *diversity* encompasses a broad range of differences. Many service providers only associate the term with *cultural diversity*, which has to do with the differences and similarities between groups of people, relating to their country of origin and their beliefs. In addition to cultural differences, however, many other characteristics are involved in diversity. For example, within a group of Vietnamese people are subgroups such as males, females, children, the elderly, athletes, parents, grandparents, thin and overweight people, gays and lesbians, physically disabled and mentally disabled individuals, Buddhists and Christians, married and single people—to mention just a few.

Diversity is a complex issue. Start your journey to better understanding by learning about how various people are similar rather than focusing on their differences. Also, keep an open mind when interacting with others and be fair to everyone. In fact, thinking about and looking more closely at diversity provides wonderful opportunities because people from varying groups and geographic locations bring with them special knowledge, experience, and value. And while people may have a lot of differences, they also probably have a lot in common. These similarities form a solid basis for successful interpersonal relationships if you are knowledgeable and think of people as individuals. As a service provider, you can benefit from their uniqueness if you simply work to get to know people on a one-to-one basis. If you fail to view people as individuals instead of just part of a group, you may *stereotype*—lump them together—and treat them all the same. This is a recipe for interpersonal disaster, service breakdown, and organizational failure because customers may label you and your organization as unprofessional or even discriminatory. The sidebar titled "Examples of Stereotypes" shows some of the stereotypical examples that some people have about various groups.

EXAMPLES OF STEREOTYPES

The following are examples of statements that some service providers might make which could demonstrate underlying stereotypes or beliefs about different groups. The challenge with such comments or views is that they may not be true, since there are exceptions in all groups of people.

- Italians use their hands a lot when talking.
- North Americans are arrogant and rude.
- People who live in mobile homes drink a lot of beer and live off welfare.
- Older people are hard of hearing, are not good with technology, and drive slowly.
- Muslims hate North Americans.
- Women are not as good at math and science as men are.
- Chinese people are good at business.
- People from the southern United States are slow.
- American Indians and Eskimos are alcoholics.
- People with disabilities cannot perform as well as someone who is not disabled.
- People from Generation Y are lazy and unmotivated.
- Jewish people are good with money.
- Men can handle stress better than woman.
- African Americans are good at sports.
- Brazilians are loud and pushy.
- People from the United Kingdom are formal and "stuffy."
- Gays are overly sensitive.

THE SCOPE OF DIVERSITY

As you have already read, there is more to diversity than many service providers realize. The world continues to grow smaller as people from various countries and groups migrate and integrate into populations. This creates opportunity and challenge in delivering effective service. The following sections address some of the changes that you will experience at some point in your career as a service provider.

Changing Demographics

The *demographics*, or general characteristics of a group in a given population, in most nations are shifting dramatically. There are approximately 6.8 billion[1] people living in 195 countries throughout the world. Within those numbers are people of various nationalities, ethnicities, ages, and racial, educational, family, and religious backgrounds. They have separate languages and differ in physical and mental abilities, sexual and behavioral preferences, and socioeconomic backgrounds, as well as values and beliefs. All these characteristics (and others) help make each person an individual and create an assortment of needs, wants, and expectations that you must recognize and address when delivering service.

As Tom Hanks said in the popular film *Forrest Gump*, "Life is like a box of chocolates. You never know what you're gonna get."[2] This statement really sums up the reality of what you can expect whenever you interact with people in your place of business. The key is that you must anticipate and prepare for all possible scenarios where diversity might be an issue.

In our highly mobile, technologically connected world, it is not unusual to encounter a wide variety of people with differing backgrounds within the course of a single day. Those service professionals who understand the changing landscape of diversity will succeed in providing positive global customer service. As an example of some of the changes that are occurring, Hispanic and other ethnic populations are growing at a very fast rate. By 2020, the Hispanic population is projected to add more people to the U.S. population than all other racial and ethnic groups combined. By 2050, that group will be the largest one within the population. The percentage of non-Hispanic whites will steadily fall from 74 percent in 1995 to 64 percent in 2020 and 53 percent by 2050, while the black population will nearly double its 1995 size to 61 million.[3] What this ultimately means is that successful service providers will need to be multilingual and be aware of not only cultural and language differences but also the value systems possessed by a variety of ethnic and racial groups in order to better serve their customers in the future.

While many nations have populations that are growing in diversity and size similar to what is occurring in the United States, others are seeing their population size decrease. For example, the overall population on the European continent is projected to shrink due to aging populations and a decline in fertility rates. Many countries in the European Union are searching for creative ways to counter this trend and deal with immigration in a more productive manner. If these countries fail to take decisive action on these extremely important issues, the political and economic influence of these traditionally powerful countries may shift dramatically by mid-century. Along with those shifts, dramatic socioeconomic changes will take place in today's less influential countries as people in these countries move up the ladder to business and financial success. These shifts have already begun in countries such as China, Mexico, and India, where in recent decades we have witnessed growth and business development. Some projections show that in many European countries "by the year 2060 . . . the working age population is projected to be smaller by almost 50 million persons compared to 2008. Over the same projection period the population aged 65 years or over is projected to increase by almost 67 million persons."[4] Obviously, this will have a significant impact on global consumer habits and service needs, since the world's economy and buying habits are so closely intertwined. Key suppliers today may lose their stronghold on worldwide exports, while other nations emerge to be political, industrial, and financial leaders. One impact is that if you fail to provide timely and quality service to your customers online, they can simply switch to another Web site and potentially find what they need there. As many people struggle to make ends meet and save money, brand loyalty often takes a back seat to savings and convenience for many consumers.

WORLD POPULATION AGE BREAKDOWN ESTIMATES

- **0-14 years:** 27% (male 944,987,919/female 884,268,378)
- **15-64 years:** 65.3% (male 2,234,860,865/female 2,187,838,153)
- **65 years and over:** 7.6% (male 227,164,176/female 289,048,221)

POSITIVE GLOBAL SERVICE ACTION TIP

Keep an open mind about all customers and avoid seeming judgmental or forming an opinion about others based on what they look like, what others have said about them as individuals or as groups, or what your perceptions or personal biases are in order to prevent a breakdown in communication and in the customer-provider relationship.

Knowledge is the prime tool in your preparation for positive customer encounters. By having a sound understanding about such aspects as the products and services offered by your organization, human behavior, and cultural, religious, and gender differences, you are well on your way to interacting effectively with any person with whom you have contact in the workplace. This knowledge comes through education and training, travel, research, and experience, and it is also gained by taking the opportunity to interact with others who appear different from you and by keeping an open mind about others. If you go out of your way to meet and learn about those who are different from you, you increase the chance that you will be successful in providing positive service to your customers.

FOCUS ON POSITIVE GLOBAL SERVICE: THE IMPORTANCE OF RELATING

Having knowledge of the population, understanding the culture, and speaking the local language are crucial to business success. People would much rather deal with an organization that understands their needs and to which they can relate.

Think of the companies and organizations in your local area that you frequently visit. Make a list of 5 to 10 of these organizations:

_____

_____

_____

_____

_____

_____

_____

_____

Next, put a check mark by each organization for each of the following characteristics:

__ Has a staff of people who represent different generations
__ Has someone on staff that speaks Spanish (or other dominant language
in your neighborhood or geographic area)
__ Has a balance of men and women working in the organization
__ Has a diverse employee base with people of various ethnic and racial
groups represented

Finally, think of the organization that you feel most comfortable doing business
with and list some of the factors that contribute to your comfort level:

_____

_____

_____

_____

_____

_____

THE IMPACT OF DIVERSITY ON BUSINESS

Since the early 1960s, numerous laws have been passed in the United States,
the United Kingdom, and many other countries that prohibit discrimination based on personal characteristics. Among others, these include
age, race, sex, color, national origin, religion, disabilities, and sexual orientation. These factors cannot be used to discriminate against someone
in the workplace. A major effect of these laws is the awareness that by
having a diverse workforce, private organizations and public institutions
can enhance their success through a philosophy of inclusiveness rather
than divisiveness and omission. In addition to providing workplace and

professional development opportunities for all workers, the laws help to integrate people of all types and backgrounds into a more cohesive workforce. For example, when the Americans with Disabilities Act of 1990 was signed into law, there were an estimated 42 million people in the United States with disabilities. That number continues to grow as the aging population develops various special needs. The legislation prohibited discrimination against people within defined categories because of their disabilities and resulted in employers and business owners having to make modifications to address the needs of people with disabilities. Job opportunities and access to services and products became available. Subsequently, other countries have passed similar laws that require service providers to develop strategies for equally serving all customers.

As a service provider, you must know and comply with various laws related to dealing with *internal customers* (coworkers, supervisors, managers, and peers) and *external customers* (people with whom you come in contact as part of your job) in a variety of protected diversity categories. If your employer does not provide training on these laws, ask your supervisor about them and do research on your own to ensure compliance and equitable treatment of others.

One benefit of complying with equal opportunity laws and building a diverse workforce is that in bringing people together from all walks of life, businesses can grow by capitalizing on a better understanding of customers and the marketplace; an enhanced brain pool from which to pull ideas, make decisions, and solve problems; and a varied source of experiences and creativity. From the executives down to those working with customers on the front line, when people identify and value characteristics and factors that make each employee and customer unique, they increase the opportunities for personal and organizational achievement.

While having a diverse employee base can sometimes lead to disagreements and differences of opinion because of perceptions, values, and beliefs, it can also contribute to a more robust understanding when it comes to overall group performance. When a group of people approach a given situation from various perspectives, they can often collectively pull their creativity together to come up with more innovative and cost-effective strategies for doing business and serving customers. This typically leads to breakthroughs in product development and service delivery, which can translate to an increase in revenue, efficiency, and effectiveness and a reduction in expenditures. In fact, an ideal team will be made up of people with different personality styles, genders, and personal and professional backgrounds. When team members are too similar in race, gender, and culture, they often think along the same lines and agree more. This can lead to being complacent and sticking to the status quo, or the "way we've always done it," rather than tapping into intellectual diversity and fresh capabilities to seek new ways of doing something.

POSITIVE GLOBAL CUSTOMER SERVICE

What is *positive global customer service*? It is recognizing that you are dealing with globally diverse and unique individuals at each contact point with a customer or potential customer and taking the time to listen effectively, respond appropriately, and address their needs. It is also taking ownership of and responsibility for your environment and customer interactions by being prepared and doing whatever it takes to help guarantee a successful outcome when dealing with customers. Positive global customer service involves being willing to do the extra little things that project a *customer-centric* attitude (e.g., answering the phone in a professional manner, returning calls and e-mail in a timely fashion, remembering little details your customers shared and then referring to those details during a conversation, or going out of your way to help resolve an issue when service breaks down). This means applying what Dr. Tony Alessandra and Michael O'Connor call the *Platinum Rule*[5] ("Do unto others as they want done unto them") in their book of the same name. In other words, instead of treating people like you want to be treated, get to know them. Find out what they like, dislike, expect, value, believe, and want; then attempt to satisfy them to the best of your ability. If you cannot provide what they need, consider getting someone else to assist who can better understand and address actual needs.

From a service perspective, when customers believe that employees are knowledgeable about various aspects of diversity and value others, those customers are likely to reward the organization with their business. Not only will they typically remain loyal to an organization that they like, but they will usually spread the word about their positive experiences. This equates to more revenue generated for the organization, which can then afford to increase salaries, expand and enhance its facilities and operations, provide training and benefits, improve the way it markets itself, and fend off competition more effectively. On the other hand, if customers believe that they are being treated indifferently and that service providers do not understand or care about their particular needs, they will potentially desert the organization and encourage their friends to do likewise. This means the potential loss of revenue and all its associated benefits.

You may have heard that one person can make a difference in the world. Well, one service representative can make a difference in the level of success that is achieved by an organization. If you are in a position where you are the first person with whom a customer or potential customer comes in contact face-to-face or via technology, you have the power to create a positive image in that person's mind. You are the face of your organization in such instances. What you do or say from the time you greet the customer until the transaction ends will cement an image in the customer's mind. Through your presence, knowledge, verbal and nonverbal cues, and attitude toward service, you can create an experience that will have the customer thinking either "Wow, this is a person (or company) whom I want to visit again" or "Where did they get that person? I'll never do business with this organization again." If the latter occurs, your organization has a problem, because research shows that dissatisfied customers will more likely tell many other people about a negative service experience than they will a positive one. This less-than-favorable word-of-mouth publicity can bring disaster in the form of lost business. And don't forget that it is your current and new customers who provide the revenue that pays for your salary, benefits, training, and much more, so you have a vested interest in ensuring that each interaction is positive.

The acronym POSITIVE may help you identify some strategies for creating or contributing to a positive global service environment. *POSITIVE* means that you should:

- Put your best foot forward. Maintain a positive approach to situations involving customers, smile frequently, and have a "can-do" attitude.
- Offer whatever level of assistance possible. In addressing customer needs and wants, go out of your way to uncover and resolve problems and to build a strong customer-provider relationship.
- Stay abreast of current industry trends and strategies for delivering quality customer service. By upgrading your knowledge and skills regularly, you will be prepared to address any type of customer situation. As well, know your products and services. Be willing and able to share their benefits with customers.
- Identify true customer needs by listening proactively. You have two ears and one mouth. Use them accordingly.
- Take the time to get to know more about your customers. Never forget that your customers are the reason for your employment.
- Invite your customers to open up and share information. Ask open-ended questions (e.g., who, what, when, how, why, and to what extent) that typically lead to more detailed responses from others.
- Verify understanding. When a customer provides information, ensure that you heard and understood it correctly before responding.
- Engage in relationship-building strategies immediately. Start with a smile (not just on your face, but in your voice and words too) and a professional greeting when meeting customers in person, over the telephone, or in an e-mail.

FOCUS ON POSITIVE GLOBAL SERVICE: BUILDING TRUST

Think of personal experiences that you have had with service providers as a customer. What did they do well from a communication, appearance, and relationship standpoint? How did that make you feel?

Take a few moments to reflect on your experiences as a customer in the past two weeks. Which ones stand out as a positive experience? In those encounters with a service provider (either face-to-face or via technology), what positive service behaviors did he or she exhibit? Capture these behaviors below and use them as a guide for creating a positive service environment of your own when working with customers.

_____

_____

_____

_____

_____

_____

_____

THE ROLE OF TRUST

In relation to customer service, trust typically equates to customer loyalty—a precious commodity sought after by many organizations. Providing positive global service can lead to acceptance, satisfaction, referrals, and an enhanced position in the marketplace by helping establish trust and relationships with current and potential customers. *Trust* is a crucial element of a positive global service environment, because without it, you have no customer-provider relationship. Trust is not just confidence that you will provide quality products and services at a fair price; it goes deeper than that. From a customer standpoint, trust might involve believing that you and your organization have your customers' best interests in mind when creating or providing products and delivering services. From a service provider standpoint, it might be believing that customers are not out to "rip off" your organization by returning for a refund or replacement of products that they purchased and subsequently used or abused. Trust involves both parties being able to expect a win-win outcome based on mutual respect and collaboration during a business transaction.

In order to build and maintain trust, it is crucial that you *under-promise and overdeliver* so that customers are pleasantly and consistently surprised with the level and quality of products and services they receive. For example, you might tell a customer that something he or she ordered typically takes two days for the warehouse to send; however, you might ask staff to expedite the process and get the order out the same day because the customer told you the item was a birthday surprise for a relative. Never tell customers that you can do something that you are not certain you can do. Tell them what you *can* do, not what you can't do, and remember that it can take years to build trust but only an instant or single event to lose it. By raising customer expectations and failing to follow through, you can quickly destroy any level of trust that you and your organization may have taken a long time to establish. Once lost, trust may never be regained to the previous level, no matter what you do to make amends. This is why customers sometimes desert organizations even when problems are resolved. Often, the organization does just enough to correct the problem, but does not compensate the customer for inconvenience or frustration and time wasted. This can lead to the customer feeling undervalued or underappreciated.

POSITIVE GLOBAL SERVICE ACTION TIP

In order to regain your customer's trust when service breaks down, refer to your policy on service recovery and use the following steps in order to rectify the situation:

- Apologize sincerely.
- Gather enough information to understand what happened and identify the cause of the problem.
- Take immediate action to correct the problem.
- Offer some sort of restitution for the error (e.g., a discount coupon for a future purchase, a partial refund, free shipping, or something else that is in line with the degree of inconvenience).

- Repeat your apology.
- Thank the customer for bringing the issue to your attention and for giving you the opportunity to correct the issue, and also offer thanks for the customer's understanding and patience.

In a global service world, there are potential relationship "minefields" that can cause problems related to trust. This is because for customers from many countries (including Brazil, China, and Mexico), building a strong interpersonal relationship is extremely important and in many instances must be accomplished before business is conducted. For example, in *relationship-oriented countries*, it is not unusual to have a number of meetings with people in an organization before coming to an agreement. Lunch, dinner, and office meetings often occur for weeks before an agreement or important decision is reached. In such cultures, someone's word is like a verbal contract, and violations are not taken lightly. For that reason, if you are doing business with a customer from a relationship-oriented country, you must recognize the need to engage in some degree of conversation prior to asking for a buying decision or getting straight to business. This can present difficulty for call center representatives who are constrained by talk times or other controls or in environments where staff has been downsized to a minimal server level. In such instances, before coming into contact with a customer, it is wise to discuss with your supervisor the degree of flexibility you have in terms of the time and ways you have to deliver service. By better understanding the operational guidelines for your job, the chances of creating a problem with customer trust or violating organizational policy will be reduced.

Another potential problem is that you can negatively impact the *customer-provider relationship* if you bring up certain topics to individuals from some cultures. For example, it is potentially inappropriate for a male service provider to directly address or compliment the wife or daughter who accompanies a male customer from a Middle Eastern culture without the man's permission. This might be perceived as rude or disrespectful. Similarly, asking about a man's wife or daughter could be viewed as an unwelcome intrusion. Such cultural nuances may seem unimportant if you are from a different culture, but you must remember that people leave a country; they do not leave their culture. It is part of their personal background and value or belief system and should be respected.

FOCUS ON POSITIVE GLOBAL SERVICE: IDENTIFYING TRUSTWORTHY ORGANIZATIONS

Take a few minutes to list industries, organizations, and professionals that you generally trust and with which you enjoy doing business.

_____

_____

_____

Why do you have a level of trust with these industries, organizations, or professionals?

_____

_____

_____

Now create a list of industries, organizations, and professionals that you generally distrust and with which you do not like doing business.

_____

_____

_____

What caused you to distrust these industries, organizations, or professionals?

_____

_____

_____

How can you use your responses above to deliver better service to your own customers and more effectively build trust with them?

_____

_____

_____

ADDRESSING CULTURAL VALUES

Many service providers take customer values for granted. This is a mistake. *Values* are the "rules" that people use to evaluate issues or situations, make decisions, interact with others, and deal with a variety of situations. People often use their value systems to guide their thinking and help determine an appropriate course of action. Each group and subgroup will typically have accepted values and traditions that they honor. This might be a special handshake or greeting or something more overt like the way someone dresses or behaves in a given situation.

From a customer service perspective, values often strongly drive customers' needs and influence the buying decisions that they make. Values differ from one culture to another, depending on the culture's views on ethics, morals, religion, and many other factors. For example, if customers perceive clothing as either too sexy or too conservative, they may

POSITIVE GLOBAL SERVICE ACTION TIP

Always project a positive service attitude, and always be personable and willing and able to answer questions about your organization's capabilities. There are only two types of people you will ever meet in the future . . . customers and potential customers. Either someone currently uses your products or services, or he or she is a potential user. If you keep this fact in mind every time you meet someone when you are in the workplace or are standing in a line to get a sandwich, cash a check, or transact whatever business you might have, you are on your way to delivering positive global customer service.

not purchase the items. Or they may not buy a house because it's in the "wrong" neighborhood.

Although many *cultures* have similar values and beliefs, specific *cultural values* are often taught to members of particular groups starting at a very young age. The values of each group may differ, but that does not mean that any group's values are better than another's; they are simply important to that particular group. Someone's values may not always have a direct bearing on customer service, but those values can have a very powerful influence on what the customer wants, needs, thinks is important, and is willing to seek or accept.

Values can also influence your perceptions and actions when serving others. For example, if you have a negative perception of someone from a specific country because of news reports, personal experiences with another person from the country, or stories that you have heard from others, you may send unconscious nonverbal signals that could offend the person. If you are conscious of value differences, you can better understand your customers and avoid conflict or misunderstandings in dealing with them. The key to positive global service success is to be open-minded and accept that someone else has a different belief system from yours that determines his or her needs and that your belief system is not necessarily "better." With this in mind, you should strive to use all the positive communication and needs identification strategies that you can when interacting with customers in order to satisfy them.

Your goal is to provide positive global service to your customers. To achieve this objective, you must be sensitive to, tolerant of, and empathetic toward all customers. You do not need to adopt their beliefs, but you should adapt to them to the extent that you provide the best service possible to all your customers. This is where the Platinum Rule of service that you read about earlier comes in handy.

The following sections focus on some specific values that customers might exhibit based on their beliefs.

Approach to Modesty

Often a sense of *modesty* is instilled into people at an early age (more so in females), and a customer can display modesty in many ways. Modesty may be demonstrated by covering the mouth or part of the face with an open hand when laughing or speaking. In some cultures (e.g., Quaker and Muslim), conservative dress by women is one manifestation of modesty. For example, women may demonstrate modesty and a dedication to traditional beliefs by wearing a veil or headdress. Such practices are often tied to religious and cultural beliefs that originated many generations ago. Modesty takes another form in the nonverbal communication cues used by some customers to send messages. For example, direct eye contact is viewed as an effective communication approach in the many Western cultures, and lack of eye contact is sometimes perceived to suggest dishonesty or lack of confidence to someone from those cultures. However, in many countries (India, Iran, Iraq, and Japan), direct eye contact is often discouraged, in particular between men and women or between people who are of different social or business status, for it might be considered disrespectful, inappropriate, or rude.

As a service provider, you should be aware that you might inadvertently offend someone from a different culture through your work environment. For example, the magazines in your organization's waiting room may contain advertisements with scantily clad models, and the television may play programs or commercials with sexual situations, depending on the channel. To avoid potential problems, be sure to create an inoffensive work area.

Perceptions of Gender Roles

Closely related to modesty are perceptions and expectations related to *gender* roles that men and women should assume in a business setting. In some cultures, women are still limited in opportunities to participate in business or in relationships with men in the workplace. Although gender roles continue to change throughout the world, authority and decision making are often clearly established male prerogatives within many cultures, subcultures, or families. For example, in many Middle Eastern, Asian, South American, and European countries, women have often not gained the respect or credibility in the business environment that they have achieved in many parts of North America. In some countries it is not unusual for women to be expected to take a "seen-and-not-heard" role or to remain out of business transactions. In Korea and other Pacific Rim countries, it is reportedly rare for women to participate in many business operations. Men often still have higher social status than women in a number of countries (at least in public settings). You do not have to agree with these beliefs and practices, but you will need to take them into consideration when interacting with customers from countries in which these practices are common.

Often, customers who have lived or worked in Western cultures for longer periods will acculturate and may not take offense to more direct behaviors between men and women that are meant to convey friendliness and to engage customers (e.g., smiling, engaging in small talk about families, or offering compliments on dress).

POSITIVE GLOBAL SERVICE ACTION TIP

If you notice a customer is avoiding eye contact or seemingly being evasive, consider the possibility that there may be a cultural reason rather than assume the customer is being dishonest or lying. Certainly, if you suspect illegal intentions, call your risk management staff or a supervisor; however, do not unnecessarily force the issue or draw undue attention to a customer's nonverbal behavior, actions, or cultural dress.

Expectations of Privacy

A person's culture, personality, size of immediate family, and place where he or she grew up will sometimes affect that person's approach to communicating with others and sharing information, especially between sexes. Often, *expectations of privacy* will vary from one country or region to another. For example, some people who are British, German, Australian, Korean, or Japanese may display a tendency to disclose less personal information than many North Americans do. The reality is that some people are just more open and appear friendlier than others. Customers who fall into this category may tend to talk about virtually any topic with you or with others that they hardly know. Many other customers may be more reserved and private and less willing to share personal information or life experiences, especially in a business interaction. For this reason, you should recognize that because of their expectations, they may not actively engage in small talk that is not directly related to the business at hand. If you encounter such customers, respect this preference and stay focused on gathering only the information you will need to address their specific issues and concerns.

This should not be construed to mean that you should totally avoid small talk; just keep it under control and watch customer reactions closely. Talking about the weather, traffic, or some other impersonal topic might be fine. Avoid controversial topics that might be emotional hot buttons to other people (e.g., politics, religion, or perspectives on birth control). Otherwise, you may make some customers feel uneasy, and they may even complain to a supervisor or others. Their discomfort in such instances might stem from the fact that if you are conducting business in a Western culture, when someone asks a question or shares information, there is often an expectation that the other party will reciprocate. Reluctance to respond may be perceived as being unfriendly or even rude, thus making some customers feel uncomfortable.

POSITIVE GLOBAL SERVICE ACTION TIP

If you tend to be the type of person who is very gregarious and talks freely about virtually any topic, you may want to limit this a bit in the global service environment. Stay focused on the business of serving your customers in an expeditious and professional manner. Keeping your conversations centered on satisfying the customers' needs can accomplish this.

Forms of Address

Customers' preferences for a particular name or *form of address* can have an impact on your ability to effectively deal with them. Many North Americans have a reputation for priding themselves on their informality and the corresponding tendency to use first names when talking to others. People from some countries may see this as rudeness, lack of respect, arrogance, or overfamiliarity. For example, people from a number of cultures (including those from many European countries, South Korea, and Argentina) stress formality in the business environment and place importance on the use of titles and family names when addressing others. If a Westerner called a customer from a more formal culture by just the person's first name without permission, it might result in an irritated or outright angry customer.

Often, personal preferences in use of names are based on cultural and personal values. Many people have been taught from a very early age to respect older people and people in certain professions. For example, in cultures of countries (e.g., Japan) in which there is a distinct hierarchy based on age or position, titles such as *sensei* (teacher) or *san* (Mr., Mrs., Ms.) are often used as a show of respect. If you start a conversation with customers and immediately cause friction by incorrectly addressing them, you may not be able to recover. Moreover, informality or improper use of family names could send a message of insufficient knowledge of or concern for the customer as an individual or as someone who is important to you.

POSITIVE GLOBAL SERVICE ACTION TIP

Depending on where you do business or where your customer is from, it is best to use a more formal approach with a title (e.g., Mr., Mrs., Ms., or Dr.) and the customer's surname when you first meet him or her, since you will not know preferences.

Conflict Resolution

Whenever two people come into contact, there is the potential for misunderstanding and conflict. In a customer-provider situation, conflict should be avoided whenever possible. The easiest way to avoid potential problems and relationship breakdowns with your customers is to become familiar with various cultures and the way in which positive communication and interactions typically occur. Additionally, strive to recognize your own biases toward other people and groups and keep your personal preconceptions in check. If a disagreement occurs, though, you should be familiar with basic *conflict resolution* strategies that might be used to quickly resolve the situation and salvage the customer-provider relationship. You will learn more about these techniques in Chapter 9, which addresses service breakdowns.

Certainly, there may be times when a customer might seem to initiate conflict through a negative attitude toward you or your organization, perhaps because of a previous experience the customer had with you or a different service provider. In such instances, remember not to retaliate or do anything that might escalate the situation. While offering a flippant or off-the-cuff response might make you feel better, it will likely raise your customer's level of emotion and could lead to a complaint to your supervisor, lost business, or even violence. Such behavior might also be interpreted incorrectly by others who witness it, and you could end up looking like the perpetrator, especially if your customer's original behavior was not seen by others. Use the positive communication techniques that you will read about later in this book. In doing so, you can potentially display empathy and understanding while preventing the appearance of disagreeing with or doubting your customer.

Often, the way customers deal with conflict or emotion is a result of their culture or subculture and is based on their behavioral-style preference (e.g., whether they tend to be people- or task-focused). Anthropologists have categorized cultures into two types or groups: *individualistic*, in which people focus on individual goals (e.g., as in Western cultures), and *collective*, in which people are viewed as part of a group and the focus is on group achievement or success (e.g., Japan or Native American cultures).

Members of individualistic cultures are likely to take a direct approach to conflict and openly deal with a situation one-to-one. People from collective cultures may address conflict indirectly. In these cultures, an informal mediator is often used to negotiate or intercede when communication breaks down in order to prevent embarrassment for those involved.

Even within subcultures of a society, there are often differing styles of communicating with others and dealing with conflict. As an example, think of your friends, peers, or coworkers. How do they deal with disagreement or conflict? Of course, regardless of culture or group, the way in which people choose different forms of conflict resolution is often based on such factors as their personality-style preferences, experience, age, and cultural background. As a service provider, you must strive to choose the correct strategy for dealing with conflict in order to prevent emotional escalation and customer dissatisfaction. The key is to listen and remain calm, especially if the customer becomes agitated.

 POSITIVE GLOBAL SERVICE ACTION TIP

Try not to take it personally when customers abuse you verbally or nonverbally. Keep in mind that when customers use derogatory language or other negative communication techniques during a conversation, they are normally mad at the organization and its policies, procedures, products, or service and not necessarily at you.

SUMMARY

In this chapter, you have been introduced to the concept of doing business in a global world in which you might encounter people who are different from and yet similar to you. You have also explored some of the possibilities for providing positive global customer service to those customers. Some key ideas include the following:

- Diversity is not just cultural; it encompasses human characteristics that are different from one's own but that occur within other cultural and diverse groups.
- In our highly mobile, technologically connected world, it is not unusual for many service providers to encounter within the course of a day a wide variety of people with differing backgrounds.
- You must know and comply with various laws related to dealing with people, both internal and external, in a variety of protected diversity categories. If your employer does not provide training on these laws, ask your supervisor about them and do research on your own to ensure compliance and equitable treatment of others.
- Positive global customer service involves being willing to do the extra little things that project a customer-centric attitude.

- Apply the Platinum Rule of "do unto others as they want done unto them."
- As a service provider, you are the face of your organization. What you do or say from the time you greet the customer until the transaction ends will cement an image in the customer's mind.
- Trust typically equates to customer loyalty—a vital element of a positive global service environment because without it, you have no customer-provider relationship.
- It is crucial that you underpromise and overdeliver so that customers are pleasantly and consistently surprised with the level and quality of products and services they receive.
- For people from many countries, building a strong interpersonal relationship is extremely important and in many instances must be accomplished before business is conducted.
- Values are the "rules" that people use to evaluate issues or situations, make decisions, interact with others, and deal with a variety of situations.
- Although many cultures have similar values and beliefs, specific cultural values are often taught to members of particular groups starting at a very young age.
- The key to positive global service success is to be open-minded and accept that someone else has a different belief system from yours that determines his or her needs.
- Often, a sense of modesty is instilled in people at an early age (more so in females), and a customer can display modesty in many ways.
- You do not have to agree with beliefs and practices related to gender roles, but you will need to take them into consideration when interacting with customers from countries in which these practices are common.
- Strive to recognize your own biases toward other people and groups and keep your personal preconceptions in check. This can help reduce the potential for disagreement.
- Often, expectations of privacy will vary from one country or region to another.

CHAPTER

2

Identifying and Addressing Consumer Behavior

Customers learn behaviors as children and often repeat them as adults. As a service provider, you cannot control how they act; however, you can control how you act and respond to them.

KEY CONCEPTS

After reading this chapter and when applying concepts learned, you will be able to:

1. Explain how the economic conditions in the world have impacted customer service.
2. Describe how consumer behavior has changed and what organizations are doing to address those shifts in today's global economy.
3. Define some of the factors that are influencing customer service today.
4. Discuss the impact of customer loyalty on you and your organization.

5. Identify ways to manage customer needs, wants, and expectations.
6. Use knowledge of behavioral styles to establish and maintain more powerful customer-provider relationships.
7. Exhibit the core elements of positive customer service when dealing with people inside and outside your organization.

As the world continues to change politically, economically, techno-logically, and in many other ways, so do the people you serve. Values and beliefs are evolving in various cultures, and that is affecting what people want. Customer perceptions about when and how products and services should be delivered are also changing. The impact of this shift can be seen in the way that companies attempt to address customer expectations and the advertisements they use. For example, in past advertisements FedEx stressed, "When it absolutely, positively has to get there overnight, call FedEx," Burger King touts that you can "Have It Your Way," and Enterprise Car Rental emphasizes that "We'll pick you up."

With the proliferation of the Internet and the millions of Web sites now online, service is available 24 hours a day, 7 days a week, and 365 days a year. All this feeds the goal of customer satisfaction and provides a vehicle for organizations to be more competitive in a global marketplace. There is virtually nothing that a customer might want that isn't a mouse click away.

THE IMPACT OF THE ECONOMY ON SERVICE

A number of economists have estimated that the global recession took hold at the end of 2007. In reality, there were underpinnings of the problem at the beginning of the new century and earlier. These economic changes have brought worldwide financial havoc with them and caused many con-sumers to severely curtail buying and change their saving and spending habits, perhaps forever. Unemployment has skyrocketed around the world, and entire governments have been brought to the edge of financial collapse. Couple these issues with dramatically changing world demographics, changing cultural values, and many other political, lifestyle, and ecological shifts and you have a prescription for organizations to revamp the way that their products and services are delivered to customers.

Why individuals and certain consumer groups buy, and what they buy, has been studied by marketing experts for years, with the goal of trying to more accurately predict patterns and needs that can be addressed by manufacturers and service providers. Each demographic entity has its own special patterns of behavior and spending which you should be aware of in order to better handle customer needs and wants.

Because of changing demographics and consumer behavior patterns, many organizations are continually adapting and refocusing their approach to serving customers and marketing their products and services. Organizations are keenly interested in many things related to customer behavior. Among other things, they want to know:

- Who is buying?
- What are they buying?
- What triggers their buying habits?
- When are they buying?
- How much they are buying?
- Why do they buy one product or service over another?
- How are they making purchases and buying decisions?
- What are they doing with the products they purchase?

All this information allows organizations to better target and serve current and potential customers and can assist you and other front-line service providers in better addressing the needs and wants of your customers. The reality is that your customers do not stop needing and wanting products and services just because the economy slows down or jobs start going away. They still make purchases, but they do it in a more cautious manner by selecting things that are most important and in many cases more affordable. Because of that, brand loyalty often goes by the wayside as customers seek out products and services that address their needs and perform as well at a lower cost. This is where your product knowledge and service skills come in handy. By being able to effectively discuss the differences and value added by your organization's offerings, you can often persuade customers to switch from their preferred brand or vendor and buy from you.

SHIFTS IN CONSUMER BEHAVIOR

Overall, the buying power of various ethnic groups in the United States has grown. According to one study by the University of Georgia's Selig Center, "Over the 18-year period (1990–2008), the percentage gains in minority buying power vary considerably by race, from a gain of 337 percent for Asians to 213 percent for American Indians to 187 percent for blacks. All of these target markets will grow much faster than the white market, where buying power will increase by 139 percent."[1] Other sources contend that women are also a force to be reckoned with in the retail environment. Female consumers account for a majority of buying decisions on consumer products and services in many areas, including everything from automobiles to health care. Many of the increases described are due to more representation of these groups in the workplace and at higher professional levels (e.g., management), higher education levels, and better access to workplace opportunities for minorities (e.g., training, promotions, and transfers).

Other diverse groups are also having a major impact on global markets, especially in the United States, where one marketing firm "estimated the buying power of gays and lesbians [to] exceed $835 billion and projected the gay and lesbian population to exceed 16.3 million people by 2011."[2] In addition, people with disabilities spend billions of dollars on goods and services. Some estimates for online spending by this group alone top $10 billion a year. Add to these numbers the demographic of the newest generation of shoppers—*Generation Y* (also known as *Millennials, teens, tweeners,* and *twenty-somethings*), born between 1978 and 2000 with nearly 84 million members in the United States alone. According to Kit Yarrow and Jayne O'Donnell in their eye-opening book *Gen Buy: How Tweens, Teens and Twenty-Somethings Are Revolutionizing Retail*, this demographic group spends over $200 billion a year, and it is estimated that in their lifetime, their consumption will top $10 trillion.[3]

Obviously the recession slowed the amount of sales being made worldwide. Even so, with the types of economic power being wielded by various ethnic, age, and other diverse groups, service providers should plan accordingly and be prepared to meet the needs of each group of customers. That means gaining knowledge about values, beliefs, motivators, history, and other factors that can influence someone's behavior and perceptions, especially related to those of diverse categories. For example, there is a potential for distrust when some people of different cultures or groups with a history of negative relations (e.g., Caucasian and African American or North American Indian, Chinese and Japanese, Israeli and Palestinian, Christian and Muslim) come together. As a service provider, if you are aware of potential negative perceptions, you might modify your approach to a given situation.

POSITIVE GLOBAL SERVICE ACTION TIP

Spend time researching spending habits for the various customer groups that you most often serve so that you can identify potential patterns of consumer behavior. Once you have done this, work to create an atmosphere where all customers feel comfortable with you and recognize that you are striving to address their unique needs and wants while serving them.

FACTORS INFLUENCING CUSTOMER SERVICE

There is no doubt that the world population and workplaces are changing. Unlike the past, there are now likely to be a higher number of older customers with whom you will interact in the course of your daily job activities. Depending on the country and method in which you deliver service, there is also more opportunity for you to encounter more consumers than ever before who are female, disabled, or non-native language speakers; who are from different socioeconomic backgrounds; or who possess a variety of other diverse characteristics from societies around the world. Add to this mix the constantly changing technological innovations being made and adopted in organizations to aid customer service professionals, and your job has gotten more complex than ever before. All these shifts are having a profound impact on the way that you deal with your customers.

Successful companies develop and implement proactive, strategic approaches for providing customer service that takes into account all the changes taking place. They train employees in effective service and include strategies for interacting with customers who have diverse backgrounds.

If you work for such an organization, you have probably seen such changes. Various forms of technology have likely been embraced, updated approaches for dealing with all types of customers and their needs and preferences have been instituted, and partnerships with other groups (e.g., customers, vendors, complementing organizations, and, in some cases, competitors) have been formed in order to add assets, products, and services that can strengthen the organization and add value for customers. Additionally, such a visionary organization has made adjustments in the way that it does business and delivers products and services. For example, instead of having a *help desk*, which traditionally only provided reactive service when something broke down or the customer had a problem using your products or services, you now have a *service desk* that anticipates potential customer issues and needs. Such planning helps to inform and show customers that your organization does care about meeting their needs. To also help to prepare you and your peers, the organization likely invests in new technology and trains you how to effectively use the features of the system and software. It also provides you with training on various aspects of dealing with customers appropriately and efficiently (e.g., on policies and procedures, customer service topics, interpersonal communication, diversity, conflict resolution, time management, and behavioral styles) and on product knowledge and skills that allow you to ask pertinent questions or offer suggestions during each interaction with customers or potential customers.

IMPACT ON CUSTOMER LOYALTY

As the economic condition of the world continues to shift, it has many implications for your customers. One major issue is that many customers are no longer attached to the idea of using one organization to meet their needs. In addition to seeking higher value, they want personalized service that addresses their needs and expectations.

Customer loyalty is an emotional rather than a rational thing. It is often based on how effectively you and your coworkers deliver positive global customer service and is supported by sound service policies and procedures and solid-quality products and services backed by a customer-friendly guarantee.

For any organization to be successful in gaining and retaining customers in today's competitive global business environment, the organization must project a customer-centric approach to service. It must also be perceived as having the best interests of its customers at heart; not just its own bottom line. Going back to what you read in Chapter 1, people must trust an organization and its service representatives before they will do business with it, especially if they are from countries in which relationships play a big role in doing business. This can often be the deciding factor when a customer has a concern or question about an organization or its products or services.

A key point for you to remember in serving others is that today's consumers are far more educated and informed than at any point in history. They are also more selective, have more choices, and are more demanding than their predecessors. With the proliferation of the Internet and social media, people can access information almost instantly from virtually anywhere. As a result, customers are savvier and better prepared to make buying decisions. Gone are the days when consumers got most of their information from an advertisement or had to depend on a salesperson to educate them. According to Forrester Research, "Over the past three years, [consumers] have become more likely to research products online and less likely to be influenced by advertising. Even worse . . . the percentage of consumers who think price is more important than brand name has steadily increased."[4]

THE IMPORTANCE OF CUSTOMER LOYALTY

For almost four decades, the research firm Technical Assistance Research Program (TARP) in Arlington, Virginia, has conducted various studies to determine the impact of customer service. The following extracts from a number of their studies have revealed that:

- It will cost an organization five times more to acquire a new customer as it will to keep an existing one.
- On average, 50 percent of consumers will complain about a problem to a front-line person. In business-to-business environments, this jumps to 75 percent.
- For small-ticket items, 96 percent of consumers do not complain or they complain to the retailer from whom they bought an item. For large-ticket items, 50 percent complain to front-line employees, and 5 to 10 percent escalate the problem to local managers or corporate headquarters.
- At least 50 percent of your customers who experience problems will not complain or contact your organization for help; they will simply go elsewhere.
- Customers who are dissatisfied will tell as many as 16 friends or acquaintances about a negative experience with your organization.
- The average business loses 10 to 15 percent of its customers per year because of bad customer service.

Source: R. W. Lucas, *Customer Service Skills for Success,* 5th ed., Burr Ridge, IL: McGraw-Hill Higher Education, 2011.

FOCUS ON POSITIVE GLOBAL SERVICE: RETURN POLICIES MAKE A DIFFERENCE

Take a look at the following return policies from actual online booksellers, and then answer the questions that follow.

COMPANY A
Returns must meet the following criteria:

a. Books must be received within thirty (30) days of the invoice date. Please allow one week for shipping.
b. Books must be received in salable condition. Damaged books will not be accepted for credit.
c. Refunds will not be made on videotapes and software unless they are defective at the time of purchase. Please notify [organization's name] of any such defects within ten (10) days of the invoice date.

Return Shipping Information

Returns must be shipped to [organization's name and full address].

Any returns not shipped to the above address will not be credited and FULL PAYMENT for shipping will be the responsibility of the shipper.

All charges incurred in returning materials, including customer's charges, if any, are the responsibility of the shipper.

Ensure that your returns are not lost or damaged.

Comments and Feedback

We value your opinion! If you need to return any of the enclosed material, please take a minute to let us know why. Your comments and suggestions will help us better meet your needs in the future.

COMPANY B

To err is human; to return is just fine . . .

Already read the book? Pages printed upside down? The package arrived bruised, battered, and otherwise weary from the trip? Actually, the only reason you need to return an item bought from us is this: You're not satisfied . . .

Having a chance to talk with our customer helps us learn and improve our service. It is also an opportunity to demonstrate the [organization's name] customer policy: YOU'RE RIGHT!

What do you feel is the goal of the first policy example? Explain.

_____

_____

_____

_____

What do you feel is the goal of the second policy example? Explain.

_____

_____

_____

_____

Which company do you feel really had its customers' best interests in mind when it developed the policy? Explain.

_____

_____

_____

_____

Source: Lucas, R. W., *Customer Service: Skills for Success*, 5th ed., McGraw-Hill Higher Education, Burr Ridge, Il, 2011.

MANAGING CUSTOMER NEEDS, WANTS, AND EXPECTATIONS

Many people often confuse needs with wants. A *need* is an internal motivator or driver that someone requires and that typically can be categorized as either primary (things vital for survival, such as food) or secondary (a specific type of food). In addition to the things that people must have, there are many things that they desire (e.g., jewelry). These are called *wants* and are often generated through advertising, peer pressure, or an internal motivator that makes people feel that they must have something. Marketers prey on this feeling of "must have" to sell their products and services. There is also a gray area between needs and wants that relates to items that people rely on heavily to obtain their needs. An example of this might be transportation (e.g., car, bus, or subway) that allows them to get to work to make the money to satisfy their needs and wants. As a service provider, it is important for you to understand how cultural and individual values impact needs and wants and to know the difference so that you can better assist your customers in fulfilling what is important to them. If you are familiar with *Dr. Abraham Maslow's hierarchy-of-needs theory* of motivation (see Figure 2-1), you can relate it to the service experience and recognize that until people have met their basic (biological and physiological) needs, they cannot focus on higher levels of need.

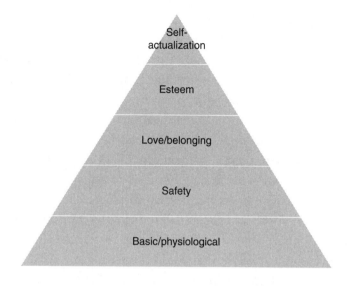

Figure 2-1 Maslow's Hierarchy of Needs

Coupled with needs and wants are customer *expectations*, which are preconceived ideas about your organization, products, or services. Cultural background, beliefs, advertising, and publicity are just a few of the many factors that influence a customer's expectations. The interesting thing about expectations is that they are like an ocean—they ebb and flow, continually changing. For example, if someone reads an article about the newest smart phone with all the latest applications or the newest trendy toy for children at Christmas time, he or she might expect to have to stand in a long line to purchase it, pay more for the item because it hasn't been discounted, or perhaps even find it difficult to get one. On the other hand, a year after the release of such items, the customer would expect ease of accessibility and a much reduced cost, especially for the technical items because they become obsolete quickly.

Related to expectations about service, customers (and many service representatives) have been conditioned through books, articles, training, news reports, and experience that "The customer is always right." For that reason, many people feel that if they raise their voices, curse, and demand to see a manager or conduct themselves in some similar manner, they will ultimately get what they want. In such instances, you may have to call upon all your training, patience, and professionalism to avoid becoming emotionally charged and responding inappropriately. The reality is that while you should treat all customers as the most important thing in your day while interacting with them, there are some instances when their behavior and expectations might dictate that you cannot adequately serve them to their level of expectation because of your lack of skills or due to a policy that prohibits a requested action. In such instances, the assistance of a coworker or supervisor may be required. Your coworker or supervisor may have additional knowledge or authority to help resolve the situation. The key is to let customers know what you can do—and not what you can't do. And if you have to say no, do so in a manner that allows them to feel that they were a part of the decision process and got something that they wanted, even if it was only a rational explanation of why they did not get what they requested.

You will read some strategies for handling such situations in Chapter 4. Below you'll find some common customer expectations that you might encounter.

POSITIVE GLOBAL SERVICE ACTION TIP

Be conscientious and prepared to think like customers in order to satisfy their needs, wants, and expectations. The easiest way to find out what customers want, need, or expect is to ask them.

Anticipating Customer Needs

Providing products and services that your customers do not value or appreciate is bad business. That is why you should strive to better understand consumer behavior and what customers want and need. To achieve this, organizations use a variety of information-gathering strategies. Some of the more common include:

- Asking customers to describe their service experiences through the use of on-site feedback forms or online or mailed surveys.
- Doing an on-the-spot survey following a sale or transaction, in which you ask a customer how well the product or service received met his or her needs and expectations. Follow-up surveys are useful as well.
- Employing focus groups, made up of a sampling of customers, where you gather information in response to specific product- and service-related questions.
- Analyzing sales, marketing, service, and other types of reports to help spot trends and make adjustments to policies and procedures.
- Keeping track of all bids or proposals to determine the acceptance and sales percentages and analyzing them to determine if there are patterns for the ones that were not successful.
- Reviewing marketing data that have been collected through interviews and research to help determine shopping and buying patterns for your customer demographics.

COMMON CUSTOMER EXPECTATIONS

On any given day, you may have customers contact you in regard to your products or services. Many of these customers do not have extreme expectations and can be satisfied in a relatively quick and easy manner. Some of the expectations are addressed by service providers, while others are handled by the organization.

Interpersonal Expectations	Strategies for Addressing
To feel welcome	Enthusiastically greet customers in a positive manner with a smile (whether face-to-face or on the telephone) and use your customers' names several times.

Interpersonal Expectations	Strategies for Addressing
To feel comfortable	Take the time to allow customers to talk about nonbusiness-related topics without pressuring them. Help relieve anxiety by smiling and communicating in a calm, nonthreatening manner. When customers have to wait, provide them with an inviting service environment that includes a comfortable place to sit, reading material, and refreshments, if possible.
To feel appreciated	Treat customers as if they are the most important people in the world. Go beyond what might be expected, provide special offers, and remember any special details, such as family members' names that they've previously told you. Thank the customers at the end of their transactions and follow up to ensure you met their expectations.
To feel understood	Listen actively and carefully—do not interrupt when customers are speaking. Ask pertinent questions, provide regular feedback, and be empathetic to their needs.
To feel important	Remember and use their names from memory, elicit their opinions about service improvements, and generally show that you value their business and ideas.

Product and Service Expectations	Strategies for Addressing
Easy access	Ensure that customers know how they can get in touch with service providers, place orders, get information, and provide feedback—and that they are able to do so without difficulty.
Quality products and service	Provide only the best-possible items and support to customers by using reputable suppliers and training employees to offer above-average service and product knowledge.
Safety	Ensure that all products have been tested for safety and that any potential problems are rectified quickly and effectively before customers encounter them.
Delivery as promised	Ensure that you provide what you advertise and promise, delivering it when you promise it and in the manner in which you promise it. Customers do not like unpleasant surprises. Make sure that your products match the images and descriptions in your advertising and on your Web site.
Competitive pricing	Comparison-shop for comparable products and services to make sure that what you charge customers is reasonable and equitable. Have a policy for price matching, if necessary.

Professional problem solving	Put the mechanisms in place to help quickly identify and resolve issues related to products and services. This process should empower frontline employees to handle issues without having to contact a supervisor and should be seamless to customers.

THE ROLE OF BEHAVIORAL-STYLE PREFERENCES IN CUSTOMER SERVICE

One major factor that often determines the outcome of any customer-provider service interaction is the behavioral-style preferences of both you and your customer. *Behavioral styles* are observable actions that you and other people exhibit when dealing with tasks or people. As people grow from infancy, their personalities form based on their life experiences and the environments in which they are reared. These become the basis of their behavioral-style preference(s). Some researchers believe that by the time people reach the first grade, their behavior is formed for life.

For you to be effective as a service professional, you will need to understand human behavioral-style characteristics. By becoming more proficient at identifying your own behavioral characteristics and those of others, you will better be able to create and maintain positive relationships with your customers. Self-knowledge is the starting point.

Just because customers say or do something differently from the way that you would doesn't mean that they are wrong. It simply means that they approach situations from a different perspective. Positive relationships are built on accepting the characteristics of others. Since many people won't always act the way you want them to, in order to provide positive global service, you need to adapt. This does not mean that you must make all the concessions when behaviors do not mesh. It simply means that although you do not have control over the behavior of others, you can control your own behavior to deal more effectively with your customers.

Many self-assessment questionnaires and much research related to behavioral styles are based on the work begun by psychiatrist Carl Jung and others in the earlier part of the twentieth century. Jung explored human personality and behavior. He divided behavior into two "attitudes" (introvert and extrovert) and four "functions" (thinking, feeling, sensing, and intuitive). These attitudes and functions can intermingle to form eight psychological types; knowledge of these types is useful in defining and describing human behavioral characteristics.

From Jung's complex research (and that of others) have come many variations, additional studies, and a variety of behavioral-style self-assessment questionnaires and models for explaining personal behavior. Examples of these questionnaires are the Myers-Briggs Type Indicator and the Personal Profile System. Several organizations allow you to complete free surveys online.

Although everyone typically has a *primary behavioral pattern* to which he or she reverts in stressful situations, people also have other character-istics in common and regularly demonstrate similar behavioral patterns. Identifying your own style preferences helps you identify similar ones in others.

FOCUS ON POSITIVE GLOBAL SERVICE: IDENTIFYING YOUR BEHAVIORAL STYLE(S)

As a quick strategy for identifying your primary and any secondary behavioral styles, make a copy of this page and then complete a brief informal assessment of your style(s).

Step 1. Read the following words and phrases and rate yourself by placing a number (from 1 to 5) next to each item. A 5 means that the word accurately describes you in most situations, and a 1 means that the word doesn't describe your behavior well. Before you begin, refer to the completed sample assessment that follows.

• Consistent	• Fun loving	• Calculating
• Detail-oriented	• Loyal	• Popular
• Competitive	• Quality-focused	• Patient
• Optimistic	• Decisive	• Logical
• Relaxed	• Enthusiastic	• Objective
• Nonaggressive (avoids conflict)	• Sincere	• Talkative
• Practical	• Accurate	

Step 2. Once you have rated each word or phrase, start with the first word and put the letter *R* to the right of it. Place an *I* to the right of the second word, a *D* to the right of the third word, and an *E* to the right of the fourth word. Then start over with the fifth word and repeat the *"RIDE"* pattern until all words have a letter at their right.

Step 3. Next, go through the list and count point values for all words that have an *R* beside them. Put the total at the bottom of the list, as shown in the completed sample assessment below. Do the same for the other letters. Once you have finished, one letter will probably have the highest total score. Each letter describes a primary style preference, and the one with your highest total score is your natural style tendency.

If *R* has the highest score, your primary style preference is rational. If *I* has the highest score, you exhibit more inquisitive behavior. *D* indicates decisive, and *E* is an expressive style preference.

If two or more of your scores have the same high totals, you likely put forth similar amounts of effort in both these style areas.

Most people have a primary and at least one alternate style of behavior. Keep in mind that this is only a quick indicator. A more thorough assessment, using a formal instrument such as a questionnaire, will be better at predicting your style preferences.

Source: R. W. Lucas, *Customer Service Skills for Success*, 5th ed., Burr Ridge, IL: McGraw-Hill Higher Education, 2011.

SAMPLE COMPLETED BEHAVIORAL-STYLE ASSESSMENT

5	Consistent	*R*
2	Detail-oriented	*I*
3	Competitive	*D*
2	Optimistic	*E*
5	Relaxed	*R*
3	Nonaggressive (avoids conflict)	*I*
3	Practical	*D*
3	Fun loving	*E*
5	Loyal	*R*
1	Quality-focused	*I*
1	Decisive	*D*
2	Enthusiastic	*E*

5	Sincere	R
1	Accurate	I
5	Calculating	D
1	Popular	E
5	Patient	R
3	Logical	I
1	Objective	D
4	Talkative	E
Total	R = 25 I = 10 D = 13 E = 12	

Source: R. W. Lucas, *Customer Service Skills for Success,* 5th ed., Burr Ridge, IL: McGraw-Hill Higher Education, 2011.

Human behavior is complex. For that reason, you would be doing yourself and your customers a disservice if you attempt to use your interpretation of behavioral characteristics and cues as absolute indicators of the type of person with whom you are dealing. While everyone shares some of the characteristics listed for all four behavioral-style categories, both your experience and your comfort levels with others help you better understand and adapt to the behavioral style of your customers. Generally, most people are adaptable and can shift style categories or exhibit different characteristics depending on the situation, if they so desire. For example, if you are more introverted [high inquisitive (*I*) style] and are more comfortable working alone or with tasks, you can still interact well for a short period of time with an internal or external customer who is very outgoing and personable. Similarly, if you are more of an extrovert [high expressive (*E*) style] who enjoys talking to anyone about virtually any topic, you are able to control that behavior and focus on specific detailed tasks when the occasion calls for it.

POSITIVE GLOBAL SERVICE ACTION TIP

Learn more about your behavioral style and your customers' styles by taking the time to obtain one or more of the commercial self-assessment surveys available on the Internet (e.g., Personal Profile System or Myers-Briggs Type Indicator).

Each person should be valued for his or her strengths and not be looked down upon because of what you perceive as a shortcoming. In a customer environment, each contact has the potential for contributing to your success and that of your organization. By appreciating the behavioral characteristics of people with whom you interact, you can avoid bias or prejudice and better serve your customers. An important point to remember is that there is no "best" or "worst" style.

Remember when dealing with your customers that even though they have a primary style, they may demonstrate other style behaviors too. If you become familiar with all style characteristics, recognize them in yourself, and observe how others display them, you can begin to learn how to better adapt to various behaviors. When interacting with others, remind yourself to watch their overall actions and behavior in order to get a better perception of their style preferences rather than react to one or two actions. Also, keep in mind that these characteristics are generalities and not absolutes when dealing with others. People can and do adapt and change behavior depending on a variety of circumstances.

The following lists of characteristics can help you become familiar with some behaviors displayed by people with each primary behavioral style.

R: Rational Behavioral Style

People who have a preference for the *rational behavioral style* may tend to:

- Avoid conflict and anger.
- Avoid situations that draw a lot of attention.
- Wear conservative clothing with muted colors and accessories.
- Wait in one place for periods of time without complaining, no matter how irritating it is.
- Exhibit congenial eye contact and facial expressions.
- Seek specific or complete explanations to questions ("That's our policy" does not work well with an *R* customer).
- Employ brief, businesslike handshakes.
- Phrase opinions as questions rather than statements (e.g., "Do you think this would be a better choice?").

- Choose small-group or solitary activities over large-group or interactive ones.
- Like to be on a first-name basis with others.
- Listen and observe more than talk.
- Communicate more in writing than face-to-face.

I: Inquisitive Behavioral Style

People who have a preference for the *inquisitive behavioral style* may tend to:

- Rely heavily on facts, times, dates, and practical information to make their point.
- Use formal titles and last names as opposed to first names. They may also stress the use of full names for themselves, not nicknames.
- Prefer to communicate via e-mail rather than face-to-face or on the telephone.
- Ask specific, pertinent questions rather than make statements of their feelings.
- Be very punctual and time conscious.
- Use cool, brief handshakes, often without a smile.
- Keep their personal life separate from business.
- Wear well-coordinated but conservative clothing and accessories.
- Carry on brief conversations.
- Use closed-ended questions (e.g., "Did you know that . . . ?" or "Have you checked . . . ?").
- Be diplomatic with others.
- Prefer solitary leisure activities (e.g., reading or listening to relaxing music).

D: Decisive Behavioral Style

People who have a preference for the *decisive behavioral style* may tend to:

- Be assertive and direct in their approach (sometimes overly so).
- Display a seemingly overconfident or arrogant demeanor.

- Say what they think, often without considering the implications or impact.
- Ask specific, sometimes blunt questions and give short, straight answers.
- Talk rather than write about something.
- Be in motion a lot and move quickly.
- Prefer active, competitive leisure activities.
- Display symbols of power to demonstrate their own importance.
- Wear clothing that tends to be very stylish and professional. Image is important to the decisives.
- Work consistently toward finding solutions to problems or issues.
- Have functionally decorated but seemingly disorganized offices (all items have a purpose and are not there to make the environment more attractive).
- Be solemn and use closed, nonverbal body cues (e.g., crossed arms or hands on hips).
- Have firm handshakes and strong, direct eye contact.

E: Expressive Behavioral Style

People who have a preference for the *expressive behavioral style* may tend to:

- Display an outwardly friendly, positive attitude.
- Use animated, free-flowing gestures when talking.
- Speak loudly and expressively with a wide range of emotion.
- Use direct eye contact and an assertive, warm (often two-handed) handshake.
- Smile and use open body language (e.g., hands waist high or higher and lots of gestures).
- Stand close when talking face-to-face.
- Share feelings and express ideas easily with anyone who will listen.
- Talk rather than write about something.
- Change topics or get distracted when talking.
- Use informal nicknames and first names when communicating.

- Seek out excuses to socialize or talk with others.
- Avoid boredom or routine.
- Miss deadlines and dislike timelines.
- Create or propose projects.
- Like action-oriented, people-centered, or group-oriented leisure activities.
- Wear trendy, bright, or unusual clothes and jewelry.

The important thing to remember about the different style categories is that there is no right or wrong style. No one style is better than another. We all have all four style preferences to some degree; however, we exhibit or revert to our primary style when in stressful or pressure situations. By recognizing the behaviors, you can start to identify them when others exhibit them, and you can then potentially adapt to their behavioral needs. But like any other aspect of diversity, do not stereotype and treat someone exhibiting certain behaviors in a predetermined manner. This is a formula for a service and relationship breakdown.

CORE ELEMENTS OF POSITIVE GLOBAL CUSTOMER SERVICE

No matter what behavioral style or demographic group you are dealing with, there are specific strategies that you can use to ensure customer satisfaction. Often the approaches you use to service delivery will be based on your customer, the industry, organizational values, and your own personal training and experience. The important thing to remember is that most people react well to some core elements of positive global customer service. These components help customers achieve what they want and need. Figure 2-2 shows how some of the core elements can impact your customer.

Empathy

Customers want to have their needs and wants understood, and they want you and your organization to take a proactive approach to fulfilling their

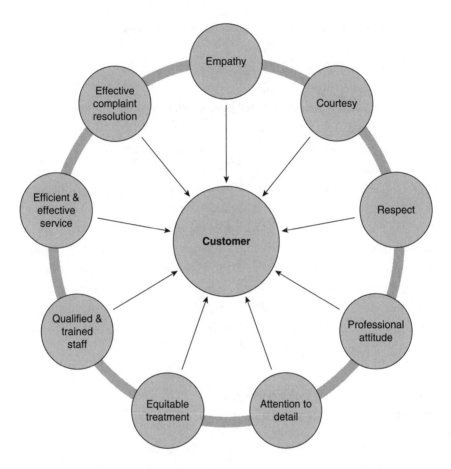

Figure 2-2   Core Elements of Positive Customer Service

expectations. This is especially true when something goes wrong with products or services in the mind of a customer. It does not matter what you think about a perceived breakdown. If a customer believes something did or did not occur, either positively or negatively, then it happened and you will have to address the customer's perception and emotions and the accompanying issues. The last thing you want to do is get into the old schoolyard game of "did not–did too" with a customer who has a perceived problem. You will *not* win in such situations and risk angering the customer, losing business, and generating negative word-of-mouth publicity as the story of the event is shared with others later.

When you empathize with your customers, you attempt to understand what they are going through emotionally by pulling from your own experiences and background and then responding appropriately. In a global world, empathy may be difficult sometimes. The challenge is that people bring with them cultural or personal experiences or backgrounds. In such instances, you may have no frame of reference from which you can relate to what a customer is feeling or experiencing. Even so, there are some standard things that you can do or say when service breaks down or customer expectations are not met. If you listen intently and if you use positive, open nonverbal cues and offer empathetic comments, you can help create an atmosphere of understanding and assistance. Treating each customer and each situation as unique will make your life and your customer's a lot easier.

POSITIVE GLOBAL SERVICE ACTION TIP

Do not confuse empathy with sympathy when dealing with customers. The first is your attempt to put yourself mentally in your customers' position and try to imagine how they might be feeling or why they are acting in a specific fashion. The ultimate goal is to show that you understand their issue or where they are coming from emotionally. Sympathy implies feeling sorry or having pity or concern and can cause a negative reaction from customers if they perceive you are exhibiting sympathy.

Courtesy

Many people have been taught that it is nice to say "please" and "thank you" when interacting with others. Having good manners indicates respect, which goes a long way in sending positive interpersonal messages and setting an amiable tone when interacting with customers. Even though customers may not really always be right, you should treat them as if they are crucial to your success . . . because they are. While it may sometimes be difficult to remember to be courteous when situations become tense or emotionally charged, you should go out of your way to maintain your composure and be polite when dealing with customers. If you feel that you cannot maintain your composure, simply excuse yourself and get a coworker or supervisor to step in, if that is possible.

Courtesy can be a powerful tool in any situation, but especially in those in which tensions, stress, or emotions are potentially high (e.g., medical facilities, town meetings, some government offices, customer service desks, courtrooms, or car impound lots). Remember the old adage to "kill them with kindness" when things start getting out of control or you feel your blood pressure rising.

Respect

Respect is a deeply rooted personal value for many people, taught at a very young age. Depending on where people were born and grew up, they often receive guidance on the importance of respect for the elderly, property, and authority. Such values drive how people deal with others and the situations in which they find themselves throughout any given day. Think about how you react when someone cuts you off in traffic. Your thoughts or reactions are often based on your values, just as the thoughts and actions of others are based on their value systems and life experiences.

As a service provider, it is crucial that you value and respect your customers and their points of view whenever interacting with them. Use patience and empathy and work toward negotiated win-win situations in which customers get what they need from their encounters and so do you and your organization. Take ownership of situations and act in a professional manner. Some common indications of respect include:

- Keeping an open mind
- Taking time to listen to your customer without interrupting
- Attempting to empathize and understand the customer's true issue or point of view
- Negotiating to a win-win situation so that neither side feels it "lost"
- Being honest and sharing what you can do for the customer, not what you cannot do
- Trusting that your customer is not out to cheat your organization
- Communicating in an assertive but nonthreatening and open manner

- Creating a feeling of collaboration versus competition with your customer
- Avoiding intimidation or coercion to get your way

Professional Attitude

When you come into contact with a customer at what Jan Carlzon, CEO of SAS Airways, years ago called a *moment of truth* (the point where the customer and service provider first come into contact either face-to-face or on the telephone),[5] it is crucial that the instant be a pleasant and memorable experience for the customer. Anything less is courting disaster from a service standpoint. Simple efforts like smiling, listening, using a customer's name, and projecting a "can-do" attitude make a world of difference in setting a win-win environment where the customer gets what he or she wants, needs, and expects, and you and your organization get what you need from the encounter—current and future business.

Attention to Detail

Positive global customer service is based on your having the necessary product and service knowledge and your then making the effort to prepare and deliver service right the first time. It is sometimes the little things that make a difference in how a customer perceives service. Your customers should not have to spend additional time contacting you or returning to your place of business to correct a problem that your organization created. For example, consider what might happen if you worked for a bank and keyed in improper amounts for deposits that customers made. Some officials from the bank's main office would then later have to call or visit your branch to research the error and get it resolved. Chances are good that the bank would not be happy. In addition to just the time it takes to resolve the issue with your bank, cascading issues could develop in such an instance. Customers might end up with overdraft fees from your bank, while other issues could develop with their creditors. Any secondary issues would take time to resolve, and your customers would become very frustrated and angry with your organization. All this can often be avoided if you and other service providers focus on each job task and do not allow things like e-mail, other customers, or coworkers to distract your attention.

Equitable Treatment

Have you ever stood in line or at a service counter only to have someone else walk up to ask a "quick question" that turns into an entire conversation? Have you ever found out that someone else got a better deal than you did from an organization? How did these situations make you feel? Probably not valued, respected, or equal. These are the types of events that can turn a current or potential customer against an organization. That's why it's important to exhibit fairness when dealing with all customers. In most situations, it would be appropriate to ask the interrupting customer to wait his or her turn; or direct the customer to another service representative for assistance; or perhaps listen until you realize the issue is not simple, then ask the person to take a number or wait in line out of fairness. Of course, all these should be done politely, with a smile, and in a professional manner.

If you are like many people, one big area of irritation is having a service provider stop helping you to answer a ringing telephone while you wait. When dealing with a customer, the service provider should typically let any incoming calls go to voice mail, barring special circumstances. Out of fairness, if someone has waited his or her turn for service, the person should not be "put on hold" while you attend to someone who called rather than came in for service. Every organization should have a policy on how to handle ringing phones when servicing other customers. You must know how to handle such situations *before* they occur rather than risk alienating customers. If you are unsure, speak to your supervisor.

Qualified and Trained Staff

As author Jim Collins stressed in his bestselling book *Good to Great*,[6] it is important that organizations hire the right people, put them in the correct jobs, and train them in order for the employees and the organization to excel. Customers should have to expect no less than a competently trained workforce when they contact your organization. After all, they are spending their time, effort, and money to patronize your business, so they should receive value for their investment.

While many organizations are generally scaling back on employee training, sales and customer service training sessions are often still being provided. This is because most managers realize that service is not "nice to do"; it's actually a key strategic initiative that must be delivered by highly motivated, knowledgeable, trained service representatives. Anything less is an invitation to lost business and revenue and ultimately to failure.

Employees should consider volunteering for any professional development training that will add to their knowledge and skill base. If your organization provides educational assistance, it is also wise to consider college courses that add academic credentials to your background. At the very least, go to the library to check out books and conduct Internet research on topics related to key terms highlighted in this chapter. For example, if you searched the phrase *customer service* on YouTube.com, you would find dozens of short videos that deal with various customer service situations and topics.

The important thing to keep in mind is that while all the techniques available can help, each customer is unique and requires specialized care. Use the basics of listening to your customers to determine their needs, wants, and expectations and then use an appropriate service strategy to satisfy them.

Efficient and Effective Service

Customers are no different from you in the way that they value their time. In some cultures in the Middle East, a delay is often anticipated because of the way that people view time. In many Westernized cultures, though, time is equated to money. There is often little patience for missed deadlines and delays.

While most people expect that there might be a slight delay in getting service during business hours or at a busy business location, they often do not tolerate what they consider undue delays. They recognize that most organizations have scaled back staff in today's economy and are trying to do more with fewer human resources. Still, that does not excuse negligence or lengthy waiting periods.

Your challenge as a service provider is to recognize each customer in a timely manner and provide service to the customer as quickly and efficiently as possible. Face-to-face, this might mean holding up one finger and smiling to indicate that you see the customer and will attempt to be with him or her shortly, or it might mean answering all calls within four rings or having an answering system to take a message. If these goals should become a regular problem, you might truly be understaffed, and the issue should be brought to your supervisor's attention immediately.

When waits are obvious or necessary, share the reason with your customers as soon as it's known so that they feel respected and informed and can make a decision on whether they care to wait. For example, if you work in a restaurant and there is a water pipe break that shuts down kitchen operations, give your customers an option to reschedule and then compensate them for their inconvenience by offering a discount on their current or future visits. Unless there will be a lengthy delay, most people will opt to wait and will appreciate the discount. They will also appreciate the opportunity to participate in the decision-making process, which can have a soothing effect and reduce the chance that you will soon have to deal with an irate customer. If you are not certain of your level of empowerment related to what you can offer in such instances, speak with your supervisor in advance so that you are prepared should the need arise.

POSITIVE GLOBAL SERVICE ACTION TIP

When approaching your supervisor with a service-related problem, have one or two suggestions for resolving the issue in mind. This shows that you are a professional who sincerely cares about your job and customers and are not just complaining.

Effective Complaint Resolution

Most effective service organizations have policies and procedures for dealing with customers when things go wrong. If yours does not, suggest to your supervisor that it become a subject for discussion at your next team or departmental meeting. An important point to consider when customers complain is that they are helping you and your organization to identify an area that is not meeting their needs, wants, or expectations. In effect, they are providing you with an opportunity to fix something that is broken and to salvage the customer-provider relationship. Seize such opportunities to practice your courtesy by thanking them and then listen carefully as they explain the issue. Once you are certain that you fully understand what went wrong, set out to apply sound problem-solving strategies to resolve the issue as quickly as possible. Don't forget to ask your customers if the action(s) you took to rectify a problem following a service breakdown resolved it to their satisfaction and what else you can do to assist them. Also, make sure to thank them for bringing the situation to your attention and for giving you the opportunity to fix the issue.

THE IMPACT OF TECHNOLOGY

In addition to the personal element of positive global customer service, organizations have discovered that there are many opportunities to enhance service delivery through the use of technology. No one piece of equipment has done more to revolutionize customer service than the personal computer. Coupled with the Internet, it has revolutionized the way people communicate and do business. Future possibilities are limitless. According to the Web site Internet World Stats, as of June 30, 2010, there were almost 2 billion (27.6 percent of the world population) Internet users around the globe (see next page).[7] Think about the potential if only 1 percent of those people did business with an organization and spent only $10 a year . . . that is $2 million in sales! No wonder many organizations are investing time and money into technology-based systems and hiring and training people to deliver service via technology.

WORLDWIDE INTERNET USERS (AS OF JUNE 30, 2010)

Here are some data from a recent study on global Internet use:

- Asia—825 million
- Europe—475 million
- North America—266 million
- Latin America and the Caribbean—205 million
- Africa—111 million
- Middle East—63 million
- Oceania and Australia—21 million

With a computer and a network, organizations of all sizes have been able to reach out and capture customers who were not attainable in the past. Through the Internet, any business can now let people all over the world know of its products and services. Small companies can appear larger and compete with bigger organizations that have more staff and resources. Often the deciding factor in the success level of an organization comes down to the quality of the service that its staff provides.

Many organizations have realized the power of the Internet and have rushed to capitalize on ways to attract and hold customers through technology. This venture into electronically delivered service and sales has been termed *e-commerce*. According to the Web site Whois Source, as of August 1, 2010, there were over 121 million active domain names. Many of those belong to organizations and businesses that sell products and services to individuals (*business-to-consumer*, or *B2C*) and other organizations and businesses (*business-to-business*, or *B2B*) all the time. As a result, e-commerce sales in the first quarter of 2010 amounted to 4.0 percent (over $38 billion) of total retail sales of $960 billion.[8]

From a service standpoint, using technology often means that an organization needs to take a multifaceted approach to attending to customers. In addition to face-to-face service, customers often have a variety of options, such as toll-free numbers, fee-based 900 numbers, and fax, texting, Web site, and e-mail systems, all of which are staffed by representatives in a *customer care center*. These people should be available around the clock to answer questions, take orders, solve problems, and provide various services or support to people who call, write, or fax.

With all the technological advances available to support customer service, it is still important to remember that many customers appreciate old-fashioned, personalized, face-to-face customer service. Contrary to what many service providers believe, though, it's not just older customers. Factors such as the ages of your customers, their educational and socio-economic backgrounds, their comfort levels with technology, and their behavioral-style preferences can influence whether or not they would rather deal with a person or technology. Some people are *high touch* (preferring assistance), while others are *low touch* (preferring to serve themselves); therefore, offering a variety of service delivery systems is smart business. Successful service organizations realize that each customer is unique, and so they provide flexibility in offering service and support through a variety of means. Whether service is delivered face-to-face or via technology, there is often no substitute for a dedicated, knowledgeable, and well-trained employee to assist when needed. You and your peers are the lifeline of your organization and have to take responsibility for quality service in order to help make it successful and satisfy your customers.

POSITIVE GLOBAL SERVICE ACTION TIP

When connecting with customers via technology, do not forget that projecting a positive attitude in your written or spoken words is just as important as when you are dealing with them face-to-face. It's more so in many cases, because when your customers do not see you, they can only draw conclusions about you based on their interpretations of your words or tone of voice.

SUMMARY

In this chapter, you have read about many of the changes that are impacting consumer behavior as well as techniques and strategies for enhancing customer-provider relationships. Some of the key concepts that you investigated include:

- Women, teens, gays, lesbians, and various minority groups have become virtual financial powerhouses in the area of consumer spending.

- It is estimated that in their lifetimes, members of the Generation Y consumers group will spend over $10 trillion on goods and services.
- Successful companies develop and implement a proactive, strategic approach to providing customer service in order to react to all the changes taking place.
- Customer loyalty is an emotional rather than a rational thing.
- A need is an internal motivator or driver that someone requires; wants are things that customers desire
- Expectations are preconceived ideas about your organization, products, or services.
- Common interpersonal expectations include feeling welcome, comfortable, understood, respected, and important to the service provider and his or her organization.
- Common product and service expectations include easy access, quality, safety, competitive pricing, professional problem solving, and an effortless return policy.
- Behavioral styles are observable tendencies (actions that you can see or experience) that you and other people exhibit when dealing with tasks or people.
- The four categories of behavioral-style preference are rational, inquisitive, decisive, and expressive.
- Just because customers say or do something, or react, differently from the way that you would, doesn't mean that they are wrong. It simply means that they are different.
- Although everyone typically has a primary behavior pattern, people also have other characteristics in common and regularly demonstrate similar behavioral patterns.
- Often the approaches you use to service delivery will be based on your customer, industry, organizational values, and personal training and experience.
- Core elements of positive global customer service include empathy, courtesy, respect, professional attitude, attention to detail, equitable treatment, qualified and trained staff, efficient and effective service, and effective complaint resolution.

- In addition to the personal element of positive global customer service, organizations have discovered that there are many opportunities to enhance service delivery through the use of technology.
- No one piece of equipment has done more to revolutionize customer service than the personal computer. Coupled with the Internet, it has revolutionized the way people communicate and do business.
- From a service standpoint, using technology often means that an organization needs to take a multifaceted approach to attending to customers.
- With all the technological advances available to support customer service, it's still important to remember that many customers appreciate old-fashioned, personalized, face-to-face customer service.

CHAPTER

3

Creating a Professional Service Image

It only takes a split second for a customer to decide whether to do business with you and your organization.

KEY CONCEPTS

After reading this chapter and when applying concepts learned, you will be able to:

1. Describe what makes a positive first impression.
2. List some of the benefits of a positive first impression.
3. Explain some of the factors that help create a professional image.
4. Exhibit professional dress standards in the workplace.
5. Discuss the importance of relationships in delivering positive global service.
6. Use neurolinguistic programming (NLP) to strengthen relationships with customers.

7. Demonstrate professionalism through words and actions.

8. Create a professional work environment to support positive global service efforts.

Customer service is viewed as a dying art by many people. Ask someone to relate any customer service story to you and he or she will likely pick a negative one. A study of 800 respondents by Max Impact Corporation in Rochester Hills, Michigan,[1] found that the majority of people believe that service either is getting worse or no longer exists (see Figure 3-1). In many instances this can be attributed to the lack of training provided to service professionals or to a poor attitude on the part of the customers or the person serving them. Whatever the cause, your goal should be to consciously strive to increase the level of service that you provide to your customers. This starts with the first impression that you make.

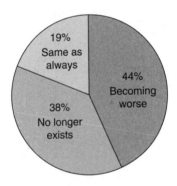

Source: Max Impact Corporation

Figure 3-1 Customer Service Survey Results

MAKING A POSITIVE IMPRESSION

First impressions are crucial and often lasting. Because of this, ensure that the one you make is the kind that will bring customers back rather than send them to a competitor. While a bad impression may not be impossible to undo, it is certainly easier to get off on the right foot with a positive one instead of having to figure out how to recover from a service breakdown.

In many instances what customers first hear on the telephone, experience through e-mail or fax, or encounter face-to-face can have a definite impact on how they view you and your organization. Researchers, funded by the National Science Foundation, found that exposure to someone's face can create an almost instantaneous and lasting impression. "As minimal an exposure time as a tenth of a second is sufficient for people to make a specific trait inference from facial appearance. Additional exposure time increases confidence in judgments and allows for more differentiated trait impressions."[2] Another study at the University of Minnesota Duluth found that "it can take as little as three minutes to determine how a relationship will progress."[3]

From the time you first come into contact with a customer until the time a transaction ends, you are sending messages about yourself and your organization. In his bestselling book, *Service America,* Karl Albrecht relates how former SAS (Scandinavian Airlines) CEO Jan Carlzon defined a service *moment of truth* as "an episode in which a customer comes into contact with any aspect of a company, however remote, and thereby has an opportunity to form an impression."[4] This observation is important to remember. Think about times when you walked into a restaurant and wondered about the cleanliness of the kitchen based on the state of the restroom. To ensure that you and your organization do not come under such customer scrutiny, do your best to see that the first impression and all other aspects of a customer experience are superior and promote quality positive global customer service.

Benefits of a Positive First Impression

Some typical benefits from a positive first impression include:

- Encouraging return business
- Helping generate referral business
- Saving on advertising dollars because you do not have to keep replacing existing customers
- Potentially reducing costs because customer complaints go down and service recovery efforts do not have to be employed

- Expanding profitability overall as more customers stay, new ones come in, and expenditures are reduced
- Increasing the likelihood that customers will overlook or forgive minor errors or service breakdowns because they like you and your organization

Your degree of professionalism and enthusiasm when you greet customers can leave them feeling excited about working with you and your organization or feeling indifferent and unsure about continuing a relationship. When customers and potential customers first come into contact with you through any means, they do an almost instantaneous assessment of you and your organization. Preparation, conscious effort, and a sincere desire to serve others are required in order to create a positive impression in all these areas. A failing grade in any of these can mean a relationship breakdown, lost business, and potential negative results for you in the form of poor performance ratings.

While you may have greeted dozens of other customers on a given day and possibly answered the same questions or shared the same information numerous times, it is the first time your customer has heard it. Treat each customer with the same enthusiasm and professionalism as the first. One story that illustrates this point involves a cast member at Walt Disney World in Orlando, Florida, where millions of guests from all over the world visit each year. Many speak languages other than English. This cast member was assigned to assist guests near the entrance to Cinderella's Castle. As you can imagine, the one question that she answered dozens of times within the span of an hour was, "Where are the restrooms?" Not very exciting for her, but each time she reminded herself that while she had told dozens of others where the restrooms were before, this is the first time that she had shared the information with a specific guest. Therefore, each time, she smiled graciously and greeted her guests, and then, rather than pointing and explaining directions, she walked them through the castle to show them the facilities on the opposite side of the building. Along the way, she engaged the guests in small talk, shared information about the castle, and got to know a little about them. How do you think this made them feel? How would you have felt about your experience?

With her simple actions and personal approach, the cast member was able to project a positive first impression and provided positive global customer service to each guest.

FOCUS ON POSITIVE GLOBAL SERVICE: POSITIVE FIRST IMPRESSIONS

Think about the experiences you have had with customer service representatives in the past week when you called or visited an organization (other than a government entity), went through a drive-through, or contacted them via the Internet or e-mail.

What positive factor(s) stands out in your mind?

_____

_____

_____

_____

What negative factor(s) stands out in your mind?

_____

_____

_____

_____

Would you patronize, visit, or contact the organization again? Why or why not?

_____

_____

_____

_____

Would you refer others to the organization? Why or why not?

_____

_____

_____

_____

THE ROLE OF PERSONAL APPEARANCE

Through your *appearance* and *grooming* habits, you project an image of yourself and the organization. The way that you appear to others is a major part of making a first impression. Organizations often have policies for grooming, mode of dress, and other aspects related to employee appearance. Even if yours does not, you should follow traditional business fashion and grooming standards for your industry. If you are unsure what that entails, it is usually safe to dress or groom as your supervisor and peers do rather than try to stand out as an individual. Also, consider how your customers are dressed and how they might react to your appearance and then adjust accordingly. In a multicultural world, you also have to remember that people from many cultures have specific expectations related to employee appearance. While some cultures take a more relaxed approach and allow "business casual" dress in the workplace (e.g., the United States, the Philippines, Australia), others are more formal, and customers anticipate a higher degree of dress and grooming (e.g., the United Kingdom, Venezuela, Poland, Germany, China). In the more formal countries, you may be severely judged based on fashion mistakes, and a customer's impression of you and your organization could be negative as a result. It is always wise to err on the side of conservatism when dressing for work.

Personal Appearance and Grooming

The way in which you present yourself through grooming and hygiene and through your manner of dress sends a powerful message of either professionalism or indifference. Before you leave home for work, make sure that your shoes are shined and maintained, your clothes are clean, pressed, and in good order, and your appearance is professional. For example, your clothing, grooming, and choice of jewelry or other accessories could send a negative message to some people based on their cultural beliefs or personal preferences. It is crucial to be able to distinguish between what is appropriate and inappropriate for the workplace and to adhere to appropriate standards. This is because, even though you provide attentive, quality service, your customers will be evaluating your appearance upon first contact and will form an opinion. Their opinion may make the difference in whether they will continue to patronize your organization or go to a competitor.

Hygiene

While each cultural group may have its own interpretation of what is acceptable related to *hygiene*, failing to follow culturally acceptable hygiene practices based on where you are employed might result in a perceived offensive appearance and negative reactions from customers and co-workers. This is because you will often be interacting with customers from cultures different from your own, and those customers will be applying their own cultural norms when judging you. Effective hygiene habits are crucial for successfully building strong interpersonal relationships and providing quality levels of service.

No matter what your job, there is little excuse for neglecting basic hygiene. People generally recognize that service providers who work in certain jobs are going to encounter more dirt and grime than others. Even so, most people have a negative reaction to someone who does not employ standard hygiene practices or take pride in his or her personal appearance. Such people are often perceived as inconsiderate, lazy, or simply dirty.

Keep in mind that customers do not have to continue to do business with you and your organization. With few exceptions, if they judge you, your coworkers, or your employees to be offensive in any manner, they can easily find an alternative source for the products and services they need. Another thing to remember is that without customers, you do not have a job. The bottom line is that good hygiene and attention to your personal appearance are crucial in a service environment.

A number of grooming trends have been perpetuated by what many actors and fashion models wear and how they look. For example, a lot of male actors and models sport a one- or two-day beard stubble in their professional and private appearances. While some people may think that this looks sexy in movies, it has little place in most professional work environments and often sends a message of someone who did not get up in time to shave that morning before coming to work. Likewise, many studies show that prominent *tattoos* and visible *piercings* (e.g., ear, nose, eyebrow, tongue, cheek, or other visible locations) are becoming more commonplace. In many instances, though, tattoos and piercings not only raise some eyebrows but also can cause a negative customer reaction based on stereotypes of people who have such things. Often, these reactions are from older customers, for example, baby boomers (born between 1946 and 1964). Since this group is one of the largest market forces, their views should be considered if you want to be a successful service provider. Covering tattoos or not wearing body jewelry while at work is a simple fix to prevent negative reactions from some customers.

One final area to consider about hygiene is that although good hygiene and grooming are important, going to an extreme through excessive or unusual use of makeup, cologne, hair color, or perfume can create a negative impression and may even cause people to avoid you. This is especially true related to strong scents, because many people have allergies or respiratory problems.

POSITIVE GLOBAL SERVICE ACTION TIP

Have a candid conversation with your supervisor and ask for constructive feedback related to how he or she perceives your typical appearance. If possible, make any adjustments your supervisor recommends.

Clothing and Accessories

In recent years, the management of many organizations integrated *casual Fridays, dress-down days,* and *business casual* into the workplace in an attempt to adapt to the changing values of today's workforce. If your organization has done so, remember that the word *casual* should not be interpreted as "sloppy." An example of how such casual dress policies are used can be seen in many U.S.-based high-tech and graphic-arts work environments. These industries often have a large number of younger, technically savvy employees, and recruiting is often very competitive for new applicants. One inexpensive means of attracting and keeping such employees has been to allow them to wear jeans, T-shirts, sandals, and, in some companies, shorts to work. Unfortunately, like a number of seemingly good ideas, this trend toward being a bit lax is now starting to slowly reverse in many organizations because some employees have taken the concept of "casual" to an extreme. As a result, employees have begun to negatively affect the workplace and the opinions that many customers have of some organizations. This realization often comes when important clients from countries that have differing values and perceptions of what is appropriate dress in the workplace visit and provide negative feedback to managers on what they see. To them, such a casual approach to dress is an indication of a casual approach to doing business. In an economy where every customer counts, organizations are definitely looking for ways to attract and keep this precious commodity, and so they are having to rethink what image is being presented to their customers.

A mistake made by many workers, especially those early in their careers as customer service professionals, is that they must spend their entire paychecks on expensive clothes and accessories to impress managers, coworkers, and customers. In fact, doing this might work against you if you fall into this category because others might view you as immature and unable to effectively manage your money. This might make them doubt your professional capabilities.

Work clothing does not have to be expensive, but it should be well maintained and appropriate to your work setting. No matter what type of clothing is designated in your organization, you can project a positive, professional image by simply wearing clothing that is clean and pressed and shoes that are polished. Certain types of work clothing and accessories are acceptable, while others are inappropriate. If your organization does not have a policy outlining dress standards, always check with your supervisor before wearing something that might deviate from the standards observed by other employees or that might create an unfavorable image to your customers.

 POSITIVE GLOBAL SERVICE ACTION TIP

If you are in doubt about appropriate attire, many free publications and videos are available on the Internet to help you select the right clothing, jewelry, eyeglasses, and accessories for your workplace. You can also check with your company's human resources department and your local public library or bookstore for more information.

FRIENDLINESS AND COURTESY

Relationships are such an important part of doing business in many countries (e.g., Bolivia, Japan, Panama, the Philippines) that getting to know your customers in a relaxed fashion rather than rushing directly into a sales pitch can often make the difference in their reaction to you. For example, if you were working as a service professional in a clothing store and noticed a woman (this example applies equally to a man) who appeared to be from a different culture, you might approach her with small talk while she is looking through a rack of clothing. You could ask what she thinks of a certain color as she browses through various pieces. You might then offer your perception of the garment. Once you have identified that the woman speaks a different language or has a foreign accent, you could ask where she is from and open a dialogue about her country or some other related aspect that may get her to open up and talk. Later you can start to subtly probe about whether she is looking for anything specific or how you might assist her.

The following strategies can help foster successful customer-provider relationships:

- **Smile.** Unlike many other nonverbal cues used around the world, the smile is one of those, with a few exceptions, that can universally signal friendliness or friendship and acceptance. Use your smile to make customers feel welcome in face-to-face and telephone meetings. Since people cannot see you and may never have met you when they call your organization, your smile on the telephone can positively impact your voice tone and may make the difference in how they perceive you and your organization when they call.

- **Make eye contact.** Simple eye contact can alert customers to the fact that you see them and are ready to respond to their needs, answer questions, or assist them if needed. Just keep in mind that members of some cultures and subcultures (Asian, Hispanic, African American) view prolonged or direct eye contact as being potentially intrusive, intimidating, challenging, or arrogant. It is often helpful to smile as you look at your customers, when appropriate. In some situations this lightens the mood and helps reduce the chance that customers might feel that you are trying to "stare them down" or that you are trying to intimidate or push them to a decision.

- **Greet customers by name.** In his book *How to Win Friends and Influence People*, Dale Carnegie stressed that the sweetest sound to a person's ear is his or her own name.[5] Simply by using your customer's name, you may put your relationship on a positive track and help solidify a sale or transaction in a manner that will help ensure satisfaction as well as future and referral business.

  Typically, you should ask for a person's name early in your conversation if he or she has not provided it. Use the name immediately in a response in order to help remember it, and then periodically use it during your transaction or discussion. Because some cultures prefer a more formal approach in doing business with strangers, make sure that you use the person's title (Mr., Ms., Mrs., or Dr.) and last name unless he or she gives you permission to do otherwise in order to avoid offending the person or appearing presumptuous or arrogant. This is especially true when someone is senior to you in age or status (e.g., the CEO or a senior manager from your organization) or has earned credentials or rank (e.g., a general in the military, ambassador, politician, or doctor). Doing these things also ties in to the concept of respecting your customers.

To avoid overuse of someone's name, it is appropriate in the United States to use the less formal "sir" or "ma'am" to concur or address a point with your customer. For example, "Yes, sir, we can get that to you by 6 p.m. today," or, "No, ma'am, I have not heard of that brand before." You can intersperse these terms throughout with the customer's name to sound more conversational.

Building Rapport

When working with customers, your goal should be to build *rapport* and trust with them. You should create a situation in which you are both on the same wavelength and have a feeling of understanding one another completely. By achieving this level of comfort with others, you will more likely be able to effectively elicit their true needs or concerns and provide excellent positive global service.

One strategy that you can use to develop rapport with customers is to apply concepts from the field of *neurolinguistic programming* (NLP). This approach has been used for years by salespeople, counselors, business and medical professionals, and many others. The cofounders of the process (Richard Bandler and John Grinder) focused on interpersonal communication and studied individuals who possessed the ability to quickly bond or develop rapport with others. The authors' goal was to try to learn what techniques those individuals used to form relationships in a relatively short period. The following are some of the basic rapport-building strategies that you might apply when interacting with your customers or potential customers. You will note that the strategies recommend that you mirror what your customers are doing. Bear in mind that the key is to be discreet and not make it apparent that you are doing this. Do not immediately follow their moves; otherwise, it will be obvious, and they may think you are mocking or making fun of them and become offended.

- **Mirror your customer's posture or body positioning.** Stand, sit, or walk like your customers to some degree. By mimicking their *posture* or *body positioning*, you potentially form a subconscious connection with them that may ease stressful situations like complaint handling, sales, or counseling. For example, if they sit erect or lean forward, casually follow that posture after a short period.
- **Match their gestures.** *Gestures* can send powerful positive or negative messages. For that reason they should not be overlooked as a vehicle for building and supporting stronger customer relationships. If customers cross their legs while seated or fold their arms, you should eventually do likewise. This is done for the same reasons that you match their posture and body position.
- **Respond and communicate in a similar manner.** If customers tend to use pauses between thoughts or ideas, try doing the same to some degree. If they have rapid or slower speaking styles, match your tempo to theirs. This will not only potentially aid understanding, but can help create mental "You're like me" reactions from your customers. Matching the *rate of speech* of customers is crucial to understanding. People from southern rural regions of the United States often speak more slowly than their counterparts in the North or West because of the more laid-back approach to life in their areas.

   If you ever listen to people from other countries speaking their native languages, you will also likely note distinct differences in how fast they talk compared to how fast you talk. This is not a bad thing, only different. Adjust where possible, and when communicating in your native language rather than theirs, slow your speaking rate slightly and make sure that you pronounce each word correctly and enunciate every word distinctly. If necessary, you might also try writing words or messages down neatly or using images. This might help, because many people can read and understand words from other languages but may not be able to say them.
- **Use the same terminology.** In using NLP in therapy sessions, some therapists will feed back words or terms used by their clients

in order to show that they are listening but also to get on the same linguistic level with them. You might do likewise with your customers. For example:

CUSTOMER: "I've called two times about a problem with the lamp I bought and yet the issue still exists."

YOU: "I apologize for the inconvenience of having to continue to deal with this issue. What specific problem exists with the lamp?"

CUSTOMER: "The on-and-off switch does not work all the time."

YOU: "Exactly what do you mean by 'does not work all the time'?"

CUSTOMER: "When I get up in the morning and turn the lamp on before I get out of bed, the light usually comes on, but later, when I try to turn the lamp off, the lightbulb stays lit."

The reason that NLP often works is because people tend to gravitate toward those with whom they can relate or who are just like them. By assuming postures and language similar to those of your customers, you can potentially get to a point where they form a mental relationship with you.

FOCUS ON POSITIVE GLOBAL SERVICE: RAPPORT BUILDING

Consider instances where you met someone and quickly realized that you were alike or had things in common. Create a short list of these characteristics or factors and later use it as a checklist for building skills that you will use to enhance relationships with your own customers.

What are some of the things that made you like or feel you could trust the other person?

_____

_____

_____

RELATIONSHIP-FOCUSED COUNTRIES (PARTIAL LISTING)

The following are examples of countries in which building a relationship with customers before transacting business is a crucial part of the service process.

Bangladesh	Indonesia	Myanmar	Saudi Arabia
Brazil	Iran	Pakistan	Singapore
China	Iraq	Philippines	South Korea
Colombia	Japan	Poland	Thailand
Egypt	Kuwait	Qatar	Turkey
Greece	Malaysia	Romania	Vietnam
India	Mexico	Russia	

- **Show respect.** Everyone has an opinion. While your customers' opinions may not be the same as yours, they are still important to them and must be respected. Failure to _respect_ your customers can lead to animosity, resentment, and problems in your customer-provider relationships. An easy way to demonstrate that you value their perspectives is to ask for their opinions and allow them input in any decision making, especially when things go wrong. You may already have a solution or two in mind, but you can make it appear that they are making the choice by saying to them something like, "We could do either _____ or _____ to resolve this. Which do you think would work best?" By giving options and providing an opportunity to become involved in the process, you help ensure that they will take ownership of the solution and likely be more satisfied.

- **Use good manners.** Basic expressions of *good manners* such as "please" and "thank you" are simple tools for demonstrating that you value and respect your customers. Unfortunately, many service providers seem to be lacking in such common civilities these days. Whether it is a result of negligence on the part of caregivers who did not require these rudimentary courtesies from their children or a lackadaisical or poor attitude on the part of service providers, failing to demonstrate basic good manners can lead to relationship breakdowns. Make sure that you use these simple, socially acceptable courtesies when interacting with your customers. People recognize and appreciate the little things that you do, and such courtesies can sometimes mean the difference in how people perceive you and your organization. Something as simple as "Could you please take a number," or "Have a seat, and I'll be with you as soon as I finish with this customer," or "How may I assist you?" recognizes your customers, alerts them to your intentions, and increases the possibility of a positive service outcome. Your final opportunity to help ensure customer satisfaction comes with a sincere "Thank you for calling [shopping with] [name of organization]. I look forward to assisting you again soon" at the end of a transaction or conversation.

- **Be patient.** Serving others can be a stressful job at times, especially when you are overworked or understaffed or are dealing with less than pleasant customers. Even so, you should demonstrate patience by listening to what your customers have to say to the point where you understand their issues or can assist them effectively, continuing to maintain your professionalism at all times and making an effort to provide quality positive global customer service.

   When communicating with people who speak other languages, have a speech or learning impediment, are indecisive, or have some other reason that they speak slowly, listen carefully and allow them to speak. If you interrupt them or offer your ideas or advice too quickly, you may cause them to lose their train of thought, offend them, or come across as being pushy or unconcerned about their needs.

PROFESSIONALISM

Professionalism is demonstrated in many ways and has different definitions for many people. The key for you is to present an image that you and your organization are proud of. Professionalism is not locked to your job title. It is more about your attitude toward the job, your organization, and your diverse customer base. It is also about the quality of your work and the personal ethics that you display in dealing with others.

- **Demonstrate enthusiasm.** If you are excited about your job and enjoy working with customers, it will show through your attitude, tone of voice, nonverbal cues, and level of energy that you demonstrate when interacting with others. Typically, customers respond positively to people who take an interest in their jobs and are knowledgeable, helpful, and willing to go beyond what customers have come to expect from many service providers. Even if you are having a bad day, do not project that to customers. That will only increase your chances of magnifying the stress that you are feeling. If you have a negative experience with one customer and then make your dissatisfaction or frustration apparent to the next customer, that person may become agitated or react negatively. You will then have to deal with that situation and become frustrated further, and so on.

 POSITIVE GLOBAL SERVICE ACTION TIP

If you have a negative customer interaction and are feeling agitated or stressed, allow a coworker to handle the next call or customer, when possible. This will allow you some time to cool off so that you will not transfer your negative feelings to the next customer. Take a short restroom or water break, walk around, talk to someone about a non-work-related topic, and just clear your mind before getting back to delivering positive global service to the next customer.

- **Show confidence.** Many customers look to service providers to be subject-matter experts related to their products, organization, and industry and expect them to deliver quality service. You should demonstrate that you are up to the task through use of words and nonverbal messages (e.g., posture, gestures, and facial cues) and through your knowledge of your organization and its products and services. With more information, you will project confidence when dealing with customers and will be better equipped to respond to customer questions and to make better decisions about a correct course of action to help meet customer needs, wants, and expectations. When communicating directly with customers through any means, always listen, show interest, be responsive, and project an image of professionalism and confidence.

POSITIVE GLOBAL SERVICE ACTION TIP

Read manufacturer information sheets about your products, visit the manufacturers' Web sites for additional information related to their companies, understand the functions of departments within your organization and how processes work, read industry-related magazines and articles, and continue to ask questions of your supervisor and peers in order to learn more about areas related to your job.

- **Remain focused on service.** Many service providers make the mistake of forgetting why they are at work. That is to do their job and service customers professionally in an effective and efficient manner. Your central focus should be on creating a positive environment in which customers can satisfy their needs and experience positive global service. When you are in a retail environment and customers are not present, get change for your register, walk around and restock items on shelves, pick up debris, or clean up any messes. If you are in a service environment, you can still straighten magazines, organize work areas, file folders or papers, get forms ready for customers, replenish office supplies, or perform other functions so that when customers call or come in, you are ready to shift your full attention to them without distractions. All these actions are important in projecting a positive and professional atmosphere that nonverbally tells customers that you value them and are ready to serve.

WORK BEHAVIORS TO AVOID

There are a number of things that you might do that can irritate customers or cause them to form a negative opinion of you or your organization. The following is a partial list of actions that you should avoid at all costs when customers are present or on the telephone.

- Bringing up sensitive topics for discussion with a customer (e.g., politics or religion)
- Performing administrative tasks (e.g., filing or working on the computer)
- Waiting until you run out of currency, coins, or forms before getting more
- Not having your computer booted up and software activated and ready to access before the start of business
- Interrupting service for one customer to deal with another's question
- Discussing personal problems or complaining about *anything* to another customer or coworker
- Conveying a sense that you are overworked or do not have time to deal with the customer's needs
- Talking about or disrespecting a competitor

Identify Yourself

Many customers like doing business with people they know or with whom they can form a relationship. By sharing your name along with a greeting whenever you come into contact with someone face-to-face, on the telephone, or in writing, you generate goodwill and start the process of bonding with your customers. These are important steps in helping develop a trusting environment in which customers are more likely to share information and be receptive to your ideas or suggestions.

- **Give a business card.** The simple act of handing a business card that identifies your organization, your position, and your contact information can go a long way to identifying you as a professional. If your organization provides cards, carry them with you in a protective case to keep them clean and unbent so that you can help promote your organization to people that you meet in lines at supermarkets or in other venues. Your job does not end when you leave the front door of your organization. Take ownership for helping to promote the organization and your job. Why would you do this? Because new customers bring revenue that pays your salary and benefits and helps the organization stay in business. In a down economy, your help may mean the difference between being employed and waiting for an unemployment check.

    People from some countries feel that their business card is an extension of them (e.g., Japan and Korea). For that reason, if someone from one of those countries gives you a card, he or she will present the card to you by holding both corners so that the person's name faces you, give a slight bow, smile, and make indirect eye contact with you. You should do likewise when sharing your card with the person. Receive cards with your right hand, since some cultures view the left as unclean because it is used as the toilet hand. Upon receiving the card, note the name and title and remember it for use as you talk; then place it on the table in front of you so that you can refer to it as you meet. Never put the card face down, write anything on it in the person's presence, put it in your pocket, or staple it to a piece of paper (use a paper clip instead). All these are potential signs of disrespect. You should also not ask for two cards without explaining your reason (e.g., you would like to pass one along to a colleague); otherwise, your customer may be concerned that you are likely to lose one of them, which is also a potential insult.

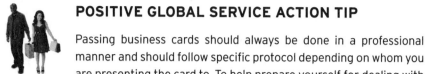

POSITIVE GLOBAL SERVICE ACTION TIP

Passing business cards should always be done in a professional manner and should follow specific protocol depending on whom you are presenting the card to. To help prepare yourself for dealing with people from various cultures and to learn the proper etiquette for using business cards, review online sources or books related to doing business in other countries or cultures. One excellent source is the book *Kiss, Bow or Shake Hands: The Best-selling Guide to Doing Business in More Than 60 Countries* by Terri Morrison and Wayne Conaway.[6]

- **Use a name tag when appropriate.** Have you gone to a restaurant, hotel, grocery store, post office, or department store lately? If so, you may have noticed that employees in all those areas typically have one thing in common—name tags. If your organization provides you with a name tag, wear it with pride where your customers can easily see your name and remember it. If your organization does not provide name tags, always introduce yourself upon meeting customers and suggest to your supervisor that the company get name tags for employees.

  One good reason for wearing your name tag is that some customers may speak a different language and not understand what you say, but they can read what is on the name tag. Even with a name tag, you should always verbally share your name with customers, because some people have visual deficits and may not be able to read it, or they may be auditory learners and better retain information that they hear.

  Getting on a friendly name basis with customers can put them at ease and may make them less likely to get upset if something minor goes wrong. They can also remember your name and ask another employee to find you if they have a question or need something else, and they can use it in providing positive feedback on their experience to your supervisor or others. Without identifying yourself to your customers, you cannot begin

to form that positive first impression that you read about earlier
or develop a trusting relationship.

• **Use a friendly, welcoming manner on the telephone.** When
someone calls your organization, you should follow established
guidelines for greeting customers. At a minimum this typically
includes a greeting, your organization's name, your name, and an
offer to assist. This may sound like, "Good morning. Thank you
for calling ABC Company. My name is Lawanda Jones. How may I
direct your call?" (or "How may I assist you?").

  This simple opening communication should be delivered
in an unhurried, upbeat, and professional manner as you smile,
since smiling can affect the tone of your voice. One thing that
many telephone service professionals have done for years is to put
on the wall next to their telephones a small mirror or button that
says "Smile" or has a smiley face to remind them to smile as they
answer the telephone.

Build Credibility

Credibility and believability are crucial aspects of the quality service
equation. This is especially true when a problem arises or a customer raises
a concern to you. The manner in which you respond and handle the situation will often determine a customer's opinion about you and your
organization.

A key element of credibility is your knowledge of the organization's
products and services. You must be able to adequately and professionally
communicate information about them to your customers. Otherwise, you
potentially lose credibility in the eyes of your customers. For example, if
you are a food server and a customer asks a question about the ingredients
of a specific item, you should be able to respond to that query with accurate
information. In the food service industry, this not only is good service but
is directly related to liability if a customer is not given an accurate account.
This is because some people have serious food allergies where exposure to
some ingredients could lead to illness or even death.

When something goes wrong, you need a strong knowledge of the
organization's policy and the level of authority that you and others have

in resolving the issue. If you lack this knowledge or the customers sense that you are unsure or hesitant, they may doubt your credibility, become angry, or demand to speak to someone who has the authority to resolve the problem.

In no case should you ever attempt to lie or "fake it" when it comes to answering questions or handling a problem that arises. You will likely be found out, and the customer will not only be incensed for being deceived but also likely to make unrealistic demands to correct the situation. You and your organization will lose credibility and trust and will probably lose the business of that customer and also everyone else who hears the story. If you cannot answer a question or handle a given situation, escalate the issue to a supervisor or ask for assistance from a knowledgeable coworker.

- **Assume responsibility.** You do not have to be a supervisor or manager to assume responsibility for helping a customer or handling a situation. You probably would not search for a supervisor or someone to deal with a fire, so it makes no sense that you would take such action when a customer needs assistance. Unless you are specifically prohibited from performing certain functions or it violates policy, law, or legal guidelines, you are probably safe assuming control of a situation and doing what needs to be done to provide positive quality customer service. There is an old adage that goes, "It is easier to apologize later than to ask for permission first." If an issue has never occurred before and you know how to resolve it professionally and within the parameters described above, go for it. Your customer will likely appreciate the fast, efficient service, and your supervisor may applaud your initiative and resourcefulness.

  When things go wrong, you should assume responsibility. For example, even if you did not create a problem for a customer, you represent your organization when the customer brings it to your attention. Apologize, determine what the issue is and what the customer expects you to do about it, and then handle the situation quickly and professionally. Your goal is to salvage the customer-provider relationship and "make the customer whole" again by compensating him or her for inconvenience and time or financial loss. If this requires higher approval, bring the matter to the attention of your team leader or supervisor.

- **Exhibit high ethical standards.** In a world that has been racked by high-profile violations of corporate *ethics* (e.g., Enron, WorldCom, Tyco International), many customers often assume that you and your organization are out to cheat them or "rip them off." Within your organization, there is also likely a sense by many employees that they cannot trust management or the organization to look out for their rights or provide for them, while managers distrust employees to perform their duties, protect organizational assets, or do the best-possible job.

The bottom line is that when customers perceive unethical behavior, there is a good probability that they will not remain loyal to your organization if something goes wrong, especially if they believe that the error occurred because you did not act in a professional manner or that an act was intentional.

One ethical challenge that you face is, again, the result of different cultures: because of differing values, some people do not view certain actions as being unethical. Since some countries have a wide gap in the distribution of wealth, it is not unusual for people on the lower end of the socioeconomic scale to perceive it as a legitimate option to take small items from a large multinational organization or employer. Thus, you have unethical employees and customers who "take" small items with little or no remorse. This does not mean that the behavior is acceptable. Wrong is wrong, and stealing or acting unethically carries with it personal, civil, and criminal penalties in many instances. Avoid such temptations and report others who participate in these acts and you should do well in creating a service environment that meets the needs and wants of your customers while serving your needs and those of your employer.

There are a number of actions that you and others can take to demonstrate high ethical standards:

- Keep your word, and stay away from activities that might be questionable (e.g., allowing a friend to benefit from

your employee discount when purchasing a product or
service).

— Strive to act in a professional manner at all times.
— Take credit for only that which you are responsible and
   actually accomplished.
— Report unethical activities to the appropriate level in your
   organization based on existing policy. If you are unsure about
   this, ask your supervisor how to handle such instances before
   they occur.
— If you are not sure whether an action is unethical, avoid
   doing it.

• **Be responsive.** In today's global business world, people expect
that you will provide products or services in a timely manner and
better than your competition. Fail to do those things and you risk
losing customers. By being prepared and having readily available
all the knowledge and tools you need to do your job, you are ready
to serve. Go out of your way to be efficient and to deliver what
you promise before or when you promised it. This will go a long
way to boosting your esteem in the eyes of customers. If you are
unsure that you can meet a promise or deadline, do not make the
commitment, because customers will hold you accountable.

CREATE A PROFESSIONAL WORK ENVIRONMENT

Customers form opinions about your organization based on many factors,
one of which is the appearance of your workplace environment. Take ownership for improving the image of the facilities and surrounding areas.
If you spot some area of maintenance that is below standard (e.g., paint
chipping off a wall, lightbulbs burned out, trash cans overflowing, or a
soiled area on a carpet), make sure to let the maintenance department or
your supervisor know so that someone can correct the problem. Be neat
and tidy, put things in their proper place when through with them, and
pick up anything that is out of place. These little efforts on your part send
a powerful message to others about your professionalism and about the
potential quality of service that customers will receive.

FOCUS ON POSITIVE GLOBAL SERVICE: IMAGE AUDIT

To get a feel for the importance of first impressions in an organization, conduct an image audit with the following checklist. If you do not currently have an employer, take a trip to any local business and conduct an audit of the facility using the checklist to record your impressions. Share your audit with your supervisor or the manager of the organization that you audited. Rate each item on a scale of 1 to 5, with 5 being the highest.

___ Overall appearance of the exterior of the building
___ Cleanliness (e.g., area free of debris and trash cans empty)
___ External maintenance (e.g., lightbulbs working, sidewalks free of stains and mold, paint in good condition, sidewalks and parking area free of holes and large cracks)
___ Overall appearance of the interior of the building
___ Interior maintenance (e.g., lightbulbs working, carpets and floors free of stains or spills, paint in good condition, restrooms clean and well maintained)
___ Work areas well lit, uncluttered, and free of unsightly piles of materials
___ Friendly, professional greeting received by customers upon arrival
___ Service professionals presenting a positive personal image (e.g., appropriate grooming, hygiene, and dress)
___ Service professionals knowledgeable and helpful.
___ Service delivered promptly.

SUMMARY

Throughout this chapter, you have read about what it takes to create a positive professional image and the various aspects that can influence your customer's perceptions of you and your organization. As you explored the concepts of the chapter, you found that:

- Factors like tone of voice, responsiveness, knowledge, ability to help resolve an issue, and manners (or lack of them) can often impact the outcome of a customer interaction.
- First impressions are crucial and often lasting.

- From the time you first come into contact with a customer until the time a transaction ends, you are sending messages about yourself and your organization.
- Your degree of professionalism and enthusiasm when you greet customers can leave them feeling excited about working with you and your organization.
- In a multicultural world, you also have to remember that people from many cultures have specific expectations related to employee appearance.
- The manner in which you present yourself through grooming and hygiene and your manner of dress send a powerful message of either indifference or professionalism.
- In many instances tattoos and piercings not only raise some eyebrows but also can cause a negative customer reaction based on stereotypes of people who have such things.
- If your organization has gone to casual or dress-down days, remember that the word *casual* should not be interpreted as "sloppy."
- Unlike many other nonverbal cues used around the world, the smile is one of those, with a few exceptions, that can universally signal friendliness or friendship and acceptance.
- Simple eye contact can alert customers to the fact that you see them and are ready to respond to their needs, answer questions, or assist them if needed.
- Simply by using your customer's name, you may put your relationship with the customer on a positive track.
- When working with customers, your goal should be to build rapport and trust and create a situation in which you are both on the same wavelength.
- One strategy that you can use to develop rapport with customers is to apply concepts from the field of neurolinguistic programming.
- Gestures can send powerful positive or negative messages.
- Matching a customer's rate of speech is crucial to understanding.

- Basic expressions of good manners such as "please" and "thank you" are simple tools for demonstrating that you value and respect your customers.
- Demonstrate patience by listening to what your customers have to say to the point where you understand the issue and can assist them effectively.
- Your central focus should be on creating a positive environment in which customers can satisfy their needs and experience positive global service.
- Credibility and believability are crucial aspects of the quality service equation.
- You do not have to be a supervisor or manager to assume responsibility for helping a customer or handling a situation.
- When customers perceive unethical behavior, there is a good probability that they will not remain loyal to your organization if something goes wrong.
- In today's global business world, people expect that you will provide products or services in a timely manner and better than your competition.

CHAPTER

4

Improving Interpersonal Communication Skills

No matter what language people speak, the key to effective communication is to approach each message with a desire to understand and share information appropriately with your customers.

KEY CONCEPTS

After reading this chapter and when applying concepts learned, you will be able to:

1. Explain how differences in native language might impact quality positive global customer service.
2. Describe how people from different parts of the world should be addressed from a service standpoint.
3. Define communication and identify what you need to know to effectively interact with your customers.
4. Discuss what might lead to service breakdowns and what you can do to avoid them.
5. Determine strategies for serving different types of customers.

6. Recognize how generalizations and perceptions affect quality service.
7. Apply guidelines for overcoming stereotypes.

As a service provider, you must like people, because you will come into contact with all sizes, shapes, colors, and types every day. If you prepare properly and gain knowledge about various common characteristics related to different groups, you will be able to effectively recognize what is important to the individuals within those groups.

To prepare yourself for success, get to know as much as you can about psychology and sociology, because you will be using skills in those areas when dealing with a diverse customer population. Also, master the wide array of service technologies that you can use to provide more powerful service to your clients. These include old standards like the telephone and fax machine, as well as newer methods such as Twitter, e-mail, and text messaging. By accomplishing these things, you will be on your way to achieving career success while building strong customer-provider relationships.

SPEAKING THE LANGUAGE OF THE WORLD

According to the book *Ethnologue: Languages of the World*,[1] there are 6,909 languages spoken throughout the world. The top 10 languages (in order) spoken by over half the world's population are Chinese (Mandarin), Spanish, English, Hindi, Arabic, Bengali, Portuguese, Russian, Japanese, and German.[2] With this degree of linguistic diversity it is no wonder that people have trouble communicating. Couple the language diversity with the transient nature of people as they regularly travel and relocate, the practice of offshoring (transferring jobs to other countries), and the spread of Internet use, and you are likely to encounter on any given day a customer who does not speak your primary language. It is likely that you will have a breakdown in the exchange of information and potentially in the customer-provider relationship at some point as a service provider.

The issue of communication breakdowns is further complicated by the fact that even when two people speak the same language (e.g., English), they often use different words for the same items. Even within the same country (e.g., the United States), there is often regional terminology that can be confusing.

DIFFERENCES IN WORD AND PHRASE USAGE BETWEEN ENGLISH SPEAKERS

United Kingdom	United States
Biscuit	Cracker or cookie
Car boot	Car trunk
Chips	French fries
Cooker	Stove
Hire purchase	Layaway or installment
Jersey	Sweater
Loo	Toilet
Pants	Underwear
Parcel	Package
Pumps	Tennis shoes
Queue	Line
Ring you up	Telephone
Rubber	Eraser
Silencer	Car muffler
Telly	Television
Toilet	Restroom
Twigs	Pretzels

REGIONAL DIFFERENCES IN WORDS AND PHRASES IN THE UNITED STATES

North/Midland/West	South
Bedroom slippers	House shoes
Dinner	Supper
Momentarily	Directly
Faucet	Spigot
Frappe	Milkshake
Lightning bug	Firefly
Man's wallet	Billfold
Pail	Bucket
Pit	Seed
Shopping cart	Buggy
To get ready	Fix or fixing to
You (plural)	Y'all

FOCUS ON POSITIVE GLOBAL SERVICE: DIFFERENT MEANINGS

To help raise your awareness of how people might speak a common language but use different terminology to describe similar things or activities, think about words or phrases that you have heard from your own experiences that differ from those used to describe the same thing in the country or area where you now reside or work. List them here:

_____

_____

_____

What problems have language differences such as these caused?

_____

_____

DIFFERENT STROKES FOR DIFFERENT FOLKS

The phrase "different strokes for different folks" was popularized in the song "Everyday People" by the musical group Sly and the Family Stone in 1968. That sentiment sums up how service providers should approach the diverse customer base of today. One of your biggest challenges in working with a diverse customer base is that no two people are alike, nor do they have the same expectations, needs, or wants, nor do they have the same knowledge, skills, or abilities related to communication. You will likely encounter people who have language deficits and physical or mental disabilities or other characteristics that can inhibit communication and understanding. In other cases, they may be unable to communicate effectively or may simply be too impatient to listen effectively during a service interaction. In all these instances, your goal should be to remain professional and know how to address the needs and wants of your customers. In many cases, you may have to guide the communication exchange in order to get the information that you need to service your customers.

A key point to remember when interacting with people who are different from you is that their communication styles and preferences may differ from yours. For example, many people from North America tend to be more direct and informal than people in other regions. They often make direct eye contact and may assume more businesslike postures. Many Hispanic and Middle Easterners use intense eye contact or appear to stare as they speak. In parts of the Middle East, the phrase "The eyes are the windows to the soul" is taken to heart. This glaring eye contact makes many people outside Middle Eastern cultures uncomfortable. On the other hand, people from an Eastern culture may be put off by direct eye contact or language that they might view as a sign of arrogance or disrespect in their country. They could also be offended by what they perceive is a forceful approach, since people in some countries (e.g., Japan, Korea, or Thailand) use a more indirect or vague communication style. For example, rather than simply telling you no when something cannot be done, someone from an Asian culture might agree to do what you request with no intention of following through. In Japan, there are over a dozen ways to say no without ever using the word. Customers from such cultures might create a response to your request for something in an ambiguous manner such as "That might be difficult." Phrasing it this way, they have avoided embarrassing you by denying or rejecting your request outright. Their intent is to save you *face*, or esteem, in the eyes of others who might overhear the conversation. Face is an important value in such countries. As a service provider, you should be conscious of this approach to communication when working with customers from these cultures.

Greetings also differ from one culture to another. For example, men from Western and European cultures often smile and extend their right hands to shake when meeting someone. In other cultures a bow might be more appropriate (e.g., Korea or Japan). A Middle Eastern customer might give a slight nod or bow, shake hands, and exchange kisses on both cheeks. A traditional Muslim man will often shake hands and then touch the palm of the right hand to his heart as a show of friendship. Women in many non-Westernized cultures hug or kiss other women on the cheek and are uncomfortable or forbidden to touch a male who is not their husband (e.g., Middle Eastern or Japanese). If you are a woman, do not be surprised if a Middle Eastern man avoids shaking your hand during a business transaction; if you are a man, do not expect that same male customer to introduce the women who accompany him. The appropriate way to deal with greeting your customers is to smile, greet them verbally, and pause to see what they do; then follow their lead.

POSITIVE GLOBAL SERVICE ACTION TIP

Choose one language that you do not speak and take classes in it in order to better serve your diverse customer base. Many organizations actively recruit and pay a bonus to employees who speak second languages.

THE COMMUNICATION PROCESS

Communication is a transactional process of designing, delivering, receiving, and interpreting messages that share knowledge and information through verbal and nonverbal means and via various channels (e.g., face-to-face, over the telephone, and in writing). It involves the creation of messages that allow others to extract the meaning and understanding that you intend in order to avoid confusion and encourage consensus. It also includes the interpretation of messages that you receive. Because of the diverse nature of the world, people often filter messages that they receive differently based on their own values, beliefs, education level, experiences, language capabilities, age, personalities, and a variety of other factors.

To share information effectively and efficiently with your customers, you need solid communication skills, knowledge about the manner in which people from different parts of the world communicate, and the self-confidence to interact positively with others who are not like you. Part of being successful in the service profession is to periodically self-evaluate and update your knowledge, skills, and customer service practices. Like anything else, the more often you practice your service and communication skills, the better you are likely to get at them.

POSITIVE GLOBAL SERVICE ACTION TIP

In addition to strategies like the personality-style self-assessment you completed in Chapter 2, you should seek out more knowledge about yourself. Ask people who know you well (e.g., peers, supervisor, friends, relatives, and regular customers) to provide you with regular feedback on your communication skills related to verbal, nonverbal, and listening skills. Ask them to be honest—not nice—in sharing their observations about your approach to communicating with others. Don't forget to thank them for their input, since courtesy is one of the core elements of positive global customer service.

COMMUNICATING EFFECTIVELY

Effective communication skills can lead to more positive customer-provider relationships and stronger interactions in your personal life. They can affect trust, respect, morale, productivity, job performance, self-esteem, and much more.

A failure to communicate effectively can cause conflict in a service environment. This might occur when customers interact with you or another employee and receive what they believe is inaccurate or contradictory information. For example, if one of your employees told a customer that he thought a product would be available on the fourteenth of the month, and it turned out that it wouldn't be in the store until the fifteenth, the customer would surely be upset upon arriving at your organization on the fourteenth and going home empty-handed. The customer might have misunderstood because he had poor listening skills and because he really wanted the product as soon as possible. What he likely heard was only a portion of the service representative's statement: "The latest version of our product will be released on Wednesday, the fourteenth, and be in our store the next day." Unfortunately, you now have to use your active listening skills effectively to determine the issue and then attempt to appease the customer and correct the situation.

As you will read in Chapter 9 on service recovery, there are a number of strategies to use in such instances when communication and service break down with customers. In this instance, start with a sincere apology and tell the customer what you can do to assist him. You might apologize for the misinformation and offer to have the item delivered for free on the fifteenth. In this manner, you have shown remorse for the error caused (even if it might not have been your coworker's fault). You have also shown empathy and offered a viable solution to the problem by telling the customer what you can do, not what you cannot do. Of course, you should find out the level of your personal authority to handle such situations before they ever occur by speaking with your supervisor in advance. Ask what level of authority you have to resolve such issues when they occur in the future. This will preclude you from having to go check with a supervisor when a customer situation arises.

POSITIVE GLOBAL SERVICE ACTION TIP

Ensure that you plan and deliver your messages effectively and then make sure the customer clearly understood your intended message. This will help keep you from putting yourself, your coworkers, or the organization in a situation where there might be a customer-provider breakdown.

Strategies for Avoiding Service Breakdowns

Service breakdowns cost your organization money and should be avoided whenever possible. In addition to product and service glitches, there might be interpersonal, cultural, environmental, or other factors that can lead to misunderstandings or a failure to meet customer needs, wants, or expectations. Since you are human, there is a chance that errors or mistakes will occur. Do your best to limit them, and when they happen, take proactive steps to correct the situation immediately with as little inconvenience to your customers as possible.

The following are some strategies that you might use to avoid breakdowns in customer-provider relationships.

Plan Your Messages Effectively

You must think before you speak. If you are unsure about a product, service, policy, information, or course of action, it is best to ask a customer to wait while you verify it. In the example you read in the last section, this might have prevented the problem from occurring and, as a result, the customer from being inconvenienced.

Use Positive Language

We have all known people who act as naysayers and challenge virtually every idea or suggestion that someone else offers. Such people can be a real detriment to positive global customer service if they act this way with internal and external customers. They might be simply trying to get all the information about an issue on the table before processing it and coming to a decision. In many cases they are not being malicious; they simply do not think before they speak or write something. Failing to look at your messages from the customer's standpoint can potentially lead to a customer-provider relationship breakdown.

Take a look at the sidebar "Turning Negative to Positive Language" to see how a negatively worded message might be communicated in a more positive manner. While the first example is efficient and polite, it may be perceived as impersonal, businesslike, or challenging or as an attempt to make the customers look like they are wrong. It also focuses on what the company needs, not what the customers need. The second example is more upbeat; it asks for the same information but works toward collaboration and a positive relationship. It also indicates that the organization is working for the customers and looking out for their interests.

TURNING NEGATIVE TO POSITIVE LANGUAGE

First, the negatively worded example:

> We regret to inform you that we are unable to approve your home refinance loan because you failed to provide a copy of your tax return to substantiate your income for the past year. You also failed to complete the area for your wife's employment on your application form.
>
> If we do not get this information by [date], we will assume you do not want to proceed with the loan application and we will terminate the process.

And now the positively worded example:

> Thank you for considering ABC Financial as a source for your home mortgage refinance loan. We are excited about the possibility of working with you on this deal and look forward to getting your application moving through the approval process. Please provide a copy of your tax return for last year and the name and address of your wife's employer by [date] so that we can validate income and work toward your desired closing date. If you have questions about this, please contact . . .

Avoid "You" Language

While the word *you* by itself is not a bad or negative word, it can be perceived negatively by some people based on their personality style, especially in emotionally charged situations. It might come across as sounding like verbal "finger-pointing." This is because the word can sound accusatory and potentially put someone on the defensive. For example, assume that a customer mailed back an item purchased online without contacting your organization for a return authorization number as indicated in your Web site return policy. Once the item arrives at the warehouse, you call the customer and state "Ms. Wu, I am calling because we received the product that you returned to our warehouse. You were supposed to contact us in advance to get a return authorization number before shipping the item back to us . . ." Notice that this language sounds accusatory and like a personal attack, especially in the way it uses the word *you*, and also makes an assumption that the customer made an error even before all the information about the situation has been gathered. For all you know, she might have called, gotten a number, and simply failed to reference it with the return shipment. At any rate, this approach potentially offends the customer and basically puts you in a parent-to-child communication mode where you seem to be talking down to your customer.

Monitor Customer Communication

Stay alert to verbal and nonverbal nuances in the messages your customers send. Listen for tone of voice and watch facial and body reactions to your statements and in the messages they deliver. Effective communication involves being able to "read" the other person during a conversation and respond appropriately to any subtle reactions from the person.

There needs to be continual verbal and nonverbal feedback from both parties during a conversation. This helps ensure that messages intended were accurately received. One simple strategy for providing feedback to your customers is to *paraphrase* what you think they said. For example, if a customer said, "I came into your store yesterday to look at shoes. The clerk brought out four or five boxes to show me, and I ended up buying two identical pairs of shoes in different colors without trying on both pairs. When I got home, I realized that one box had two different-sized shoes in it." In response, you should start with an apology for the inconvenience and then paraphrase to ensure you understood the message. After you paraphrase, always validate that your perception of what the customer said is correct. You might say something like, "Ms. Thornton, I apologize for the error. I know that this is frustrating and an inconvenience for you. I'll be glad to help correct the issue right away. Just to be sure that I understand the problem, you came in yesterday, bought two pairs of the same shoe style in different colors, and one pair has mismatched sizes. Is that correct?" Paraphrasing is a powerful tool for putting your customer's message into your own words and repeating it back to the customer. It serves to show the customer that you were actively listening while also helping you ensure that you heard the message correctly. That way, you do not respond inappropriately.

Speak Clearly

The manner in which you speak can impact how others receive your message. Your speed of delivery can also affect reception. People often talk in their primary language quickly and in many cases slur or use contracted versions of words (e.g., in English by dropping the *g* ending from words to create shortened versions such as *doin', gettin', seein'*). This can cause challenges for people who speak another language and are trying hard to listen, translate your message mentally, and get your intended message. Even when someone speaks your primary language, such shortcuts can create language breakdowns or barriers to understanding. Keep in mind that others do not have your knowledge or skills and may not be able to communicate at the same level at which you do. Be sure to always follow the rules of *grammar, punctuation,* and *syntax* (the ways in which words and sentences are structured) in order to facilitate sound communication. Make sure that you pronounce words correctly and enunciate each syllable of a word clearly.

Ask Questions

The easiest way to get information from your customer is to ask the right type of question and then listen to the response. There are many types of questions, but they generally fall into two categories—open- and closed-ended.

Open-ended questions typically begin with words or phrases such as *who, when, what, why, how,* or *to what degree.* They are designed to gather large amounts of information and to allow your customer to talk. You should use this type of question to discover customer needs, wants, and expectations and to identify information that will assist in resolving product or service breakdown. The following are some examples of open-ended questions:

- What are some of the features you are looking for in _____?
- In your opinion, why do you believe that _____ is so important?
- To what degree has _____ been helpful in the previous model that you purchased?

Closed-ended questions are generally used to validate information that you heard, verify information, or get an affirmation or agreement through a short response. Be careful not to ask only closed-ended question, because they cause you to do most of the talking and limit the amount of valuable information that the customer provides. This type of question typically starts with a verb, such as *can, did, is, was, should, could,* or *are.* The following are examples of closed-ended questions:

- Is this the correct item?
- Should I use the home phone number you provided as a point of contact?
- Could you please verify your home address for me?

Use Silence Effectively

Many cultures view silence from different perspectives. By understanding this basic fact, you can avoid potential service breakdowns when interacting with your customers.

Silence might result from a cultural standpoint when someone has been taught that those who are older or in a position of higher status should not be challenged in any way. For example, many cultures teach the value of respect for elders; therefore, if you are an older service provider or a salesperson dealing with younger customers, they might be reluctant to ask questions or challenge what you are saying. Similarly, the value of being humble is important in many Hispanic, North American Indian, and Asian cultures. If you tend to be more outgoing or dominant in your communication style when interacting with customers from such a culture, they may not ask questions that will help them make a buying decision or get the information they need to help resolve a concern.

Check Your Perceptions

When communicating with others, especially those who speak another primary language, you must follow the rules for effective communication (e.g., grammar, syntax, pronunciation, and enunciation) in order to be understood. Avoid jargon, slang, acronyms, and technical terms unless you define them for your customers and make sure that they understand what you are saying. If they appear puzzled based on nonverbal cues or something they say in response, repeat, clarify, or phrase what you said differently. You can also do a quick *perception check* to ensure that they received the message you intended.

Respect Personal Space Preferences

The term *proxemics,* or personal space, as coined by researcher Edward T. Hall in 1966,[3] refers to the physical distance between people in various social and business settings. Each culture has established, but unspoken, acceptable distances from which people feel comfortable interacting with one another. This space varies depending on the relationship among the people engaged in a conversation. People typically stand closer to family members, friends, and those they love than they do to business associates or strangers.

If you violate someone's personal space, you can cause uneasiness and social discomfort, which can ultimately end in customer-provider breakdowns. For example, in the United States people typically shake hands and then maintain a space of about 18 inches (approximately 45.7 centimeters) to 4 feet (approximately 1.22 meters), depending on group size, as they talk in a business setting. People from Japan tend to be more formal; as a result, following a bow and handshake, customers might look down and step back slightly to open the distance between themselves and the people they are speaking to. In contrast, some people from Russia, parts of Europe, and the Middle East tend to stand closer and in more direct contact with others during service encounters than might be comfortable for those outside their cultures. Based on the cultural values of someone's native country, the norms related to interactions with others are often different.

WORDS AND PHRASES THAT CAN DAMAGE CUSTOMER RELATIONSHIPS

Here are some words and phrases that can lead to trouble with your customers. Some sound harsh or rude, while others do not project a positive global customer service attitude. Try to avoid or limit their use.

You don't understand.	Do you understand?
You're not listening to me.	Listen to me.
You'll have to or need to . . .	You don't see my point.
I never said that.	You're wrong.
It's my opinion that . . .	Hang (or hold) on a second.
I (we) can't . . .	What's your problem?
Our policy prohibits . . .	Policy says . . .
Problem.	You are required . . .
I don't know.	No.
I'll try . . .	I need you to . . .
What you need to do is . . .	But . . .
You must, have to, or should . . .	That's not my job (responsibility).
Are you aware that . . .?	Endearment terms—e.g., *honey, baby, sweetie*

WORDS AND PHRASES THAT CAN BUILD CUSTOMER RELATIONSHIPS

Here are some words and phrases that can help build stronger relationships with your customers by putting a positive spin or tone on what you are communicating to them. Language such as this goes a long way to building trust and sending a message that you care about your customers' needs, wants, and expectations.

Please.	Thank you.
You're right.	Yes.
What I can or will do is . . .	May I . . .?
I'm sorry, or I apologize.	It was my error.
Have you considered . . .?	How may I assist you?
However, and yet (instead of *but*) . . .	It's my (our) fault.
What do you think?	Would you mind if . . .?
I appreciate . . .	I understand (appreciate) how you feel.

PERCEPTION CHECKING

To see if your perception of a customer's reaction to your message was correct, follow these steps:

1. Identify the *behavior observed.*
   Example: Mr. Bernardes, when I said it would be 7 to 10 days before we could get your new computer delivered to your home, your facial expression changed to what appeared to be one of concern.

2. Offer one or two *interpretations.*
   Example: I wasn't sure if you were indicating that the time frame doesn't work for you or if you had something else go through your mind.

3. Ask for *clarification.*
   Example: Which was it?

By giving customers an opportunity to provide input or clarify, you reduce the chance of later having dissatisfied them. You also send a message that you are paying attention to them.

SPATIAL DISTANCES IN THE UNITED STATES

- **Intimate distance: 0–18 inches.** This distance is typically reserved for your family and intimate relations.
- **Personal distance: 18 inches–4 feet.** This is often reserved for your close friends and business colleagues.
- **Social and work distance: 4–12 feet.** Usually you would maintain this space at casual business events and during business transactions.
- **Public distance: 12 or more feet.** You would probably maintain this space at large gatherings, activities, or presentations.

SERVING DIFFERENT CUSTOMERS

You can help assure service success when interacting with all customers by simply focusing on their needs, wants, and expectations and delivering the same quality of positive global customer service that you have read about up to this point. The following are some thoughts related to a number of diverse groups that may help ensure that you are serving your customers well.

Religious Customers

Some service providers have encountered service challenges as a result of their personal beliefs and lack of knowledge about people who practice different *religions* and dress or behave in a different manner because of their religious beliefs. You may have witnessed that since the 9/11 terrorist attacks in the United States, some people espouse negative views of individuals who are Muslim or are from cultures in which many women choose to wear the traditional *hijab* clothing—consisting of a scarf that covers the head and loose-fitting dress that conceals the body form—or in which men dress in traditional ankle-length garb with long sleeves, called a *thawb* in Arabic.

Because of their beliefs and the type of clothing they wear, many people from various religions and cultures often endure negative jokes, stories, events, and otherwise discriminatory actions by many people. Make sure that you do not project such negativity toward your customers either consciously or unconsciously when you encounter them. Not only are such actions ethically and morally wrong, but they are also illegal in many instances. When serving your customers, you should remember to take a proactive approach to providing quality global service to everyone with whom you come into contact.

POSITIVE GLOBAL SERVICE ACTION TIP

Research the major religions of the world that are prevalent in your country in order to better understand and relate to your customers. When the opportunity arises to interact with people from a different religion, get to know them and discuss their beliefs and culture. The more you understand people, the better you can serve them.

Disabled Customers

According to a report by the U.S. Census Bureau in 2008, of the 291.1 million people in the population, 54.4 million (18.7 percent) had some level of *disability* and 35 million (12 percent) had a severe disability.[4] These numbers are projected to grow as the population ages.

To address the needs of these people, laws that provide required accommodations and opportunities for people with disabilities have been passed in the United States [e.g., Americans with Disabilities Act of 1990 (ADA) and ADA Amendments Act of 2008] and many other countries. As a service provider, you and your organization must comply with these laws.

Depending on the types of disability that customers have, you may have to adapt your service delivery style a bit in order to meet their needs. Remember not to stereotype people because they have a type of disability. Just because someone has a sight or hearing impairment does not mean that he or she has the same degree of sensory loss as another customer with those disabilities. It is best to always ask customers if you suspect they need an accommodation or assistance rather than assuming and doing the wrong thing, which might cause offense or embarrassment.

The following are some strategies for providing services based on disability type:

- **Avoid patronizing.** Even if they have special needs, people with disabilities are basically the same as your nondisabled customers. Therefore, you must treat them the same. Avoid the appearance of "talking down" to customers with disabilities. A physical or mental disability does not mean that they should be valued less as a customer or person.
- **Refer to the person, not the disability.** Instead of referring to a person based on his or her disability (e.g., the blind man or woman) when talking to someone else, refer to the person based some other characteristic (e.g., the man or woman in the blue shirt or blouse). Better yet, simply say, "The man or woman who needs or wants . . ."
- **Ask before offering assistance.** Just as you would ask someone without a disability whether you might provide assistance, hold a door, or carry a package, do the same for a person with a disability.
- **Be respectful.** The amount of respect you show to all customers should be at a consistently high level. This includes tone of voice (showing patience), gestures, eye contact, and other communication techniques.

POSITIVE GLOBAL SERVICE ACTION TIP

Search online for resources and advocacy groups in order to educate yourself about the capabilities and needs of customers with various disabilities. Also, search for legislation related to the disabled in your country so that you are aware of requirements that you and your organization must meet in serving customers.

Elderly Customers

One of the biggest mistakes some service providers make, especially younger ones, is assuming that older people need more help or have disabilities (e.g., sight or hearing impairments). Do not make such mistakes when you are serving your customers. In fact, many older customers are in excellent physical and mental shape, are still employed, and have more time to be active now than when they were younger. Some studies show that senior citizens have more disposable income now than at any other time in history.

Often, many older customers do have preconceived ideas about what quality service looks like because of their experience, and they expect it. This is why you should strive to provide quality global customer service to them and all your other customers. Use the same sound service skills that you've been using and that you've read about thus far when interacting with these customers.

The following strategies will come in handy when interacting with older customers:

- **Maintain respect.** As you would with any other customer, be respectful. Even if the customer seems a bit arrogant, disoriented, or disrespectful, don't lose your professionalism. Recognize that sometimes these behaviors are a response to perceptions based on your cues. When this happens, quickly evaluate your behavior and make adjustments, if necessary. If an older customer seems abrupt in his or her response, think about whether you might have non-verbally signaled impatience because of your perception that he or she was slow in acting or responding.

- **Guard against biases.** Be careful not to let your perceptions about older people interfere with good service. Also, do not use age-based comments when referring to an older coworker or external customer, since these may cause people to form opinions about your level of professionalism or your beliefs regarding older people as a result. Either could cause problems in the workplace and ultimately impact service potential.

- **Answer questions.** Providing information to customers is crucial in order to help them make reasonable decisions. Even though you may have just explained something, listen to the customer's questions, respond, and restate. If it appears that the customer has misunderstood, try repeating the information, possibly using slightly different words.

- **Do not patronize.** If you appear to talk down to older customers, problems could arise and you could lose a customer or generate complaints to your manager. Customers who are elderly should not be treated as if they are senile! A condescending attitude will often cause any customer, elderly or otherwise, to take his or her business elsewhere.

- **Don't become overly familiar.** A mistake that some service providers make is that they become too familiar with their customers. In the case of senior citizens this might mean adopting references used by their accompanying children or grandchildren (e.g., *grandpa, grammy,* or *mommy*). For example, if a child referred to someone as "grammy" and then you later commented that "Grammy will probably like this" when referring to a product you are discussing, you might be perceived as rude, disrespectful, or intrusive. Or imagine how you would feel if you and your spouse or significant other were shopping and you used a pet name (*sugar* or *baby*) in front of a service provider who later said something like, "What do you think of this, Sugar?" In either instance, you have crossed the line from professional service provider to someone who assumes that you can take such communication liberties. This is not a safe assumption and might damage the customer-provider relationship.

International Customers

There are many issues to consider when interacting with people from other countries. Their experiences, expectations, communication abilities, values, and many other factors could differ from yours. The following are some things to consider when serving international customers:

- **Use humor and sarcasm cautiously.** People from various cultures have different interpretations about what is humorous or not, often based on their cultural values and beliefs and what is acceptable in their countries. Comments that focus on various aspects of diversity (e.g., religion, sex, sexual preference, weight, hair color, age, or social status) can be offensive and should not be made. In general, because humor and sarcasm do not cross cultural boundaries well, you should avoid using them with international customers. Each culture has a different interpretation of what is humorous and socially acceptable. Err on the side of conservatism and caution rather than risking offense.

- **Use nonverbal cues cautiously.** The nonverbal cues that you are familiar with may carry different meanings in other cultures. Be careful when you use symbols or gestures if you are not certain how your customer will receive them. As you will read in Chapter 5, some nonverbal cues that are common in one culture might have negative meanings in others. An example of this is beckoning by curling and uncurling your index finger. In the United States, this is a gesture intended to get someone to come to you; however, in Australia or Hong Kong, it might be used for calling animals or ladies of the evening.

THE IMPACT OF PERCEPTIONS ON COMMUNICATION

Communication with customers can break down because of conscious or unconscious views that you have about others. People often make *generalizations* about others as a result of *perceptions* they might have. In some instances, these generalizations are made out of careless disregard even though the person might know better, while in others they are based on ignorance or lack of knowledge about other groups. A good example of how some service providers might generalize can be seen when they lump together all customers who speak Spanish (e.g., Mexicans, Puerto Ricans, and Spaniards). While such people have a commonality in their base language, they are not the same culturally and do not share the same historical experiences. In fact, since most people take pride in their home countries, a customer will likely become offended if you assume that there is no difference between the groups based on their common language or make comments that show you know nothing about their cultures.

Such lapses can create a feeling that you are not knowledgeable about the world or do not care to learn about your customers. In either case you will do little to build rapport with them.

One form of such perceptions is a *stereotype*. Stereotypes are widely held beliefs that you might have of other people or groups. Stereotypes typically arise from partial truths, misinformation, and assumptions based on something that you have read, heard, or otherwise experienced in your life. There are positive stereotypes (e.g., Italians are great lovers) and negative ones (e.g., women are inferior to men at math).

When these stereotypes are negative, they can project an attitude of prejudice. Often these notions are a result of *ethnocentrism*. This is the belief that you or your own cultural group is superior to someone else or another cultural group. Negative stereotypes generally result from some life experience that taught us that certain individuals or groups have less value than we do. Unfortunately, unless you grew up in a bubble, you have experienced such teachings. Most people know on a rational level, though, that acting on negative stereotypes is inappropriate and hurtful.

Another potential obstacle to positive global customer service might be your perception about gender roles in your native culture. Because many cultures have clearly defined roles that men and women can or should assume in society, it is often difficult for some service providers to separate personal beliefs from quality service standards when interacting with a customer of a different gender. No matter what your personal beliefs might be related to gender, you must not let them interfere in the delivery of quality service in such instances.

FOCUS ON POSITIVE GLOBAL SERVICE: SUBCONSCIOUS GENDER STEREOTYPES

Many people have been conditioned since they were young children about what are considered acceptable gender roles for males and females in their culture. Often these beliefs create challenges when serving customers.

To identify potential predispositions that you may have related to gender roles that are assigned to men and women in your society, give your first impression for each term on the following page. Do not think about the word; just react by placing an *F* by words that you feel best describe females, an *M* by those that describe males, and a *B* by those that could describe both females and males. Don't change an answer later.

___ Truck driver	___ Soccer/football player	___ Skydiver
___ Airline pilot	___ Pastry baker	___ Chef
___ Baseball fan	___ Dog groomer	___ Bus driver
___ Entrepreneur	___ Service professional	___ Nurse
___ Romantic	___ Courageous	___ Emotional
___ Spontaneous	___ Impatient	___ Goal-oriented
___ Sensitive	___ Funny	___ Powerful
___ Strong	___ Competitive	___ Loving
___ Outspoken	___ Assertive	___ Talkative
___ Nurturing	___ Intelligent	___ Driven
___ Intuitive	___ Sexy	___ Critical

Once you have finished, go back and to see how many of each letter you recorded. Most people typically have a mix of all three. If you look closely and think of all the people you have known or heard or read about in your lifetime, you probably know some who fall into both categories. Therefore, if there is even one incident where an adjective could describe the gender opposite from the one that you've indicated, you may have some hidden stereotypes related to men or women and the gender roles they can and should fill. This does not mean that you are prejudiced. It simply means that you may want to work on expanding your knowledge about others and on trying to develop a more open-minded perspective so that you do not inadvertently do or say anything that might endanger the customer-provider relationship.

POSITIVE GLOBAL SERVICE ACTION TIP

Make copies of the "Focus on Positive Global Service: Subconscious Gender Stereotypes" activity and give them out to a group of your friends or peers. After all of you have completed the exercise, get together to discuss your answers and develop strategies for prevention of stereotypes in the future.

OVERCOMING STEREOTYPES

When you hold a stereotype about someone, you apply one negative example to all people in the group to which a representative person belongs. Once one example surfaces that seems to substantiate a stereotype, it may only reinforce your negative perception. As a result, the level of service that you provide might not be appropriate. You should never treat people differently based on stereotypes or even talk about any group of people in general terms. As a service provider, doing so can create a problem, because others may form an opinion about you or your organization as a result of what they hear you say. You must guard against verbalizing generalizations in the workplace; otherwise, a customer may think, "Well if he [or she] says that about ____, I wonder what is being said about me or my group when I am not around?"

Negative perceptions can cost in terms of lost customers and revenue. Remember that you have internal as well as external customers. If you use derogatory terms toward others, share offensive jokes that project stereotypes, or use noninclusive or discriminatory language, you are setting yourself up for failure. There is no room in today's workplace for what some consider as humor or prejudiced beliefs and actions. Most organizations have a zero-tolerance policy against such activities, and you could lose your job and have trouble finding a suitable alternative if you do not adhere to acceptable standards of behavior.

As a service provider, it is your job to maintain a positive service attitude toward all customers and to deliver the best-possible service that you can provide in any customer-provider encounter. No matter what your personal beliefs or feelings are about a particular person or group, you have a responsibility as an organizational representative to focus on customers in a manner that sends a positive message about your employer. Remember that you represent the organization when dealing with customers and potential customers.

There is no place in today's business environment for stereotyping. Your goal as a service provider should be to treat everyone with whom you come into contact equally and address their individual needs, wants, and expectations.

The following are some guidelines for avoiding stereotypes in a service environment:

- **Educate yourself.** Gather knowledge about various groups, religions, countries, disabilities, and other diverse elements that make up today's world. This is the major way in which you can help eliminate personal prejudices and can also help deter others from exhibiting them in the workplace.

- **Speak up about biases.** If you hear someone making a biased comment toward a specific group or individual, say something. Correct misperceptions, or simply point out that the comment is a negative stereotype that makes you uncomfortable and ask the person not to behave or talk that way around you. Silence conveys acceptance, and the last thing you need in the workplace is to have others believe that you are prejudiced or biased.
- **Interact with people on a personal level.** Take the time to get to know a little about your customers and coworkers, if possible. The more you learn about an individual or a group, the more likely you are to provide successful positive global customer service.
- **Build a diverse personal and professional network.** Think about the people who are in your current personal network of friends and family. Many times, without consciously trying, we associate with people who "look like us" or have similar interests and beliefs. If this is the case for you, consciously seek out people from diverse cultural, ethnic, racial, age, religious, socioeconomic, and other groups and get to know more about them and their values and beliefs. What you learn will help you enhance your ability to provide service to customers.
- **Experience other cultures.** If you get the opportunity to travel to other countries, take it. By visiting other cultures and interacting with people outside your own culture, you learn acceptance and start to realize why certain people might think or behave as they do. Two simple ways to experience other people and cultures on a local level is to befriend people from other cultures wherever possible and to seek out restaurants that serve the cuisine of other countries and eat there periodically. Typically, these establishments will be staffed by people from those countries. You can strike up conversations with management and servers and learn small facts about their home country.

- **Serve all customers equitably.** Even if you have strong feelings about an individual or a group, make sure that you do not let them influence your professionalism or level of service. If you feel that you cannot assist a customer because of your beliefs, politely excuse yourself and go get a coworker or supervisor to do so. If that is not an option, hide your feelings and strive to provide positive global service. Other customers may witness your efforts. Their reaction and degree of satisfaction with you and your organization will often be determined by the manner in which you handle the situation.

FOCUS ON POSITIVE GLOBAL SERVICE: AVOIDING STEREOTYPES

Think of instances in which you have heard people make derogatory comments, talk, or tell jokes about a certain group based on characteristics or factors related to the people in that group—for example, having to do with religion, body shape, physical or mental abilities, gender, sexual orientation, socioeconomic status, or ethnicity.

Did you participate in the conversation? Why or why not?

_____

_____

_____

_____

What are some of the stereotypes against others that you have heard about or witnessed?

_____

_____

_____

_____

What can you personally do to avoid or prevent stereotypes in the workplace?

_____

_____

_____

_____

Use your answers to the questions in this activity to create a personal action plan that will help you avoid generalizing or stereotyping others.

POSITIVE GLOBAL SERVICE ACTION TIP

Be ready to deal with a variety of diverse situations related to cultural beliefs by reading books, articles, and other information about various countries, cultures, values, and belief systems. To get started, visit Amazon or Barnes and Noble online and type in phrases such as "intercultural communication," "diverse communication," and "interpersonal relationships." Examine the tables of contents for the books that come up on the screen and then research additional terms you find there. This will provide you with a strong base of knowledge for understanding and dealing with people from around the world.

SUMMARY

In this chapter, you reviewed ways to improve communication and relationships with your customers. Some of the key concepts that you read about include:

- It's almost a certainty that on any given day you will interact with a customer who speaks another native language.
- People from other parts of the world, or who are different from you, will have a communications style and preferences that differ from yours.
- Effective communication skills can lead to more positive customer-provider relationships and stronger interactions in your personal life.

- Service breakdowns cost your organization money and should be avoided whenever possible. Take proactive steps to correct any situation immediately.
- You can help ensure service success when interacting with all customers by simply focusing on their needs, wants, and expectations and delivering the same quality of positive global customer service.
- Generalizations are often made about others as a result of perceptions that you might have.
- Stereotypes are typically based on partial truths, misinformation, and assumptions about another group. There is no place in today's business environment for stereotyping.
- No matter what your personal beliefs or feelings are about a particular person or group, you have a responsibility as an organizational representative to focus on customers in a manner that sends a positive message about your employer.

CHAPTER

5

Communicating Nonverbally

The unspoken nuances that accompany your words are often more powerful than anything you can say verbally.

KEY CONCEPTS

After reading this chapter and when applying concepts learned, you will be able to:

1. Explain the components of nonverbal communication.
2. Identify at least three positive and three negative nonverbal cues.
3. Describe the meaning of body language, or kinesics.
4. Create a list of various nonverbal cues.
5. Discuss how hand gestures differ among cultures.
6. Share how various facial expressions can be used to communicate effectively with customers.
7. Make a list of environmental cues that can impact customer-provider relationships.

8. Recall ways that color impacts emotion and sends nonverbal messages.
9. List differences in the way that men and women communicate.
10. Develop a list of strategies for improving nonverbal communication.

Just as with verbal communication, nonverbal cues can vary greatly around the world and often lead to misunderstandings and customer-provider relationship breakdowns. This happens because nonverbal cues such as gestures, facial expressions, stances, silence, and others are not universally the same. If you approach people from other cultures with the same nonverbal cues you use in your own culture, you are setting yourself up for failure, possible confrontation, and lost business. The only way to be fairly safe in using nonverbal cues with customers from other cultures is to study differences and remember that people from around the world communicate in various ways. In the sidebar "Focus on Positive Global Service: Multicultural Nonverbal Cue Quiz," you'll find a brief opportunity to test your knowledge of cross-cultural nonverbal communication skills.

FOCUS ON POSITIVE GLOBAL SERVICE: MULTICULTURAL NONVERBAL CUE QUIZ

Take a few minutes to indicate the message(s) that you believe the following nonverbal cues communicate based on your personal cultural beliefs and norms. You will find the answers to these questions and more as you read this chapter.

1. Making direct eye contact when talking

_____

2. Smiling

_____

3. Laughing while negotiating

_____

4. Responding with a long silence during a conversation

_____

5. Touching a customer while talking

_____

6. Patting a small child on the head as you compliment him or her

_____

7. Crossing the middle finger over the index finger or vice versa

_____

8. Using a "thumbs-up" gesture (fingers curled toward the palm with thumb projecting into the air)

_____

9. Joining the thumb and index finger to form a circle with the remaining fingers extended upward in the air

_____

10. Hugging a customer of the opposite sex in the workplace as part of a greeting

_____

11. Passing items to a customer with the left hand

_____

12. Crossing legs so that the sole of your shoe is pointed toward your customer

_____

POSITIVE GLOBAL SERVICE ACTION TIP

Watch your customer's nonverbal reactions as you communicate in order to note indications that he or she may be confused about, shocked by, or otherwise unsure of the meaning of your intended verbal and nonverbal message. If you believe miscommunication has occurred, immediately do a perception check rather than ignore the problem and potentially damage your relationship.

NONVERBAL COMMUNICATION

People have been using *nonverbal communication* for thousands of years to convey concepts and ideas, even before many had a spoken or written language. Think of the stories told by cave dwellers and other distant ancestors. In ancient times, dancing around a fire and using gestures to share stories was commonplace. Many people living in remote regions around the world still do so today. They do not have the luxury of being able to read books, watch television, or gain knowledge from well-traveled individuals. They pass along their beliefs, values, and culture from one person and generation to the next partly through nonverbal means.

In the modern world, people use a wide array of physical and silent gestures, movements, and expressions as supplementary ways to share their opinions, emotions, ideas, and thoughts. Some gestures and cues are viewed positively, and others are viewed negatively. For example, something as simple as a customer pointing to a glass filled with water on your desk and then to her mouth could let you know she wants something to drink.

POSITIVE AND NEGATIVE NONVERBAL CUES

Positive Cues	Negative Cues
Making brief or no direct eye contact (in some cultures)	Yawning
Smiling	Chewing or eating food
Facing toward the customer	Showing inattention to the customer
Nodding affirmatively (up and down in Westernized countries)	Fidgeting
Using appropriate hand gestures (based on culture)	Using inappropriate hand gestures
Effecting an open body stance or posture	Crossing arms across chest
Engaging in active listening	Placing hands on hips
Staying silent as the customer speaks	Staring blankly at the customer
Gesturing with an open hand	Interrupting
Maintaining a professional appearance	Appearing unkempt
Keeping a clean, organized work space	Having a disorganized or cluttered workspace

As a service professional, it is impossible for you to "not" send nonverbal messages to your customers. They are evaluating you based on your posture, facial expressions, body type, skin color, clothing, and many other nonverbal cues. Your goal should be to pay attention to all these factors and to communicate a message of professionalism—one that says you are alert, happy, capable, and ready to serve your customer. On the telephone, your tone and attitude should project a positive, upbeat, and professional presence that helps encourage people to continue to do business with you and your organization. When speaking with a customer face-to-face, you should avoid negative body cues—such as crossing your arms across your chest, pointing your finger at someone, or rubbing the back of your neck or the bridge of your nose—and facial gestures—such as frowning or using eye contact inappropriately as your customer speaks—and any other movement that might indicate boredom, stress, frustration, or displeasure since some cultures view these things negatively. Also, you should be conscious of nervous habits like fidgeting, which could say to the customer that you are impatient, uncertain, or otherwise not confident about a given situation (e.g., a sale).

It is important to monitor not only your own nonverbal cues but those of your customer as well. In doing so, remember that even though someone from a different culture uses a nonverbal cue similar to one that your culture uses, it may not have the same meaning. Learning to appropriately interpret and appreciate different nonverbal cues will give you a big advantage over your competition when dealing with people from various cultural and diverse backgrounds. So when you see a customer use a nonverbal cue, be careful not to assign meaning to it out of *context*. This is because the same gesture (e.g., a smile) might have different meanings based on the situation, the customer's level of emotion, the environment, the person accompanying the customer, time, the customer's cultural background, and your personal frame of reference related to the signal.

In most cases, when something goes wrong or communication breaks down because of poorly chosen nonverbal cues, the offending person either is ignorant of cultural variances or is simply not thinking about the possible interpretation by the receiver. One key to effectively communicating nonverbally is to ensure that your nonverbal messages to customers are in *congruence* with the words you use. For example, if you say, "Good morning, welcome to ABC Company," but have a frown on your face and use a tone lacking excitement, your nonverbal facial cues will likely send a negative message to your customer. Do not forget the importance of the smile and your tone of voice when communicating with customers.

Within each cultural group, there are *subcultures* based on ethnic differences, languages, social alignments, and other characteristics. Even within a given subcultural group, there are differences. For example, members of youth gangs or ethnic groups often develop their own greeting rituals that involve hand gestures and adopt specific types of clothing that identify them as a member of a specific gang. When interacting with your customers, make sure that you do not generalize and think, "Ah, they are from ____, so they mean ____ when they do ____." Always be alert to the entire message that your customer sends, including verbal and nonverbal cues. It is actually better to look for clusters of cues rather than focus on a singular one. For example, instead of just thinking that because someone nodded his head in response to a question that he agrees; listen to what he says as well. If he nods and says, "That might be possible," during a price negotiation, then you do not have firm agreement and should continue discussing.

POSITIVE GLOBAL SERVICE ACTION TIP

To get an idea of how you use voice tone and whether you inadvertently send positive or negative nonverbal messages as you speak, turn on an audio recorder for about half an hour and place it on a table as you interact with your spouse, significant other, friends, or family members. Later, listen to the conversations and focus specifically on your tone as you ask and respond to questions or share information. Are you upbeat and enthusiastic, or do you drone on or lack enthusiasm as you speak? Chances are that the way you communicate in these situations is the same as when you speak with customers. Make any necessary adjustments.

FOCUS ON POSITIVE GLOBAL SERVICE: EVALUATE YOUR NONVERBAL COMMUNICATION

To get a better idea of how you present yourself to customers nonverbally, ask a coworker to use the following guidelines and evaluate your nonverbal communication during a service transaction with a customer. Once it is over, spend some time having the coworker provide feedback on how well you did.

Body language	Does your body posture and positioning send a relaxed positive (e.g., confidence and self-assurance) or tense negative (e.g., uncertain, confused, or unconfident) message about you?
Facial expression	Does your face say, "Hello, welcome, I am able and ready to serve you," or does it show a bored, disinterested employee who is going through the motions of providing service?
Eye contact	Are you making appropriate and adequate eye contact to show interest without causing possible discomfort or offense?
Tone of voice	Does your voice project a smiling professional who sounds even-paced, comfortable, and confident?

Body Language

Many researchers have studied the use of *body language*, or *kinesics*, for years in an attempt to interpret and define human meaning from nonverbal cues. Further, some studies have found that women are more able to accurately decode the nonverbal cues of others than are men.

Julius Fast caught the attention of millions of readers with his best-selling book *Body Language*.[1] Average people became fascinated by the idea that you could know what message someone was sending by observing how he or she sat, stood, gestured, made eye contact, and moved. Since then, hundreds of books and articles have been published that share studies done in various cultures in an attempt to home in on this elusive topic. The similar conclusion from all the research is that there is no singular interpretation for any aspect of kinesics. That is the message that you must remember when dealing with every one of your customers. Treat customers as individuals, respect their cultural beliefs, and recognize that what you or they mean by the nonverbal cues that you both use is absolutely subject to misinterpretation.

How you filter the nonverbal cues of others will depend on what type of education you have, how much you have traveled or been exposed to other cultures, and which country you are from or cultural background you have. Your perspective about yourself and the pride that you have in your culture can often impact the degree of success that you will have in sending and receiving nonverbal signals effectively. People in some cultures have a very positive image of themselves and think that others share this belief. As a result, they are sometimes viewed as arrogant, insensitive to others, or cocky. For example, many view people from the United States this way. This does not mean that if you are from the United States that you should not be proud of your country and heritage; you just might want to tone down your enthusiasm and be conscious of how you come across to your customers from other countries when you communicate. Keep in mind that your goal is to deliver positive global customer service and not offend anyone. The same is true no matter what your national origin might be. The following are some common nonverbal cues that you might use or encounter when interacting with customers.

- **Chewing gum or eating.** Most organizations have policies against chewing gum or eating food while on the job or around customers. The general reason is that if you are chewing gum (or eating food), it makes it difficult for people to understand what you are saying. There is also the potential that you might accidentally spit near a customer. From a cultural nonverbal-cue standpoint, there are additional reasons not to chew. Typically, in many cultures, to eat or chew in public is considered rude and demonstrates poor manners.
- **Holding hands near the mouth.** While numerous nonverbal messages can be sent by holding your hands near your mouth, you should avoid doing so consciously. Placing your hands over or in front of your mouth can send messages of doubt, uncertainty, or embarrassment or can suggest that you are hiding something.

Also, by holding your hands near your mouth, you can potentially distort your words or muffle your voice. This creates a challenge for customers who speak a primary language different from yours or for those who are hearing impaired and rely partly on reading your lips to understand your message.

- **Keeping your "manners" in check.** Many people have been taught the value of treating a woman like a lady. In other words, to protect or respect a woman by using courtesies such as standing when a woman enters the room for the first time, pulling a chair out for her at a table in a restaurant, holding a door and allowing her to go through first, or walking on the curb side of the street to protect her from mud or water splashed by vehicles. If this is your value system, you should honor it when appropriate— for example, in after-work settings or informal gatherings with regular customers or coworkers. In the United States and other Western cultures, where women have struggled to get legal recognition of their rights and to be treated as equals in the workplace, these courteous behaviors might create problems and should typically be avoided in most instances. Obviously, if a woman (or man) were coming to a door with her arms full of packages or materials, you should offer to hold the door and allow her through first.

  Remember that the examples of the values and courtesies in the previous paragraph are not universal. In many countries (e.g., Middle Eastern, Asian, and South American), women are not afforded the same rights and treatment and often follow men or allow them to go through the door first. In some countries, they might even help a man with his coat.

- **Offering greetings.** A firm handshake is an acceptable and expected practice for men and women in Western business settings and those familiar with Western business culture. In many countries, a light handshake, nodding, bowing, alternate hand gestures, or a hug and kiss on the cheek is substituted. For example, in Latin America, men and women often embrace during a greeting, and men often follow this with a hearty slap on the back of the shoulder to another man. Still, in other countries, shaking hands between men and women is not an acceptable practice. Instead they bow slightly when greeting one another (e.g., Korea, Japan, Vietnam, and other parts of Asia). People from other parts of the world often use their own traditional greetings. For instance, in places like India and Thailand, people put the palms of their hands together as if they were praying—a gesture known as Namaste—as they slightly nod their heads and smile.

- **Leaning toward or away.** Depending on the culture and your own behavioral style, you may tend to lean either toward or away from customers as they speak. In many Western cultures, it is typical for people to lean toward a speaker when they are seated in order to hear what is being said and to indicate that they are listening and interested in what is being said. This posture is often accompanied by direct eye contact and an occasional smile, when appropriate. Depending on the relationship, this might even be accompanied by a brief light touch on the hand or forearm. When people are reflecting on what someone has said or if they want to send a more relaxed message, they often lean back in their chairs. Keep in mind that in Korea, Japan, and other more formal countries, sitting upright with feet flat on the floor and hands on the knees is an acceptable seated posture.

- **Nodding the head.** If someone is from a Westernized country, when people nod their heads up and down by raising and lowering their chins toward the chests, they typically mean that they agree, accept, or are saying yes. This is not the case in many other countries, where a head nod simply means that they are listening or are following what you say or are being polite (e.g., Japan and China). In other countries (e.g., India), people often do what some call a "head bobble," similar to the movement made by the little plastic characters with neck springs that you see on the dash of someone's car. This slight side-to-side motion while smiling might be a tacit agreement, or it could mean the listeners are simply being polite. In either instance, you have not gained their total commitment. If you are discussing prices on a product or service, you would continue the negotiation or discussion at that point with your customer. In some places (e.g., Turkey, Iran, and parts of Greece), people actually indicate yes by moving their head left to right in the same manner that people from Western cultures indicate no.

- **Passing items.** Because the left hand is used for bodily functions in many cultures in the Middle East and India, you should avoid passing business cards, food, or other items with that hand.
- **Showing the bottoms of your feet.** When some people are relaxed or in an informal setting (e.g., at a bar, restaurant, or information meeting with people or customers that they know well), they might lean back and put their feet up on a piece of furniture (e.g., on a bottom opened drawer of a desk or on an empty chair) as they talk to someone or share ideas. Such a casual posture is interpreted by some people as confidence, arrogance, or poor manners. If you assume such a posture and the bottoms of your feet point toward a customer who is not from a Western culture (e.g., Egypt, Singapore, Saudi Arabia , Sudan, and Thailand), you would be delivering a grave insult, since the foot is considered dirty and is the lowest part of the body. The implication might be that "you are lower than my foot." Likewise, you should never point or gesture toward a person or object, especially any religious object, with your foot.
- **Staying silent.** Various cultures take a different view of silence during an interaction. For example, North Americans are often viewed by people from some cultures (e.g., Asian) as talkative, aggressive, and boastful. If you are from the United States or Canada, you might view customers from Japan or China as being indifferent or lacking opinions if you are having a discussion and they seem only to be listening or hesitant to respond. In reality, many people from Eastern cultures have been taught to be reflective and quiet and to observe. If the people to whom they are talking are older or of a higher socioeconomic status, they are also taught to quietly pay respect and listen to them. This is contrary to what many people from Western cultures are often taught,

which is to speak up and voice opinions or ask questions. In either instance, there is a chance that because of misunderstanding on both sides of the conversation, there could be a breakdown in communication or the customer-provider relationship.

- **Sitting.** There are various ways that men and women cross their legs when they sit. Depending on the customer with whom you are interacting, you might possibly send a negative message if you cross your legs in a certain way. For example, many men from Western cultures assume a relaxed posture when sitting and cross one leg over the other at the knee so that their foot points either right or left. As you will read shortly, this could cause offense to people from certain cultures. The alternative way for men to cross their legs at the knee is to put one over the other so that the top leg simply hangs down or dangles. Some men are physically uncomfortable with this posture or view it as a homosexual manner of sitting, depending on their culture. As a result, they often avoid this posture. But in England and other parts of Europe, the latter posture is the culturally proper way for a man to sit, especially in a business or more formal setting.

  Women in many cultures are taught that ladies do not sit with their legs apart and that they should cross their legs either at the knees with one leg draped over the other or tightly at the ankles. In Korea and Japan, where physical balance and control of one's life is an important value, people often do not cross their legs, but simply sit "squared" in an upright or fairly rigid posture, with both feet on the floor and their hands resting on their knees as they talk.

- **Slouching.** Customers of any culture who see a service professional that they perceive to be slouching and with little enthusiasm typically form negative opinions about the employee and his or her organization. Balance and good posture are valued in many cultures.

- **Touching.** The study of touching in nonverbal communication, or *haptics*, has been used by researchers for years to better understand how people from different cultures use and react to touch. Many touching gestures have multiple meanings. Consider the reaction of a stranger whom you accidentally rub against compared with the reaction of a regular customer whose hand or arm you intentionally touch during a business greeting or handshake. Depending on their culture, people may react in totally different ways. For example, in the Middle East, people might give a loud cry and make accusations of molestation or an offense against their virtue, while in other cultures, people might not even give a second thought to the episode. Of course, the outcome scenarios might depend on the manner and context in which you rubbed against them or in which you touched their hand or arm.

  The importance of understanding how people from around the world interpret what you might consider an innocent gesture cannot be understated. For example, many adults in some cultures have a habit of patting the head or caressing the hair of a small child as they comment to a parent about how cute or sweet the child is. In Western cultures, most people would think nothing of this act. However, in countries like India, Singapore, Taiwan, Sri Lanka, or Thailand, this is a very offensive gesture, because the head is believed to be the seat of the soul. By touching it, you might be wishing ill upon the person or disrespecting the cultural belief.

  To further complicate the issue of touch, people who are more introverted or who tend to be more task- rather than people-oriented often protect their personal zones and do not like others intruding into their space or touching them, especially strangers. This is why the general rule of thumb is that in the workplace or business setting, the only acceptable touching is a professional handshake in Western cultures and the appropriate greeting in others (e.g., hug, bow, or cheek kiss).

POSITIVE GLOBAL SERVICE ACTION TIP

Get an idea of how certain nonverbal cues look to others by observing some of your coworkers or those who work in organizations that you frequent. Make a mental note of movements, postures, and gestures that draw attention positively or negatively. Consider using ones that you perceive as positive and avoiding those that you consider negative as you serve your customers.

Hand Gestures

A person's hands can be valuable tools for reinforcing an idea, a comment, or a concept if they are used correctly. Otherwise they can lead to confusion and communication breakdowns. The following are some common hand gestures that might be used or witnessed in your workplace. Consider their possible differing meanings as they relate to a customer's country of origin before using them.

- **Placing your hands on your hips or in your pockets.** In Vietnam, someone who is using this gesture while talking is usually considered arrogant or disrespectful. It is often viewed as a closed gesture indicating annoyance or defiance or an unwillingness to listen to the opinion of a customer.
- **Crossing your middle finger over your index finger or vice versa.** Often used as a symbol meaning "Wish me luck" or indicating closeness with someone—showing "we are tight"—in the United States, it is looked upon as an obscene gesture in Vietnam. Ignorance of a customer's cultural perceptions of a gesture might create an embarrassing situation if you use an inappropriate cue.
- **Pointing the index finger.** This gesture is seen as a rude, disrespectful, or threatening gesture when directed at another person in a number of countries. If you must point to something or in a customer's direction, do so casually with fingers extended and joined as you gesture with your arm extended so that you do not unintentionally offend anyone.

- **Pointing to yourself.** People use different ways to point to different areas of their body when they are talking about themselves. For example, in the United States people point their forefinger at their chest, while in Japan they point at their face and in China they point at their nose. By recognizing cultural differences, you might avoid a situation in which you project your own cultural meanings related to a customer's gesture(s). Remember, if you are in doubt, do a perception check.
- **Using your thumb and forefinger to create an O.** The symbol that stands for "okay" in the United States and some other countries actually means "zero" or "poor quality" in Vietnam and Belgium. In parts of Latin America and parts of Southern Europe, it is an insult; in Greece and Turkey, it is a vulgar sexual invitation. Even worse, in parts of Tunisia, it can mean "I will kill you." Obviously, you want to send the appropriate message based on your customer's culture.
- **Giving a thumbs-up gesture (with remaining fingers curled toward the palm).** In the United States and many parts of Europe, this gesture can indicate things are going well or okay, while in Islamic and Asian countries, Nigeria, and Australia, it is often viewed as rude and offensive. In Germany it stands for the number 1, while in Japan it signifies the number 5. Since the potential for confusion exists, you may want to avoid this gesture and the next when interacting with your customers.
- **Giving a thumbs-down gesture.** This is the opposite of thumbs up in the United States and Europe.
- **Making a V with your index and middle finger.** Using the V symbol with the index and middle finger extended upward and the thumb and remaining fingers curled toward the palm, with the palm facing outward, typically indicates victory or peace in the United States, Mexico, and many countries in Europe, as well as some other parts of the world familiar with the Western interpretation. However, in some countries, by turning the palm toward you and using the same gesture, you can send a message akin to the middle-finger gesture used in Western cultures.

Facial Expressions

By moving the muscles in your face, you can convey feelings and messages to others that let them know whether you are experiencing happiness, sadness, frustration, anger, or many other moods. As with other nonverbal cues, the interpretation of facial expressions can vary among cultures and individuals. Since the time of Charles Darwin, researchers have studied facial expressions and found that the most common ones are interpreted in similar ways by cultures around the world. It is the beliefs of individual cultures related to the appropriateness of expressing emotions like surprise, happiness, sadness, anger, fear, and disgust that change how people use and interpret such facial signals.

Because facial expressions are closely tied to human emotion, you should be careful about projecting subconscious biases that you might have toward any group, since you might unintentionally send a negative message to a customer before you realize it. For example, if you disapprove of customers who have facial piercings and tattoos, you might indicate your displeasure nonverbally with a smirk or other facial gesture.

The following are some typical facial expressions:

- **Eye contact.** Eye contact is important in maintaining the flow of conversation and for gauging your customer's response in many situations. The use of eye contact with your customers can be tricky depending on their cultural background, sex, and other factors. The rules for making eye contact vary among cultures and subcultures based on the values and beliefs of the group. In the United States, the United Kingdom, Canada, the Netherlands, and parts of Eastern Europe, direct eye contact is more likely than in other parts of the world. Many people in these areas of the world are often leery of someone who avoids making direct eye contact, and children are often taught "to look me in the eye when talking to me." People in some cultures find this concept intrusive, and it makes them uncomfortable. On the other hand, many Arabs will stand close (almost nose-to-nose) when they talk to someone of the same sex, and they make direct eye contact for long periods of time. Their goal is often to determine the other person's truthfulness and to show that they are paying attention. In addition, it is taboo for Middle Eastern women to look men directly in the eye. Like many other factors related to diversity, certain values taught by members of various subcultures in any country have an impact on the way that the people in those subcultures communicate and use nonverbal cues. Generally, it is best to follow your customer's lead with eye contact and not make assumptions based on your cultural beliefs.

- **Smiles or laughter.** Smiles are generally meant to be an indication of friendship or acceptance worldwide, so you should use them liberally when interacting with your customers. There are exceptions, though. Some people in Asia and other cultures may smile or laugh nervously when unsure, embarrassed, or angry; when they have made a minor mistake or blunder; or when they do not want to hurt your feelings. Do not interpret the smiles or laughter of your customers from these countries as agreement or acceptance in all situations. Look at all aspects of the conversation (clusters) and the context in which gestures are being used. If necessary, do a perception check to verify your interpretations.

- **Winking.** Be very careful with this gesture since it really has no place in a professional setting. While your intent might be an innocent indication that you and the other person share a common understanding or that there is a bond between you, it has potential sexual overtones and can be seen as rude and offensive, especially between sexes in many countries.

NONVERBAL ENVIRONMENTAL CUES

In addition to the nonverbal cues related directly to your person, the *environmental cues* in your workplace can also send powerful messages to your customers. To ensure that your work area is projecting a positive, professional image, conduct regular environmental surveys in order to identify any items that might be perceived by your customers as unprofessional, negative, or offensive.

Areas of concern should include the general appearance and organization of the workplace. A messy work space may cause customers to question your professionalism, ability, and commitment to serve. Granted, in some professions, keeping a work area clean all the time is difficult. However, that is no excuse for giving up on the cleanliness and organization of your area. If each employee takes responsibility for cleaning his or her area, cleaning becomes a routine event during a work shift, and no one has to get stuck with the job of doing cleaning tasks at a specific time. Also, the chance that a customer may react negatively to the work area is reduced or eliminated.

In order to make sure your work space is appealing and inoffensive to customers of both genders and from various cultural backgrounds, make sure that you eliminate any objects, posters, photos, publications, or calendars that might be offensive to anyone based on issues related to gender, religion, sex, politics, ethnicity, or professional group. Such items have no place in a professional work environment and may even violate laws. Failure to remove such material might result in legal liability for you and your organization and create a hostile work environment while costing you customers.

Sending Messages with Color

Some cultures use color in clothing to define rank or status, and certain colors appeal to some people more than others. It is important to recognize these facts if you are doing business with someone from another culture or traveling to other countries to do business. Otherwise, you are likely to make some serious cultural blunders. The sidebar "The Emotions of Color" provides some general guidance on the power or effect of certain colors on people, but there are exceptions. For example, in the United States and several other countries, black is often associated with very formal occasions or death. In other cultures, varying colors are synonymous with funerals (e.g., white in China, yellow in Mexico, and purple in Brazil). In the United States, pink is considered a feminine color, and many men will not wear it because of the perception that only women and homosexuals wear pink. In other parts of the world, yellow is perceived as a more feminine color.

Additionally, people in China consider red to be a color of good fortune or luck, while in Turkey it is associated with death.

This does not mean that you should expand your wardrobe to include items of clothing in all colors. Just be aware of the potential interpretation that customers from other cultures might derive from what you wear.

THE EMOTIONS OF COLOR

Red	Stimulates and evokes excitement, passion, power, energy, anger, intensity. Can also indicate "stop," negativity, financial trouble, or shortage. In some Eastern cultures it is worn by brides, in China it is worn to attract luck, and in South Africa it is used for mourning.
Yellow	Symbolizes caution, warmth, mellowness, positive feelings, optimism, and cheerfulness. Yellow can also stimulate thinking and visualizing. Used to indicate mourning in Egypt and to represent courage in Japan.
Dark blue	Depending on the shade, can relax, soothe, indicate maturity, and evoke trust and tranquility or peace. In the United States, blue is associated with masculinity.
Light blue	Projects a cool, youthful, or masculine image.
Purple	Projects assertiveness or boldness and youthfulness. Has a contemporary feel. Often used as a sign of royalty, richness, spirituality, or power.
Orange	Can indicate high energy or enthusiasm. Is an emotional color and sometimes stimulates positive thinking.
Brown	Is considered an earth tone that creates a feeling of security, wholesomeness, strength, support, and lack of pretentiousness.
Green	Can bring to mind nature, productivity, positive image, movement in a forward direction ("go"), comfort, growth, or financial success or prosperity. Also can give a feeling of balance.
Gold or silver	Signals prestige, power, warmth, status, wealth, elegance, or conservatism.

Pink	Projects a youthful, feminine, or warm image. In the United States pink is associated with femininity.
White	Not really a color (reflection of all colors in the spectrum). Typically used to indicate purity, cleanliness, honesty, and wholesomeness. Is visually relaxing. Used in weddings in Western cultures and symbolizes death in some Eastern cultures.
Black	Lack of color due to absorbing all colors of the visible light spectrum. Creates a sense of independence, completeness, and solidarity. Often used to indicate financial success, death, or seriousness of a situation in some cultures.

Adapted from R. Lucas, *Customer Service Skills for Success,* 5th ed., Burr Ridge, IL: McGraw-Hill Higher Education, 2011.

DIFFERENCES IN GENDER COMMUNICATION

Many researchers have found distinct differences in the way that men and women approach communication and relationships in the workplace. Some attribute this to the fact that "female and male brains develop at different rates and that boys tend to develop speech and language skills at a slower rate than girls."[2] One basis for differences in communication between the sexes is that women tend to be more bilateral in the use of their brains—often switching between left and right brain hemispheres to process information. Men tend to be more lateral in their thinking by using either their left brain hemisphere (e.g., logical, analytical, factual, and oriented toward facts and figures) or their right (e.g., creative, artistic, or expressive) based on the situation they find themselves in. No matter what country you are from, there are things that men and women do differently in communicating, especially when dealing with members of the opposite sex. You must recognize these differences and adhere to them if you want to be successful in working with a multicultural, diverse customer base.

Bestselling books by famed gender communication experts John Gray and Deborah Tannen have introduced millions of readers to the differences between male and female communication. In *Men Are from Mars, Women Are from Venus*,[3] Gray stresses that men and women might as well be from different planets because they often focus on completely different types of information when they talk. Similarly, Tannen stresses that women seek the emotional meaning of a message when talking and often focus on building rapport or equity, while men often look for the "report" or bottom line and details.[4] Because of the different perspectives, communication between the two can often break down. When you deal with customers of the opposite sex, you should strive to listen actively and to gather pertinent information that will help you provide quality global customer service. When sending messages to members of the opposite sex, you have to create ones that meet the information needs of your customers and be aware of their reactions to what you said. You also have to consider their cultural backgrounds and perceptions about acceptable relationships between men and women; otherwise, misunderstandings might arise that result in a breakdown of the customer-provider relationship.

One factor that might account for the difference in the way men and women communicate in a given country is that with rare exceptions (e.g., some indigenous tribes in Asia and Africa) societies are patriarchal, with males maintaining leadership and dominant roles in government, business, and the home. As a result of these traditional roles that have existed for centuries, women were often subservient or disempowered in the family and society; thus the male's word was final. In today's world you might encounter the remnants of these beliefs when serving customers who come from the Middle East, parts of Asia, and some of the island nations. In some instances, it is taboo for women to speak to males other than their husbands or family members. If, during a service transaction with a Middle Eastern man, you were to attempt to speak to his wife who accompanied him, even about something as innocent as the weather, you and she could face the wrath of her husband or male family member. Women do not typically speak during business transactions in that part of the world. In Western cultures, this is usually not the case. The table on the following pages summarizes some key differences in the way that men and women in the United States and other Western cultures communicate.

	Females	Males
Body	Claim small areas of personal space (e.g., cross legs at knees or ankles)	Claim large areas of personal space (e.g., use figure-four leg cross, armrests on airplanes)
	Cross arms and legs frequently	Use relaxed arm and leg posture (e.g., over arm of a chair)
	Sit or stand close to other females but further from males with whom they have no close relationship or friendship	Sit or stand away from other males but close to females
	Touch more (both sexes)	Touch males less, females more
	Nod frequently to indicate receptiveness	Nod occasionally to indicate agreement
	Lean forward toward speaker	Lean away from speaker
	Hug and possibly kiss both sexes upon greeting	Hug and possibly kiss females upon greeting
Vocal	Use high inflection at end of statements (sounds like a question)	Use subdued vocal inflection
	Speak at faster rate	Speak at slower rate
	Use paralanguage—(rephrasing someone else's message into one's own words) frequently	Use paralanguage occasionally
	Express more emotion	Express less emotion
	Use more polite "requesting" language (e.g., "Would you please . . . ?")	Use more "command" language (e.g., "Get me the . . .")
	Focus on relationship messages	Focus on business messages
	Interrupt less; more tolerant of interruptions	Interrupt more, but tolerate interruptions less
Vocal	Use more precise articulation	Use less precision in word endings and enunciation (e.g., drop the "g" in -ing endings)

	Females	Males
Facial	Maintain eye contact	Glance away frequently
	Smile frequently	Smile infrequently (with strangers)
Behavior	Focus more on details	Focus less on details
	Are more emotional in problem solving	Are analytical in problem solving, (e.g., try to find the cause and fix the problem)
	View verbal rejections as personal	Do not dwell on verbal rejections
	Apologize after disagreements	Apologize less after disagreements
	Hold grudges longer	Do not hold grudges
Environmental	Commonly display personal objects in the workplace	Commonly display items symbolizing achievement in the workplace
	Use bright colors in clothing and decorations	Use more subdued colors in clothing and decorations
	Use patterns in clothing and decoration	Use few patterns in clothing

POSITIVE GLOBAL SERVICE ACTION TIP

When communicating with customers of the opposite sex, remember that they might approach a situation differently than you do. Listen to their words, watch their nonverbal cues, and pay attention to clusters of signals that they send so that you can potentially detect when something is not working well or when a misunderstanding has occurred. In such instances you should work to correct the situation quickly.

IMPROVING NONVERBAL KNOWLEDGE AND SKILLS

If you want to be successful in dealing with customers in a global environment, then you will have to study the ways of the world and become a student of human nature. Recognize that differences exist in symbols and cues and their meanings around the world. Learn as much as you can about people and regions of the world. Do not judge your customers based on your beliefs or what you do. Accept them for who they are and strive to deliver positive global customer service each and every time.

The following is a list of strategies that can help make you more effective and confident in dealing with customers who are different from you. These are just a few. Always look for ways to become educated about various aspects of nonverbal communication in a diverse world.

- **"Listen" with your eyes.** Since words are often not as powerful as nonverbal cues, pay attention to what people do as well as what they say. Variances in multicultural use of space, body language, facial expression, hand gestures, and other cues are often open to misinterpretation. Become adept at watching for incongruent signals that do not match the words being spoken. When you see these, make sure to ask for clarification rather than assume that you know your customer's intended meaning.

FOCUS ON POSITIVE GLOBAL SERVICE: NONVERBAL OBSERVATIONS

If you have access to a mall, restaurant, or other public area where people from various cultures congregate, go there and find a quiet location in which to sit and observe in an inoffensive manner. Look for gestures, facial expressions, body postures, and general interactions between same and different sexes and between other cultures. Also watch how older and younger people interact. Be careful not to let your observations pigeonhole people, where you think, "Ah, Hispanics do this, people from the United Kingdom do that, or people from the United States always . . ." This is stereotyping and can lead to problems later on.

Make a copy of this page and record some of your observations below for future reference.

_____

_____

_____

- **Immerse yourself in other cultures.** Get to know people from other cultures on a personal level to learn how they think, what their values are, and what their countries are like from their perceptions and to gain knowledge of behaviors common within their part of the world. If you have an opportunity to travel to other countries, take it. Cruises are a relatively inexpensive way to visit several countries within a short period of time. If nothing else, make a plan to go to a different ethnic restaurant as often as possible and interact with the staff.
- **Avoid stereotyping behaviors.** As you read in earlier chapters, it is never a good idea to make assumptions about all people in a group based on your interaction with one. Keep an open mind when dealing with your customers. For example, just because a nonverbal cue was misunderstood by one customer from a country does not mean that you should abandon it in future interactions with another customer from the same country. Culture is just one of the factors that impact interpersonal communication with your customers.
- **Be aware of the cues you use.** Many people have negative or repetitive nonverbal signals that they send to others. These can sometimes be annoying and cause problems with communication. For example, you might jingle the change in your pocket or fidget with a pen or some other item while a customer is speaking. If you have the opportunity to videotape yourself interacting with customers or others, watch these videos to see if you demonstrate such bad behaviors. Fast-forwarding of the video will accelerate your gesture usage and will make it very obvious if you repeat or overuse a signal. If your company has security cameras that tape what's happening, ask your supervisor if you can watch the tape to observe your interactions with your customers for training purposes.

SUMMARY

In this chapter, you had an opportunity to learn about the intriguing ways that people communicate without saying a word and to explore how some of the common nonverbal cues that you use could be interpreted differently by your customers from different countries, cultures, genders, and backgrounds. Some of the key concepts that you read about include:

- It is impossible for you to "not" send nonverbal messages to your customers.
- When speaking with a customer face-to-face, you should avoid negative body cues and facial gestures.
- Remember that even though someone from another culture uses a nonverbal cue similar to one that your culture uses, it may not have the same meaning.
- One classic study by Dr. Albert Mehrabian in the United States found that over 93 percent of the meaning of a message can come from nonverbal sources.
- One key to effectively communicating using nonverbal cues is to ensure that your cues to customers are in congruence with, or match, the words you use.
- Always be alert to the entire message that your customers send, including their verbal and nonverbal cues.
- The hands can be a valuable tool for reinforcing an idea, a comment, or a concept if they are used correctly, in the appropriate situation, and with the right people.
- As with other nonverbal cues, the interpretation of facial expressions can vary among cultures and individuals.
- In addition to the nonverbal cues related directly to your person, the environmental cues that exist in your workplace can also send powerful messages to your customers.
- Some cultures use color in clothing to define rank or status, and certain colors appeal to some people more than others.
- Many researchers have found distinct differences in the way that men and women approach communication and relationships in the workplace.
- If you want to be successful in dealing with customers in a global environment, then you will have to study the ways of the world and become a student of human nature.

6

Listening to What the Customer Is Saying

Listen to hear your customer rather than just to answer.

KEY CONCEPTS

After reading this chapter and when applying concepts learned, you will be able to:

1. Describe a variety of ways in which active listening is important to customer service.
2. Define the four phases in the active listening process.
3. Give examples of the challenges faced in effectively listening to customers.
4. Give examples of the three factors impacting your ability to listen actively to your customers.
5. Develop strategies to improve your listening ability.

Communication breakdowns are fairly commonplace when dealing with customers. A number of factors contribute to this pattern, but one of the main reasons is that many people are not adept at actively listening to their customers and responding appropriately. Neither you nor your customer can be a passive listener if you want to have a successful dialogue. It takes an active two-way exchange of information to ensure that messages are sent and received appropriately and accurately. You cannot simply make assumptions that your customer understands what you say. Such assumptions only lead to potential customer-provider breakdowns.

A common challenge in many customer interactions is that there is a degree of complacency about listening and many service providers only go through the motions of listening. This lackadaisical attitude to listening is not limited only to frontline employees. In a survey of 129 managers,[1] three-fourths (74.3 percent) perceived themselves to be passive or detached listeners. Since there are more frontline service providers than managers, imagine what the percentage at that level looks like, especially since frontline employees often receive less training, are paid smaller salaries, and have less job experience than their supervisors. In order to do your job in a professional manner, you have to approach each customer interaction with a high degree of commitment and professionalism. You have to take ownership of the situation in order to ensure that you gather all the information needed to effectively provide quality global service to every customer.

As you interact with your customers, you will encounter many situations in which you will have to select your words carefully. Whether you are being politically sensitive, are fluent in multiple languages, are striving to be technically correct, or are just trying to use good grammar, you must be conscious of multiple messages when you communicate to others. This is because there are basically four potential types of messages sent whenever you communicate:

1. The message you want to send.
2. The message you thought you sent.
3. The message you actually sent.
4. The message the receiver understood based on his or her personal filters.

With all these possibilities, it is no wonder that customers and workers in every organization complain about listening problems. If you focus on your customers in each interaction and consider their background and needs, your chances of a successful outcome increase significantly.

FOCUS ON POSITIVE GLOBAL SERVICE: LISTENING SELF-ASSESSMENT

To get an idea of how well you perceive your own listening effectiveness, answer these questions; then score yourself. Make sure to answer based on how you actually behave, not on how you think you should behave. Place a check mark in the appropriate column.

	Always	Sometimes	Seldom
1. When customers speak to me, I stop what I'm doing to focus on what they are saying.			
2. I listen to people even if I disagree with what they are saying.			
3. When I am unsure of the meaning of a customer's message, I ask for clarification.			
4. I avoid daydreaming when listening to customers.			
5. I focus on main ideas, not details, when a customer speaks to me.			
6. While listening, I am also conscious of nonverbal cues sent by my customer.			
7. I consciously block out noise when a customer speaks to me.			
8. I paraphrase the messages I receive in order to ensure I understand the meaning of my customers' message.			

	Always	Sometimes	Seldom
9. I wait until I have received a customer's entire message before giving my response.			
10. I consider a customer's culture, gender, and age when evaluating the meaning of his or her message.			

Rating key: Always = 5   **Sometimes** = 3   **Seldom** = 0
Add your total score. If you rated:

40-50	Your listening is excellent.
30-39	Your listening is very good.
20-29	Your listening is good.
15-19	Your listening is fair.
10-14	Your listening falls in the 25 percent category identified by Dr. Ralph Nichols's study, which you will read about in the sidebar "Missed Opportunities" in this chapter.

With this knowledge about your listening, focus on the methods outlined in this chapter for increasing your listening effectiveness.

EFFECTIVE LISTENING

Listening effectively by truly focusing on what a person is saying will be the primary means by which you will determine the needs of your customers. Depending on factors like gender, communication ability, personality type, and cultural background, your customers' needs are not always communicated directly. Instead they are discernible through indirect comments and nonverbal signals. You will need to be a skilled listener in order to pick up on your customers' words and their nonverbal cues and then use follow-up questioning to probe deeper in order to determine their real needs and expectations. As a rule of thumb, a listener is responsible for 51 percent of the effectiveness in any given conversation. If you fail to adequately listen to what your customer is saying, there is a strong likelihood that communication might break down.

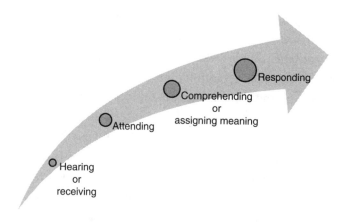

Figure 6-1   Active Listening Process

Many service providers either do not think about listening as a skill or take that skill for granted and assume everyone should be able to listen naturally. Unfortunately, this is not true. *Active listening* is a learned behavior. As Figure 6-1 shows, in order to actively listen, you must go through a *four-step process* of hearing or receiving the message, attending, comprehending or assigning meaning, and responding.

- **Hearing or receiving the message.** In the first phase of the listening process, sound waves are received in the ear and travel through the ear canal to the brain, where they are analyzed. This is a purely physiological process that requires no conscious effort on your part. It happens without your having to think about it. Unless you have a physical hearing loss or there are internal or external distracters that interfere with the message or sound, you will normally receive the sound and be able to move to the next phase of the listening process.
- **Attending.** Once the sound or message reaches the brain, the brain begins the process of deciphering what was heard and separating it from other sounds such as background noises. This is why eliminating environmental distractions is so important when

serving customers. You want to accurately receive their message so that you can come to the right decision on what to do next.

- **Comprehending or assigning meaning.** Your brain is like a computer's memory; it has millions of bits of stored information, images, sounds, smells, and other pieces of knowledge. Once you focus on a specific sound or voice, the brain takes over and attempts to match or compare it with what is stored in an effort to determine the appropriate actions necessary. Unless there is a mental disability that blocks normal functioning, the marvelous organ in your head is able to make instantaneous comparisons and determinations. Think of how your brain works when you receive a telephone call from a friend or family member whom you talk with frequently. The person typically does not even tell you who is calling when you answer; yet your brain processes the sounds received and quickly determines that you know the voice on the phone. Similarly, when a salesperson calls and begins a scripted presentation, you almost immediately identify the call as a possible sales pitch based on the caller's tone, his or her word selection, and the fact that you do not recognize the voice.

- **Responding.** The final phase of the listening process is taking action or responding to the message received. When dealing with your customers, you should always choose your words and nonverbal cues wisely. Using their personal filters, your customers will be assigning meaning to those words and nonverbal cues. If you say or do something that confuses or concerns your customers, a customer-provider conflict or breakdown could potentially occur.

FOCUS ON POSITIVE GLOBAL SERVICE: IDENTIFYING EFFECTIVE LISTENING CHARACTERISTICS

List the names of five people that you have known throughout your life whom you believe to be excellent listeners. What four words or characteristics would you use to describe each of the five people you have identified?

People   **Characteristics**

1. _____   _____

2. _____   _____

3. _____   _____

4. _____   _____

5. _____   _____

Use the characteristics that you described for these excellent listeners as part of an action plan to become a better listener. If you do not possess these characteristics, research strategies for developing them and then practice the skills until you use them flawlessly when dealing with customers. To help ensure that you are practicing the skills effectively and regularly, ask a friend, relative, or coworker to give feedback whenever you are using the characteristics or when you fail to use them.

LISTENING CHALLENGES

Communication breakdowns frequently occur because many people are poor listeners. Since listening is a learned skill, most people are left to figure out how to do it on their own or based on their parents' and friends' examples. If they do not attend college, go to professional seminars, have a good listening role model, take online or technology-based courses, or read books or articles on the topic, they have no sound grounding in the art of listening.

Diversity

When interacting with a customer who speaks another primary language, it is crucial that you listen actively and clarify anything that you are unsure about. Here's an example of what can go wrong if you fail to heed this advice.

An Asian customer called a motorcycle repair shop and explained that he had a 2009 Honda CRF50F motorcycle. He asked for what the store salesperson thought was "changes" for his model. The representative then spent several minutes discussing updates and modifications in the latest version while the customer listened politely. After a while, the customer said, "I need chainses." The representative was embarrassed when he realized that the customer was asking about the availability of motorcycle chains, not changes in design. He apologized for his error and took the customer's order.

In this instance, because of a heavy accent, and perhaps a misunderstanding by the Asian customer related to making an English word plural by adding an *es* to the end of the word *chains*, it may have sounded like "changes" to the salesperson. The error might also have been made because the salesperson did not listen carefully and did not paraphrase what he thought the customer said. Had he done so, he might have avoided giving an incorrect response and potentially frustrating or embarrassing the customer, who may have felt a loss of face or self-esteem. It's the subtle things that you have to listen for.

MISSED OPPORTUNITIES

Dr. Ralph G. Nichols, sometimes referred to as the "father of listening" in the United States, conducted a classic listening study[2] and found that the average white-collar worker typically has only about a 25 percent efficiency rate when listening to others. What this study means, of course, is that the average worker misses 75 percent of a given message during a conversation. Consider what that percentage related to poor listening habits would mean in terms of missed opportunities or lost business if you worked for a membership organization.

Opportunities	Results	Impact
100 members a day, each wanting to place a $10 order	25 orders were filled correctly	Loss of 750 orders per day ($2,737,500 lost per year)

Opportunities	Results	Impact
1,000 customers contacted the organization in one day	250 were serviced properly	750 were dissatisfied
1 million members were eligible for membership renewal in the association	Only 250,000 received their membership application after speaking with you because you got their contact information wrong	750,000 members were lost

On any given day, you will potentially be dealing with people from various parts of the world who are a different gender and age from one another and from you and have varying degrees of communication and hearing ability. These and other factors are going to present opportunities and challenges for you related to sending and receiving messages effectively. For example, if you are interacting with a customer who has a hearing impairment, you will need to adjust your message delivery style by potentially speaking louder, getting closer to the customer, or providing written information to supplement what you say. If the customer is from a culture where disagreeing with someone or complaining might cause a loss of face for either party, you may need to think of other ways to determine what the customer's issue is about and handle it appropriately.

Personal Distractions

Many of the personal barriers to listening can be better controlled than those in the environment because they are internal and are often created or maintained by you. This does not mean that all of them are easily solved. Still, by recognizing these factors, you can potentially reduce the chance of becoming distracted, irritating your customers, or providing poor service because you listened ineffectively. Some common personal distractions include the following:

- **Attitude.** Depending on how your day is going, your attitude toward your job or specific groups of people you have to deal with might be negative. If that's the case, you might find it difficult to stay focused and actively listen to a customer. If you allow your dislike for your job or perceptions about others to interfere with positive global service, you should decide whether you really want to keep your current job or perhaps find employment elsewhere. Biases or personal opinions about customers based on characteristics like your customer's age, gender, sexual orientation, or ethnicity have no place in a service environment. If you feel that you cannot provide service to a particular customer who comes in or calls, at least be professional enough to have someone else take over.

- **Circadian rhythm.** Each of us has an internal 24-hour biological clock that regulates our mood, attention span, and ability to perform at peak levels. Some people are at their peak in the morning and are able to keep their energy level up until midafternoon, while others hit their stride later in the day and go into the evening. This pattern of *circadian rhythm* affects everything from physical performance to thinking processes and can impact your ability to listen effectively. If you are a *morning person*, think of how you have felt attending classes late in the afternoon or going to an early evening meeting where the goal was to generate ideas. Were you an active participant, or did you take on the role of observer and only participate when called upon? Similarly, if you are an *evening person* and someone got you out of bed at 5:30 or 6:00 a.m. for work and then attempted to engage you in active dialogue, were you alert and attentive, or were you groggy and in a mental stupor where all you wanted to do was go back to bed? Likely, your circadian rhythm was thrown off. To some degree, this is what happens when you stay up for extended periods of time cramming for an examination, working, or traveling or when you fly across multiple time zones. When your body becomes out of sync with its surroundings or the situation, you are likely to be unproductive, frustrated, and irritable and not in a condition where you can effectively listen to your customers.

POSITIVE GLOBAL SERVICE ACTION TIP

The National Sleep Foundation recommends the following steps to help overcome jet lag if you travel on your job or are returning from vacation:

- Select a flight that allows early evening arrival and stay up until 10 p.m. local time. (If you must sleep during the day, take a short nap in the early afternoon, but no longer than two hours. Set an alarm to be sure not to oversleep.)
- Avoid alcohol or caffeine at least three to four hours before bedtime. Both act as "stimulants" and prevent sleep.
- Try to get outside in the sunlight whenever possible. Daylight is a powerful stimulant for regulating the biological clock.[3]

- **Personal irritants.** Many people have *pet peeves* that create challenges when communicating with others. Just the fact that customer service providers do not listen can set some people off. Think about the things that you do not like when interacting with others and you may identify some behaviors to avoid exhibiting when dealing with your customers. Two behaviors that cause problems in many cultures are violating personal space and eating or chewing things in public.
- **Psychological state.** Your "state of being," or how you feel, can impact your ability to listen effectively to your customers. If you are upset because of personal problems like family, finances, or health, you will likely be distracted and not ready to properly provide quality global service to your customers. Similarly, if you are angry about something, you will probably not focus full

attention on listening to what your customers need. Consider for a moment how you have reacted in the past when someone said or did something to upset you or make you angry. Did you notice a change in your voice tone or attitude? Perhaps your pulse increased and all your attention shifted to that person or situation for a few minutes. You may even have revisited the situation frequently in your mind for a period after that. All these types of reactions can take away from your ability to properly serve your customers. Typically in situations where your emotions rise, you need to get away from the situation or take time to reflect and resolve the issue before you can refocus on job activities and customers. If you fail to do this and instead attempt to serve another customer, you are likely to have a service breakdown because customers will detect your distraction through your tone of voice and body posture. This is not fair to them or your organization.

POSITIVE GLOBAL SERVICE ACTION TIP

When your emotional state rises because of personal issues or an angry reaction to a person or situation at work, take a few minutes to get away. Ask a coworker or your supervisor to cover for you while you go on a short break to clear your head. While away, do not dwell on the issues causing the reaction. Instead, read a book, take a walk, and think of positive things; focus on other issues so that when you return, you will be ready to listen to your customers effectively and deliver quality service.

- **Physical condition.** If you are not feeling well because of an illness or your energy is down, it can be difficult to project a positive global service attitude or listen effectively. There are numerous studies urging us to get at least eight hours of sleep, exercise regularly, and watch our diet. According to the National Sleep Foundation, "Researchers have found that 19.5 percent of U.S. adults are suffering from moderate to severe excessive daytime sleepiness . . . the prevalence of excessive daytime sleepiness in Europe stood at 15 percent. The study revealed that 11 percent of participants reported severe excessive daytime sleepiness—a condition more prevalent in women (13 percent) than in men (8.6 percent)."[4]

To ensure that you are ready and able to properly serve your customers and listen to their needs effectively, build in time several days a week to take a walk or ride a bicycle. Watch what you eat and stay away from the snack machines during the day. If you have an opportunity, take a 15–20-minute "power nap" during lunch or breaks to recharge your batteries. This latter strategy has been practiced in many countries for centuries (e.g., Latin America, China, and Southern Europe). All these strategies can help you perform at your peak and provide quality service.

- **Preoccupation.** Life is full of things that can compete for your attention. When you let personal distractions like your self-esteem, other people's opinions about you, personal issues, or health concerns interfere with your ability to effectively serve your customers, problems are likely to surface. When you are on the job, your focus should be preparing for and delivering seamless global customer service. Your customers should not hear about or be aware of any personal issues with which you are dealing. Quite honestly, they do not care that you are having a bad hair day, or that you are not able to pay your rent or mortgage, or that you feel like you are catching a cold. All they want is to have their needs met in a professional manner. Listen actively to each customer and address him or her individually.

- **Indifference.** This distraction relates to attitude and preoccupation. Indifference is a feeling that you might sometimes have when listening to others. The problem with indifference is that it often results in pretending to listen. Your customers are likely to quickly pick up on your inattention through your nonverbal cues and will not appreciate your less than stellar approach to service.

We all experience times where we just do not seem to have the interest to deal with some customers or situations. Often this is caused by events in our lives. For example, assume a day when you arrived late because you had car or traffic problems. As you walked into your workplace, you were greeted by a supervisor who was not happy about your being late and missing the morning staff meeting. Once on the job, your first customer had a particularly bad attitude along with what was really a minor problem that she was trying to escalate to a supervisor. Your second customer was on the phone and had a fairly complicated problem. This series of events seemed to drag on through most of the day, and by the afternoon, you couldn't really care less about whether you provided positive global service or not. We all have such days. The key is to not let one event roll over to the next; otherwise, you will find yourself taking out your frustrations through nonverbal signals and tone of voice with the next person. That only creates an unhappy cycle where the customer then becomes a difficult customer. In such instances, take a deep breath, clear your head, focus on thinking professionally, put a smile in your voice, and deal with the next person. If necessary, take a short break and get away from job tasks for a few minutes. While away, think of positive things or focus on something else other than the problems that you have encountered. When you return, be ready to listen to your customers.

External Distractions

There are some barriers to effective listening over which you have no control. These external factors can create distractions and inhibit your ability to effectively receive and attend to your customers' messages. The following are a few of the common external elements that can cause problems and that you should strive to avoid. In doing so, you will be more effective in listening to your customers and providing stellar service.

- **Physical barriers.** Based on your job requirements, you may have things that physically prevent you from adequately getting close enough to your customers to hear what they say. Desks, tables, windows, counters, or other furniture that separates you from your customers can create challenges to effective listening. Not only do such items provide limited access to your customers, but they also may send a less-than-personal service message to them. If you have any latitude in arranging items in your workspace or in positioning yourself in relation to your customers, consider a setup that allows direct access or closes the distance between you and your customers when possible. Obviously, there are some situations when this is not practical (e.g., bank tellers, drive-through or takeaway windows, or cashiers). Some organizations have realized the value of this more personal approach and set up kiosks or independent stands for their computers and registers so that customers can stand next to service providers. Often these setups are in stores in shopping malls.

By putting yourself in proximity with customers, you increase the chances of hearing them accurately. You can also help make them feel that you are collaborating as opposed to being on opposite sides of a piece of furniture in what might be viewed nonverbally as an adversarial position of "us against them." This is why interviews and meetings are often set up where people sit at right angles and next to someone as opposed to being on the other side of a table. You are psychologically partnering with customers in such arrangements.

- **Work environment.** Your work surroundings can sometimes present challenges when you are trying to listen to your customer. Many things compete for your attention in the workplace. Some common ones include telephones, e-mail, text messages, paperwork, and other people. In today's world, many people attempt to multitask. The professional thing to do is to avoid such behaviors whenever possible in dealing with a customer on the phone, face-to-face, or in an online chat. If you must address something else (e.g., answer a ringing phone because no one else is available), explain the situation briefly to your customer and ask if you may be excused for the moment or if you can put the customer on hold. If the customer says yes, do not leave him or her waiting for longer than 30 seconds without providing an update about what is happening. Where policy and situation allow, use an answering system to take incoming calls when no one else is available to do so. If customers are lining up for service, smile, let them know that you see them by holding up an index finger, and handle your current customer as quickly as possible. In such situations, you might also call for assistance from a coworker.

If you work in a noisy, hectic environment, then you may find it difficult to hear what customers are saying to you because of other people or equipment noise. In such instances, maintain a professional presence, smile, explain that you were unable to hear what they said because of all the background noise, and ask them to repeat their message. If possible, move to a less noisy location to talk. Also, avoid using a speakerphone when talking to customers since they often hear voices and background noises.

- **Visual distractions.** Since motion, color, light, and other visual elements attract attention, your mind can easily shift from your customer to someone or something moving past or in the background that is loud, bright, attractive, or otherwise competes with what you are doing. By being aware of this fact and consciously focusing your mind on what your customer is saying, you can accomplish your goal of positive service.

  Keep in mind what you have read about eye contact in various parts of the world. Just because people from a different culture (e.g., Japanese or Korean) avoid direct eye contact with you does not mean that they are not listening to what you are saying. If you are communicating with individuals from such cultures, simply look down slightly and make intermittent eye contact as you listen in order to honor their customs.

- **Semantic distractions.** When you interact with someone who speaks a native language other than your own, the chance of a communication breakdown increases significantly unless you both engage in active listening. This is because you come with different frames of reference or understanding of word meaning (*semantics*). Many common objects, ideas, concepts, actions, and other elements of the world are often defined differently in various languages. You must be conscious to use simple, one-syllable words and sentences, speak slow enough to allow clear enunciation of words, and avoid slang, contractions, and other abbreviated words or ways of communicating. Also, you must actively listen to your customers and observe their verbal and nonverbal response. If they appear confused or seem to misunderstand what you said, repeat the message or clarify it for them in an inoffensive manner. Above all, do not assume a superior posture by inadvertently sending nonverbal cues of frustration or annoyance or asking potentially offensive questions like, "Did you understand what I just said?" In such an instance, even if your customers did not understand, they are not likely to admit it. The result could be resentment, annoyance, or anger on their part and complaints or lost business for you.

Nonproductive Communication

Many factors can lead to listening breakdowns and miscommunication when dealing with customers from diverse backgrounds. Your goal is to prevent such instances whenever possible since they lead to frustration for you and your customer, wasted time, lost business, and negative word-of-mouth publicity. Some common situations that can result in these negative outcomes include:

- **Assuming a position of superiority.** If you communicate in a manner that might be perceived as judgmental, controlling, or arrogant, the customer-provider relationship will likely suffer. Remember all the things you have read about effective verbal and nonverbal communication and apply those strategies in each situation. Even if people do not speak your native language, they will receive and interpret messages through your tone of voice, gestures, facial expressions, and other cues that you send. If they perceive that you are acting inappropriately, then you are, since their perceptions are reality to them.

  To avoid any type of communication breakdown, always speak clearly and nondefensively, consider your body language and gestures, watch the reaction of your customers to what you say and do, allow your customers to speak without interrupting, provide ongoing feedback, and clarify any area that they seem not to understand.

- **Anticipating messages.** Some customer service professionals encounter problems when listening because they anticipate what their customer is going to say. In such instances they think they know what a customer is trying to say before she can finish her thought. The result is that they interrupt and provide the wrong information or answer what they think is the customer's question. In many cases they are wrong, and because of their rude behavior, they end up offending their customer. Often this tendency is a result of the service provider's behavioral style and the fact that the service provider is impatient. Many men use this approach to communication under the assumption that they are saving time and being more efficient. If you are guilty of this, you potentially send a message that you do not respect your customers and they will likely get the impression that you do not care about their needs. To avoid this perception, count to 3 slowly and silently after your customers stop talking to ensure that they have completed their thought. This can show that you were listening and have thought about what they said before responding.

- **Withholding information.** As you read earlier in this book, relationships are built on trust. This is particularly true when dealing with people from the Middle East, Latin America, and parts of Asia, where someone's word is his or her bond. Violate the sanctity of the relationship between you and your customers and you might lose their business forever. You will also probably lose that of all their friends and relatives since the story will be told to many others. Be very careful to share information about your product and services honestly and to the best of your ability. Do not manipulate or use strategies where you only provide partial information. For example, if you said that a product has a 90-day money-back guarantee but fail to tell a customer that any fees paid are nonrefundable or that labor charges are not included in the guarantee, they will likely perceive that you intentionally deceived them.

POSITIVE GLOBAL SERVICE ACTION TIP

To verify the accuracy of your perception about your own listening effectiveness, ask several people in your workplace to rate your listening abilities. Have them use the scale of *outstanding, above average, average, poor,* and *ineffective.* Once they rate you, have them provide suggestions on how to improve your effectiveness. These ratings could be done anonymously in order to get more candid feedback. Once you get the information, objectively analyze it and then incorporate it into your listening improvement action plan, as necessary.

FACTORS AFFECTING LISTENING

In a diverse business world, the question is not *will* you have to interact with a customer who is different from you, but *when.* There are numerous reasons that you and others are not able to effectively receive and respond to messages. These are some of the factors that determine how well someone listens and receives a message sent by another person.

Language Differences

In many instances, customers from other countries with whom you do business have studied your language and may be able to effectively read and understand it, but might have challenges in speaking it fluently without errors. Speaking another language can be difficult when the parts of speech and the way that letters sound differ from someone's native language. In some instances, grammar and syntax usage actually conflict even when a similar alphabet exists. For example, a native German speaker communicating in English often has trouble pronouncing the letter *w* (sounds like a *v* in German) and the letter *v* (sounds like an *f*), as in the car brand Volkswagen, which often sounds like "folksvagen" when spoken by a German. Obviously, when someone speaks with a heavy accent or pronounces words differently, you will have to ensure that you listen closely and analyze the person's message to determine the intended meaning before responding. If something does not make sense, ask the person to repeat what was said or ask clarifying questions.

The following strategies might help when you come into contact with someone who struggles with your language:

- **Be encouraging.** Speaking someone else's language can be frustrating, embarrassing, and intimidating. Show your customers that their lack of ability to speak fluently is nothing to be ashamed of. Compliment them on their efforts even if they make mistakes. Inject a bit of self-effacing humor by saying something like, "Your ability to speak my language is much better than my ability to speak yours." Throughout the dialogue, make sure that you smile and use open body posture and appropriate gestures. Listen carefully as they speak and really focus on the message they are trying to deliver if they are having difficulty.

- **Avoid judgments.** Remember that when you encounter people who are non-native language speakers or who are from another culture, their inability to speak your language or communicate effectively does not mean that they are unintelligent. Stay focused on your role in providing quality positive global service and practice active listening skills as your customers talk instead of getting distracted by their accent or the way they pronounce words. If you really cannot understand what they are saying, ask if they can write it in your language since some people can understand and write but do not speak a second language well. You might also ask coworkers or other customers if anyone speaks the customer's native language and can translate. A third option is to try speaking a different language that you have in common, if you know one, since many people from around the world speak multiple languages.

    Often, people who speak another language will start off by apologizing for their inability to speak fluently. Even when they speak a second language well, they may do this based on cultural values of being taught to remain humble, or they may feel insecure, or they may not want to cause you to lose face because you might not understand something that they say. The last point is often true of customers from parts of Asia.

- **Do not interrupt.** Some service providers have a bad habit of trying to finish other people's sentences if they are speaking slowly or seem to be struggling to find the right word. Do not do this when you are dealing with Asian customers, where maintaining esteem (face) in the eyes of others is important. You will likely embarrass and offend them by interrupting, finishing their sentence, or correcting their grammar. This is especially true if you are a woman dealing with a man or if you are dealing with an older customer from such a country. Instead, listen patiently and only respond when you are sure that your customers have finished what they want to say or when you need to answer a question that they ask you.

- **Speak slowly and clearly.** Someone's ability to receive and appropriately process your messages may be based on how slowly and accurately you speak. Take the time to slow your rate of speech slightly and enunciate words clearly. Do not take shortcuts by using jargon, slang, contractions, or terms generic to your culture that may be misunderstood by outsiders. As you speak, watch your listeners' reaction to see if there might be confusion or misunderstanding. If you note nonverbal or verbal indicators of this, do a perception check or simply ask an open-ended question like, "What questions do you have about what I just said?" rather than a closed-ended question like, "Do you understand what I just said?" This last question might even be perceived as offensive.

- **Do not pretend to understand.** If you have difficulty understanding what customers want or need because of a language barrier, admit it. Simply ask if they can either repeat or write down their message. In many instances, they are with someone who does speak your language and so can translate for you. As suggested earlier, you might also ask if anyone else present speaks your customer's language and can translate.

- **Be creative.** If you regularly have a number of customers who speak a specific language, keep a language conversion dictionary handy. For example, if you speak English and you regularly have Spanish-speaking customers come to your organization, have a Spanish-to-English and English-to-Spanish dictionary on hand so that either you or your customer can point to a word and the other can read the definition to determine an intended meaning. You might also try drawing pictures when all else fails.

Cultural Differences

In several countries and cultures, relationships are the basis for doing business. People often spend many hours together forming personal bonds and getting to know one another before ever discussing business issues. As a service provider, you must be conscious of a customer's national origin so that you communicate appropriately. For example, if you are at a business meeting with new Middle Eastern clients for the first time and immediately start asking questions like, "What is your budget for this type of product?" they may feel rushed and become defensive. Listening could suffer as a result, and you will likely end up wasting time and ultimately losing a customer.

Gender Differences

Your challenge when dealing with someone from the opposite sex is to recognize that men and women listen for different things during a conversation. For example, male service providers often strive to find out the "bottom line," listening for details that will help them make a decision about their customer's point and then interrupting with a formulated response. Often their reply is incorrect because they made assumptions about what the customer needed or wanted, and so they did not effectively gather and analyze the customer's message. On the other hand, female service providers traditionally listen with empathy, interest, and patience and allow their customers to share information, even when they deviate from the point and start sharing other information not related to their needs. Female service providers tend to listen in order to build relationships or rapport as they conduct business.

People are typically products of their environment. They learn behaviors based on the values and beliefs of their culture and society. Men tend to assume masculine, tough, or dominant roles, and women often take a more feminine, nurturing, and supportive approach when dealing with others. These cultural gender roles impact how well you and others listen and communicate. For example, because they focus on rapport and consensus building, many women often interrupt less than men, speak more precisely, and use "tag lines," or add-ons, to their statements. Examples of this include "That was a great meal, *wasn't it?*" and "This is a lovely dress, *isn't it?*" They also use qualifiers, or words that alter the meaning of words (e.g., *perhaps, only, very, maybe, really, hardly,* or *just*). For example, "The customer really did not know what she wanted" or "Perhaps I should get this in a different color."

When dealing with those of the opposite sex, remember to focus on what they are actually saying and not what you anticipate or think they will say. Adapt to their communication style and the things that they need based on your knowledge of sex and gender roles of various cultures and subcultures. The sidebar "Gender Communication Tips" provides some general tips for increasing listening and communication effectiveness between the sexes.

GENDER COMMUNICATION TIPS

The following are some strategies for communicating with customers of the opposite sex:

Men to Women
- Keep interruptions to a minimum.
- Do not monopolize the conversation.
- Listen to what the customer has to say.
- Discuss options and involve the customer in decision making.
- Engage in a mutual exchange of information and build on customer comments.
- Invest some time in "small talk" to build rapport.
- Use empathy.

Women to Men
- Get to the point or be direct and avoid excessive detail.
- Speak in short, bulleted statements.
- Avoid qualifiers or vague language.
- Ask for what you need or be specific.
- Avoid emotion (some men have difficulty dealing with it).
- Focus on problem solving.
- Be assertive.

STRATEGIES FOR ENHANCED LISTENING

Before you can properly receive the messages that your listeners have sent you, there are several things that you must do. The following are typical strategies used by effective service providers when they are interacting with their customers:

- **Prepare to listen.** In order to receive your customers' intended message meaning, you have to do some advance preparation. This includes being competent and knowledgeable about the products and services offered so that you can suggest alternative solutions to issues and questions they raise. It also entails being physically ready to serve when they contact you. As you read in this book, you should:
  — Have all necessary tools and materials at hand for quick reference
  — Be logged onto all computers and other equipment that will be used during a service interaction
  — Be fit and healthy so that you are mentally alert and can listen more effectively
  — Eliminate any other distractions or tasks when serving a customer
  — Focus exclusively on your customers
- **Stop talking.** Contrary to what some people think, it is not possible for the human brain to do two tasks with equal effectiveness simultaneously. You cannot listen and focus on what your customer is saying to you when you are entering data into a

computer, writing information down, or focusing on other people or tasks. The problem that many people have, especially men, is that they listen for key concepts or ideas and begin formulating a response while their customer is speaking, rather than focusing on the verbal and nonverbal cues being sent by their customer. In effect, they are simply waiting for a break so that they can talk. This is why they often have to ask their customer to repeat what was said or they answer partially or incorrectly.

The challenge when dealing with some people who have a hearing deficit, speak another language, or have a mental disability is that they need a bit of time to take in your messages, reflect on them, and formulate a response before speaking. Those who do not speak your primary language might need time to mentally translate what you said into their language and then formulate their response into your language. Depending on their level of language fluency, this might take several seconds. Additionally, in some cultures (e.g., those of Japan and Korea), silence is valued and is not uncomfortable for most people. Do not feel a need to quickly fill the silent void. Wait for your customers' responses.

- **Guide decision making.** In some instances, you may have to provide options for people rather than asking a blanket question like, "What do you think about what I just said?" Instead, you might say something like, "Ms. Patel, I really want to assist you in resolving this issue. Perhaps we could try _____ or _____. Which do think would work best?" She might choose one or offer a third option in response. Notice that in addition to offering choices, this approach uses a "qualifier" (*perhaps*). As you read earlier, women often use this style of communicating, so if you are a male service provider using this word, you might subconsciously be able to get onto a similar communication wavelength with your customer. Some women call this "getting in touch with your feminine side" when men do it. If you are a female service provider speaking to a male customer, then you may want to eliminate the qualifier and take a more direct approach. For example, "There are two options, Mr. Howard: ____ and ____.

Which do you think would work best for you?" Once you offer the choices, stop talking and wait for a response.

POSITIVE GLOBAL SERVICE ACTION TIP

Once you have stopped talking, count from 1 to 5 silently as you wait for a response from your customers before asking a follow-up question or adding additional information. During that time, watch their nonverbal cues for signs of recognition or confusion caused by what you said. If appropriate, ask what questions they have about what you just told them.

- **Listen objectively.** There are customers with whom you will have some degree of discomfort or dislike for a variety of reasons. Your goal as a professional service provider should be to overcome these feelings, listen openly, identify and solve any issues that they have, and then answer their questions and provide quality service. Treat all customers impartially and fairly and you will go a long way in your career while helping your organization succeed and building a solid reputation as a professional. Always try to work through differences or biases rather than letting them get in the way of professional service.

- **Avoid controversy.** When you openly disagree with your customer, you potentially create a losing proposition for everybody. Not only is your customer watching how you handle the situation, but others may be doing likewise. Think about a time when you were a child on the playground and you and a friend got into an argument that escalated into a shouting match, yelling "Did not" and "Did to" over and over. Who won? The answer is no one. The same will be true in the workplace. If a customer accuses you or the organization of lying, deceiving, or otherwise being wrong, maintain your professional composure. Acknowledge the possibility that it was your organization's fault, apologize, and inform the customer of the correct information or response. You have to hold your temper in check and do the professional thing when dealing with some customers. If you ever feel that this is not possible, excuse yourself, leave the area, and regain your composure; or if you have the option of getting someone else to handle the customer, ask for assistance.

- **Take notes if necessary.** If an issue is complicated or you will have to follow up with the customer or someone else, take notes so that you capture key points and information correctly and so that you can later verify what you said when you get back to your customer. These notes might be on a pad of paper or on your customer service management software system. Make sure you verify information like phone numbers, e-mail addresses, and physical addresses or other key details as you listen.

- **Ask pertinent questions.** At various points in a conversation with your customers, you may have to interject a question as they pause or finish an idea. Use open-ended questions (e.g., who, what, when, how, why, or to what degree) to elicit additional information and details and closed-ended questions (e.g., do, can, will, shall, or could) to verify, validate, or gain agreement to what has been said.

  When you ask questions, be sure not to format them in a way that sounds like you are being critical—for example, "You really do not want two of the same colored item, do you?" This could come across as a challenge to your customer's judgment.

SUMMARY

As you read this chapter, you were exposed to numerous concepts related to the importance of effective listening when interacting with your customers. In addition to identifying the elements involved with effective listening, you read about how men and women and people from various cultural backgrounds approach listening differently. You also encountered strategies for enhancing your listening ability. Some key points from this chapter include:

- Neither you nor your customer can be a passive listener in a successful dialogue. It takes an active two-way exchange of information that includes verbal and nonverbal feedback.

- Listening effectively by truly focusing on what is said will be the primary means that you will use to determine the needs and wants of your customers.
- Dr. Ralph G. Nichols found that the average white-collar worker typically has only about a 25 percent efficiency rate when listening to others.
- Diverse customer backgrounds impact listening behaviors.
- Depending on how your day is going or what your attitude is toward your job or toward specific groups or individuals, you may find it difficult to stay focused and actively listen to a customer.
- Many factors can contribute to someone's inability to hear.
- Many people have pet peeves that create challenges when communicating with others.
- If you are upset because of personal problems, you will likely be distracted and not ready to properly provide quality global service to your customers.
- Many things compete for your attention in the workplace. Some common ones include telephones, e-mail, text messages, paperwork, and other people.
- When you interact with someone who speaks a native language other than your own, the chances of communication breakdown increase significantly, unless you both engage in active listening.
- If you communicate in a manner that might be perceived as being judgmental, controlling, or arrogant, the customer-provider relationship will likely suffer.
- Some customer service professionals encounter problems when listening because they anticipate what their customer is going to say.
- Do not manipulate or use strategies where you only provide partial information.
- Listening values differ from one country to another. This often causes communication and relationship breakdowns when dealing with customers.
- Your challenge when dealing with someone from the opposite sex is to recognize that men and women listen for different things during a conversation.

- In some instances, you may have to provide options for people rather than asking a blanket question.
- When you openly disagree with your customers, you potentially create a losing proposition for you, them, and your organization.
- If an issue is complicated or if you will have to follow up with the customer or someone else, take notes so that you capture key issues and information correctly.

CHAPTER

7

Managing Time to Your Advantage

Today's customers often demand service 24 hours a day, 7 days a week, and 365 days in an average year. Effective global service providers strive to meet their expectations.

KEY CONCEPTS

After reading this chapter and when applying concepts learned, you will be able to:

1. Specify ways in which people and cultures may perceive time differently.
2. Describe the concept of time reality.
3. Discuss how different cultures have different perspectives related to the concept of time.
4. Define monochronic and polychronic time systems and explain why they are important to service providers.
5. Share the impact of your time allocation on customers.
6. Use the strategies learned for effective time management to better serve your customers.

7. Exhibit the strategies for effectively prioritizing tasks.
8. Identify techniques for managing time efficiently when you travel to customer sites.

Your *personal perception of time* may differ from that of others. For example, if you are looking forward to a vacation or other special event, time often seems to drag on. If you are in a hurry or are late for an event, time seems to fly by, putting even more pressure or stress on you.

Often the situation or the people involved in a given interpersonal scenario will dictate how each person perceives time. For example, many college students in the United States go by an unwritten standard that if their professor is late, they should wait a given period of time before assuming that class is canceled. If it's a full professor, the class might wait 15 minutes. If the instructor is an adjunct or associate professor, the students might only wait 10. In the workplace, however, you would be wise to wait at least 15 to 30 minutes before assuming cancellation of a meeting if you are scheduled to meet with a customer or a member of senior management.

Cultural perceptions of time differ as well. For example, some individuals grew up in a household or cultural environment where one or both parents had a lackadaisical attitude toward punctuality and were often late. If this was the case in your home environment, the chances are that you may not be as punctual as someone who learned early on that being on time was an important personal value. Depending on the situation and who's involved, this may or may not be an issue. In some cultures, being late by as much as an hour is acceptable. The higher a person's status, the longer you might have to wait for the person. In the United States and other monochronic societies, 5 to 10 minutes is an acceptable wait time if someone is late, unless the person is high ranking in an organization, government, or military. The logic in such cases is that because of the demands on their time and the level of decisions in which they are typically involved, senior-level people are more likely to be detained by unscheduled meetings, telephone calls, or other unexpected business that might cause tardiness.

In different societies, the view of time varies greatly, creating some real challenges for service providers unaware of the differing perceptions. For example, in the United States and a number of other developed nations, time is often considered a tangible commodity that can be saved, spent, divided, or made up. Business professionals often attend seminars and classes on "time management" in an effort to identify time wasters and increase their effectiveness and efficiency by better harnessing time. They have calendars, personal digital assistants (PDAs), wristwatches, computers, and other electronic devices, and formal meetings are often regulated by Robert's Rules of Order.[1]

On the other hand, customers are also often in a hurry, and they want service "now." This expectation and preoccupation with time is fed by rhetoric common throughout various cultures. Sayings such as "Time flies," "Faster than a New York minute," and "Time is money" communicate the perception that many people from certain countries have of time. The Germans and Swiss are even more time conscious than people in the United States, and punctuality is almost akin to a religious belief for many of the people in those countries.

In other countries and cultures, the activity or person that someone is dealing with, not the clock, determines the action. In such cultures, involvement or engagement with people and interpersonal transactions are stressed more than adherence to a preset schedule or agenda. There is typically no firm start or end time to a meeting or event. The essence of their cultural values revolves around taking one's time, being patient, and not hurrying to accomplish tasks in life. Quotes such as "With time and patience the mulberry leaf becomes a silk gown" and "Take care of your minutes and the hours take care of themselves" define the attitude that many people in Asia, the Middle East, Latin America, and some European countries have regarding time usage. Their approach to life is much slower, and they focus on personal-life over work-life issues.

As a service provider, you may encounter someone whose view of time differs significantly from yours. You must learn to adapt to better serve your customer. Many cultures view the past, present, and future differently and may place more or less importance on them than others outside their culture do. This may put a strain on the customer-provider relationship if you are not aware of or willing to make concessions for the differences.

Implications of time-perspective differences vary greatly. In countries like China, if you are late for a business meeting, you might cause your customer to lose face or to feel disrespected. In other countries, you might be expected to wait for your customer, even when you have a set appointment time. For example, if you are in sales and travel to other parts of the world, you might arrive expecting a meeting at a certain time and date, only to find out that the person you are supposed to meet is out of the office or on vacation even though you called the week before to verify the appointment. Always verify meetings multiple times and in writing before proceeding to them, especially if your customer is from outside your culture. Keeping subordinates and foreign businesspeople waiting for an extended period of time even when there is a scheduled appointment is not uncommon in many countries (e.g., Middle Eastern countries) when a higher-level executive is involved. Expect this and be prepared to wait patiently.

When dealing with customers from another culture who frequent your organization, you may find that they show up late for appointments. To compensate, you have to decide whether to build in some flexibility to your schedule or to turn the customers away when they arrive late. Obviously, the latter could mean a breakdown in the customer-provider relationship or lost customers. As you read through this chapter, you will explore how time is perceived and how you might maximize it to provide quality global customer service to all your customers.

TIME REALITY

No matter what country or culture you are from, the fact is that everyone has the same 24 hours in each day. You get no more or less, and you cannot buy, trade, or sell it. In many cases, some people just appear to have more time. The difference is that some people are better at managing and using their time than others.

Based on your cultural perception of time and factors like your home and work environment, stress may increase because of your difficulties in using time effectively. For example, if you work in an environment such as sales, manufacturing, or a call center where you are held accountable for production rates and work at a hectic pace, time can seem like your enemy. In these environments, employees often complain that they have to work extended amounts of overtime or on weekends in order to meet established goals or standards. A frequent by-product of this push to do more in less time is that they have little time to do creative planning, to take personal breaks, or even to think before they speak to customers.

Another challenge with time occurs if you have a personality type in which you take on too many projects simultaneously or have trouble saying no when others ask you to help out with tasks, to volunteer, or to help with personal issues. In such scenarios, your own projects often get put aside, and stress levels rise as you do other things.

The examples you just read about demonstrate the need for a good system to manage time effectively. Even if you can squeeze out a few minutes here and there, those precious minutes can help you efficiently deal with your *time reality*—what you need to do to ensure your ability to work efficiently and to more effectively serve your customers or accomplish other tasks.

FOCUS ON POSITIVE GLOBAL SERVICE: PERSONAL PERCEPTIONS OF TIME

Based on your personal work and home situation, time might seem either to slowly drag on or to speed away in various situations. Here are some examples of both. Add your own personal examples at the end of the lists in order to get a better view of how you perceive time.

Slow Time Passage

Sitting in a doctor's or dentist's waiting room

Waiting on hold on the telephone with no music or announcements

Standing on line at an amusement park ride

Standing in a checkout line at the grocery store

Waiting for public transportation

Rapid Time Passage

Being on a date with a spouse or significant other

Taking a vacation, holiday, or weekend getaway

Eating at a favorite restaurant with friends

Going on an amusement park ride

Taking an examination in school or for a license

Slow Time Passage	Rapid Time Passage
Waiting for popcorn at a theater when the movie has already begun	Speaking with a professional who bills based on time (e.g., plumber, accountant, lawyer, or consultant)

CULTURAL TIME PERSPECTIVES

For years, anthropologists have studied the use of time in various cultures to try to better understand why some people view it differently. The perspectives people have of time are often based on religious dogma. For example, in the United States where the Puritans brought ideas of efficient use of time and a focus on the future, the culture developed to where today people focus on making changes and moving forward at a fast pace and getting more done with less. Entire industries (e.g., fast food) have developed to support this driving mentality. The challenge is that because the United States has become such a melting pot of diverse people who have brought with them their own religious and cultural values, conflict with time usage sometimes erupts among people from various subcultures. Within the U.S. population, many different groups have brought religious and cultural values with them that focus on revering the past or that concentrate on the present as opposed to the future.

As an example of how time-perception differences are common, ask people from various cultures or subcultures what they perceive an

POSITIVE GLOBAL SERVICE ACTION TIP

If you interact with customers outside your own cultural group regularly, you should do research on how people from those cultures perceive time. This will help you prepare to effectively handle situations where customers are either early or late for meetings and social events.

acceptable time for being late to an appointment might be. You will likely receive very different responses. For example, people from Germany or Finland often pride themselves on being some of the most punctual people in the world and are normally early or on time for meetings and social events. Late arrival is considered rude and potentially insulting. In parts of Great Britain and North America, being 5 minutes late for a meeting might be acceptable, but 15 minutes or more would definitely be considered late and possibly rude, depending on the event and the person with whom you are scheduled to meet. In the Pacific Island, Middle Eastern, and many African cultures, tardiness of 30 minutes or more is perfectly acceptable for a business meeting in many instances.

Just as in business situations, if you invite international customers to a dinner meeting or social event, you can anticipate that they will arrive at different times. This is sometimes based on their cultural backgrounds and values. For example, someone from Japan or Korea might arrive half an hour early, a guest from the United States or England might come 5 minutes early, a Honduran might show up 30 minutes late, an Italian could be up to 2 hours late, an Ethiopian might be even later, and someone from Vietnam might not come at all; your Vietnamese customers only accepted your invitation to be polite and to avoid causing you to lose face if they said no. If you ever host such an event, make sure that you specify your expectations in writing in order to avoid confusion or embarrassment to guests. For example, your invitations might specify that dinner will be served at 7 p.m. sharp.

With people immigrating throughout the world, it is highly likely that at some point you will attend meetings with people from different cultures, invite them to an event that you are hosting, or be their guest. Before such engagements, you would be wise to do some research on the culture of the people you will meet with and their perception of time to avoid potential problems.

The manner in which time is handled in the workplace often differs among cultures as well. In the United States a five-day workweek from 8 a.m. to 4 p.m. or 9 a.m. to 5 p.m. is common. Employees in some industries work different shifts (e.g., midnight to 8 a.m.), and overtime at the end of a work shift or on weekends and holidays is normal and in some cases required. Many workers get vacation or holiday time as an employee benefit, but some people take few or no days off during the year. This might be because of their workload or the perception that they are expected to "put in the extra hours" in order to succeed in their career or maintain their job, especially in an economy where many people have been laid off. In other countries, people often take a less dramatic view of time or the need to spend excessive portions of their life at work. In many parts of the world (e.g., numerous European countries), four-day workweeks are common, and employers typically give employees four or more weeks of vacation or holiday leave per year. Employees are often required to take the time off to "recharge their batteries" or enhance their personal motivation and energy so that they will be more productive on the job. Additionally, in many South and Central American countries, a midday break closes businesses and government offices while people relax or even take a nap.

On a personal level, the amount of time that someone spends with another is a significant nonverbal signal. For example, if you meet with a higher-level customer or manager and he or she allocates more than 30 minutes for the get-together; the message is that you and what you have to say are valued and believed to be worth the time investment.

FOCUS ON POSITIVE GLOBAL SERVICE: PERSONAL TIME EXPERIENCES

Think of interviews or meetings that you might have experienced in the workplace, at school, or elsewhere, and then answer the following questions to get a better sense of how you reacted to the time allocation of others and how it made you feel. Since many people will likely react the same way you did, use your responses as a guide for allocating time and dealing with your customers, coworkers, employees, and others during a given day.

At previous job interviews, were they brief encounters of less than 30 minutes, or did they last for longer? What were the outcomes?

_____

_____

_____

When you were interacting with a sales or service professional recently, how much time did the person spend with you? Explain whether you were satisfied or dissatisfied with the encounter.

_____

_____

_____

TIME SYSTEMS

In regard to time, cultures are often categorized as treating time either as a tool to be manipulated and used to accomplish more or as an entity that provides enjoyment and opportunity to build and enhance relationships with others. The two systems of time perception are termed _monochronic_ and _polychronic_.

Monochronic Time

A _monochronic_ time system is one in which people take a linear view of time, where events are typically present- or future-focused. Tasks are completed one at a time, and events are scheduled or segmented sequentially into precise, small units. Planning is a crucial step before starting anything. Work projects, home improvements, travel, family events, and vacations all require gathering information and developing a schedule or time-usage plan in advance. Under this system, time is typically arranged, categorized, and managed with a start and end time. Germany, Canada, England, Switzerland, the United States, and Scandinavia are some examples of monochronic societies. People in these societies place a paramount value on being punctual, completing tasks, and getting the job done. These cultures are committed to regimented schedules and may view those who do not subscribe to the same perception of time as being lazy, inconsiderate, or disrespectful.

For people in the United States and other monochronic nations, time is viewed as a precious resource not to be wasted or taken lightly. Daily and future events are often planned in meticulous detail, with many people following strict schedules tracked with written and electronic scheduling tools. These schedules show appointments that we must arrive at by specific times, as well as seminars, meetings, classes, and work schedules. Even entertainment is scheduled with start and end times (e.g., television shows, concerts, or amusement park trips). All this is done in the name of efficiency, with little concern for the interpersonal relationships that might be impacted through such strict compliance with time. In his book *The Silent Language*, Edward T. Hall states, "Not only do we Americans segment and schedule time, but we look ahead and are oriented almost entirely toward the future. We like new things and are preoccupied with change . . . Time with us is handled much like a material, we earn it, spend it, save it, waste it."[2]

POSITIVE GLOBAL SERVICE ACTION TIP

If you are a service provider dealing with customers from a monochronic society, plan in advance, be on time, and focus all your attention on one customer at a time. Do not get distracted by other tasks or people.

Polychronic Time

Polychronic refers to a time system in which people take a circular view of time, or perceive that time is reoccurring, with one season or cycle leading to the next and one year evolving into the following. Memories are not left behind but are revisited when you get back to the same point, season, or time as that of the previous year.

Multitasking by working on several things or talking to multiple people at once is a common occurrence in polychronic societies as people take a more fluid or casual approach to scheduling time and accomplishing tasks. They value relationships, patience, human interaction, and honesty above task completion and speed or efficiency. Flexibility and a sense of relaxed purpose dominate meetings and interactions with others. Meetings could involve a dozen or more people all connecting individually with others in the room simultaneously as they cement relationships with no urgency to get to the point or come to an immediate agreement. If individuals from a monochronic society were to find themselves in such a situation, they would likely to be stressed, frustrated, and anxious since their focus is often on getting to the point, making a decision, and moving on to their next meeting or project. The best advice for you in such instances if you are not polychronic is to go with the flow, focus on relationship building, and let the process take care of itself. Otherwise, you risk alienating your customers and being labeled as impatient, arrogant, and inflexible. All this can lead to damaged relationships and lost business. For example, suppose you offer customers in your store assistance only to be told that they are "just looking." Allow them to do so after informing them that you are available should they need your assistance, and keep an eye on them and be ready to assist if needed. If they want to engage in conversation, participate briefly as long as it does not distract extensively from providing service to waiting customers.

Many Native American, Latin American, and Middle Eastern cultures use a polychronic system of time in the workplace and for their social lives. These cultures are much less focused on the preciseness of accounting for each and every moment and more focused on the relationships between people. For these cultures, people drive activities, rather than time. The concept of standing in line waiting one's turn is a very foreign concept and typically not followed. Neither is the value of "don't talk when someone else is talking" that is often taught to children in many monochronic cultures. In a business place or market, it is quite common in polychronic countries for multiple customers at a time to push forward and talk over one another as they vie for the service provider's attention. As might be expected, such practices can cause problems when customers from these cultures visit monochronic ones. For example, Walt Disney World in Orlando, Florida, in the United States touts itself as being "The Happiest Place on Earth." Even so, when students from South America swarm to the amusement park each year during their holiday season, it is not uncommon for arguments and even physical confrontations to erupt between them and mono-chronic guests. They often push people aside to join friends as they try to move to the front of a line in which people have been standing in the hot sun with their screaming children for up to an hour. In many cases, these students are not intentionally trying to be rude. They are simply doing what their cultural norms have ingrained in them without considering the consequences.

Cultures that are polychronic are deeply rooted in tradition rather than in task accomplishment. Such cultures place more value on the phases of the moon, seasonal cycles, a flexible pattern of local life, and the calendar of religious festivities rather than the fixed elements of a clock. Instead, their culture is more focused on interpersonal relationships. They have no problem being late for an event if they are with family or friends, because the relationship is what really matters. As a result, poly-chronic cultures have a much less formal perception of time. They are not ruled by precise calendars and schedules or singular events. Instead, people from polychronic cultures often handle multiple items or people at a time and schedule several appointments simultaneously. For that reason, sticking to a set schedule is highly unlikely. There are many stories of businesspeople from monochronic countries (e.g., the United States) visiting clients in Japan or the Middle East after exchanging numerous letters, e-mail messages, and phone calls with the expectation that they were going to "close the deal." They arrived only to find that days of meetings and social functions proved to be only an introduction or relationship-building experience. They then had to fly back a second or third time to get to a point where business was actually discussed and an agreement finally negotiated.

When dealing with a customer who comes from a polychronic society, you can expect to be kept waiting on many occasions. You may be expected to wait beyond your scheduled appointment time or to even step aside and wait while a subsequent customer's needs are met. If you travel for business and find yourself in such situations, it might be better to have an open-ended ticket in your pocket and avoid scheduling more than one meeting a day with different clients.

POSITIVE GLOBAL SERVICE ACTION TIP

If your customers are from polychronic cultures, take your time during interactions and meetings. If appropriate, consider offering refreshments and allow relationships to flow naturally without seeming to push people toward a decision or being in a hurry.

TIME ALLOCATION

Even though some managers and organizations would like to be able to dictate exact time periods that you should spend with a given customer, this is not always possible. Certainly, there need to be standards for providing service to customers in order to ensure that service providers are available to address all their needs. However, established guidelines for *time allocation* should provide acceptable ranges in which service is delivered and against which your performance is measured. If you find that periods established in your organization are not realistic or that service is suffering as a result, speak with your supervisor and make some positive recommendations for improvement. Before you do so, though, check with coworkers to see if they are experiencing the same challenges to rule out some problem area that you are experiencing. It may be that you are unaware of some aspect of your job or equipment that sometimes slows your *rate of service delivery* or the amount of time you spend with your customers. If you find that peers are meeting established standards, ask them to share with you their approach to serving their customers or speak to your supervisor about possible additional training. The key is to be efficient and effective in your efforts.

POSITIVE GLOBAL SERVICE ACTION TIP

The amount of time you spend with customers often sends subliminal messages of how you perceive their importance. Reevaluate your work habits and patterns continually to see whether you can accomplish tasks in a more timely fashion.

FOCUS ON POSITIVE GLOBAL SERVICE: TIME ALLOCATION

The way you treat customers can significantly impact your success as a service provider. As you read earlier in this book, customers generally want to feel that they are welcome and respected and that they can trust you and your organization before they will do business with you.

Assume that you are a salesperson in an exclusive clothing store where you are used to dealing with older, more established customers who dress very professionally and are well groomed. A teenage male customer with shoulder-length hair, cutoff jeans with holes in them, sandals, T-shirt, and backpack comes in and begins to browse. You do not know that his father is a bank vice president, his mother is a college professor and internationally known author, and the young customer recently inherited over a million dollars in a trust fund from his grandmother who recently passed away. His father shops in your store regularly, and the young man is there to buy several shirts and ties for his father's birthday.

You approach the young customer and ask, "May I help you?" with little enthusiasm and without smiling while giving a disapproving look as you scan the store for other more polished customers to serve. Right then, a well-dressed older woman wearing a suit approaches you, and you greet her warmly with a smile and welcome. You subsequently abandon the young man after telling him to let you know if he needs anything. You then follow the woman around and attentively assist her for the next 10 minutes. During this period, the young man waits for assistance and finally leaves to go to another shop in the mall.

How do you think this young customer feels about you and your organization at this point? Explain.

_____

_____

What is the likelihood that he will relate the story to his parents and friends?

_____

_____

What are potential outcomes from this situation?

_____

_____

ALLOCATING TIME FOR INTERNAL CUSTOMERS

Internal customers are as important as external ones since they provide the products, services, and support to you and your department that allow you to deliver positive global service to your external customers. Since they also depend on you for support, you should treat them with the same respect as you would someone from outside the organization. Unfortunately, we sometimes forget this important point, and when someone in the organization asks for assistance, we almost feel that the person is taking advantage or putting a burden on us. If you send negative verbal or nonverbal messages, such as closed body language, facial gestures, ignored requests, procrastination, or failure to follow through as promised when a coworker approaches you for help, you can project an attitude that your coworker is unimportant.

Additionally, failing to act or delaying your response in such instances could be perceived as a lack of concern or professionalism. Moreover, it is important to recognize that the amount of time you allocate to individuals can send a powerful message. For example, if you fail to work cohesively and collaboratively with coworkers, you potentially send nonverbal messages that you are not a team player. Such actions could haunt you when a coworker who feels wronged or disrespected relates your behavior to peers or possibly to a supervisor. Also, if you need your coworker's support in the future, you may well be met by reluctance.

FOCUS ON POSITIVE GLOBAL SERVICE: TIME ALLOCATION WITH INTERNAL CUSTOMERS

Assume that a coworker comes into your work area and says that she needs to speak with you. After inviting her to sit down, you continue to fumble through a file on your desk and tell her that you have only a few minutes to talk because you are expecting an important call. Your coworker starts to explain that she needs some information that you have in order for her to respond to a customer right away. As she speaks, your phone rings, and you hold up an index finger to ask her to hold on a minute. You subsequently ask her to excuse you while you take the call.

Your coworker leaves, and from her cubicle next to yours, she can overhear your conversation. She waits for over 15 minutes as you carry on a telephone conversation. From your laughter, comments, and tone of voice, she concludes that you are on a personal call. She waits patiently but then has to go to another meeting and is unable to call her customer back with the requested information.

What impact might this instance have on your working relationship with your coworker? Explain.

_____

_____

How would you feel if a coworker treated you in this manner? Explain.

_____

_____

Explain what impact your actions might have on external customers and the organization.

_____

_____

_____

TIME MANAGEMENT STRATEGIES

No matter whether you are from a monochronic or polychronic society, you will still have to interact with customers with both cultural perspectives. The challenge is to adapt to each person's unique needs and expectations while accomplishing your goals and those of your organization. The following are some thoughts on how you might blend your approach to time with that of your customers:

- **Plan ahead.** If you wait until an emergency exists, the chances that you will be able to stay in your comfort zone with regard to time lessen significantly. Learn to build flexibility into your schedule while also being aware of any pending deadlines that your customers might have. In some instances, you might have to let the customers know that you cannot meet their expectations. In such situations, be prepared to offer an alternative or to compensate them for their inconvenience or frustration, if that is appropriate.

- **Meet customer needs.** While something may not seem important to you, or when an announced or assumed customer time frame does not necessarily fit into your schedule or perception of time, recognize that the customers are the ones paying the bills. Customers are the reason you have a job and your organization exists. Respect their needs and try to accommodate their schedules and desires whenever possible.

- **Learn to prioritize.** In today's business world, life has become much more hectic and pressing in most parts of the world. This is putting a strain on service providers and forcing service professionals to reexamine their personal and cultural values related to time. A focus on balancing work and personal life has become an important issue for many people. To aid you in the workplace and reduce your level of stress, consider what must be done as opposed to what would be nice to do on a regular basis. Look for systems or ways to group tasks and events so that you meet your needs and those of your customers. Take care of the absolutes and put off some of the nice to-dos until a later time. You will read some specific strategies to accomplish this later in this chapter.

- **Manage technology.** Many people are now surrounded by technology that did not even exist in the workplace a number of years ago. As a service provider, you likely depend heavily on it to provide quality global service to your customers. The challenge is to become proficient in the technology and ensure that you use it to its fullest potential. Your customers should not have to be inconvenienced because you do not know how to transfer a call, cannot locate something in a database, or are inexperienced with new software installed on your computer. Make sure that you receive training and the information needed about your systems before a customer contacts you.

  Do not let your technology dictate the way you work. For example, if you are typing documents or entering data into a computer, do not have your e-mail or smart phone set to alert you every time a message arrives. If you do, ignore the alerts. Instead, schedule a period each hour or whenever is appropriate to check and respond to messages.

- **Practice delegation.** You do not have to do everything yourself. If there are tasks that others are better qualified or more efficient at doing, allow them to perform those tasks while you take on ones that you have the knowledge or skills to better perform. Delegation is not just a management function. Speak to your supervisor or team leader and arrange to work with teammates to decide who is best suited for specific tasks; then divide up those jobs accordingly. This will free you up to potentially spend more time with your customers.

- **Break tasks into small chunks.** Sometimes large chores seem overwhelming and can lead to frustration and stress. Look for ways to break common tasks into smaller chunks that can be done in bits throughout the day or week. This makes them more palatable while allowing you to work at a more even pace. For example, if your job requires you to return calls or respond to customer e-mail messages each day, set aside a period of time to do this in each hour during an appropriate portion of the day (e.g., from 8. a.m. until noon or noon until 5 p.m.). If you have large amounts of data to enter into your computer, determine what periods of the workday tend to be slowest in relation to customer contacts and work on this task during those periods.

POSITIVE GLOBAL SERVICE ACTION TIP

Research articles and Web sites related to time management. Try to develop a list of at least 10 different time-saving strategies other than the ones described in the text. Also, develop a list of time wasters in your personal life that ultimately can affect your ability to perform effective customer service. Create an action plan to eliminate the wasters.

PRIORITIZE TASKS EFFECTIVELY

Because of downsizing, new technology, lack of training, and increased competition, many employees feel squeezed to their maximum capacity in today's global workplace. If you find yourself in this situation, it may not be any comfort to know that you are not alone. What can help is developing an efficient system to prioritize job tasks and a tool that allows you to determine how to better use what time you do have available. By *prioritizing time* and setting up a schedule for events, activities, and work and personal tasks on a daily, weekly, monthly, and yearly basis, you can potentially reduce your stress level. You can also appear more professional and ready to deal with customers and job tasks instead of looking like you are constantly in a crisis mode where you scurry from one task or customer to the next.

Many time management experts suggest that a way for you to better manage responsibilities rather than them controlling you is to create a daily list of important tasks or activities and then assign a value to each. The key is to consistently prioritize your tasks each day. You might do this at the end of the day or the first thing in the morning when you arrive. The value of doing it the day before is that you avoid the potential of a customer or crisis waiting for you when you arrive that would prevent you from doing it in the morning. Make sure that you review your schedule frequently to ensure that you do not forget an event or activity.

Priority-Setting Standards

There are three *prioritizing standards* or guidelines that can help you in determining which tasks should be done first. These standards can assist you in developing a more realistic list of activities that should be your daily priorities. Just make sure when you create your list that it is possible for you to attain the goals you set for yourself. Build in some flexibility for dealing with customers and situations that take more time or come up unexpectedly and need to be addressed. Otherwise, you might become discouraged and give up on your system.

Use the following standards as a guide when setting your priorities.

Timing

In order to be realistic about what you can accomplish, objectively analyze each task based on your current knowledge, skills, responsibilities, and past experiences. Once you begin a task, there must be enough time to finish it; otherwise, you should seek additional resources in the form of technology, coworkers, or external resources (e.g., temporary workers or consultants) to assist you. Should such a situation arise, go to your supervisor or team leader for guidance. If the challenge is because of your current workload, share that information and ask for assistance in restructuring a task or reassigning some tasks to others.

Be realistic about the time it will take to complete a task. Make sure that you schedule enough time, plus a little extra, on your daily planning sheet. Also, consider your personal circadian rhythm or peak periods of performance. Try to schedule your most strenuous, stressful, or time-consuming tasks when you are at your best so that you are more likely to be successful or get more accomplished.

Personal Judgment

Since you know best what your own personal abilities are, what needs to be accomplished on any given day, and what other projects are pending, you are often the best person to decide the order in which you approach each task. Be logical when trying to create a prioritized list of items and avoid being overly optimistic related to how much you can do. Always build in a bit of flexibility to handle unexpected customer issues, assignments, or problems that might occur. Remember that your goal is to provide positive global service while reducing your stress level.

In prioritizing items, make sure that the ones that have the most impact on customers and others are placed higher on your list. Should you determine that you have more high priorities than you have time, you may need to ask for help or guidance from your supervisor, team leader, or a coworker. Often, the act of simply asking for assistance helps build stronger relationships with others because they might feel that you value them and trust their opinion enough to ask. The key is not to make a habit of doing this and to sincerely thank people for their assistance. You would not want it to look like you are trying to pass along your responsibilities or work to them. In addition to asking for assistance internally, consider other options that might provide assistance in accomplishing your tasks or goals. For example, there might be technology, consultants, outside vendors, or even customers who are able to provide information, products, or services that can come in handy.

Relativity

Assigning priorities is a matter of relativity, or what is most important. Some tasks and projects are readily rated higher than others. Since you are dealing with customers, a smart approach would be to ask, "What will add the most value for my customers?" Also, ask yourself, "What is the best use of my time?" Unfortunately, many service providers focus on tasks that they enjoy doing, or they fill their daily schedule with frivolous or easy tasks. This produces a hollow feeling of accomplishment, for they may get a lot done and enjoy doing it, but they have not added a lot of value to customer service or the organizational goals. Keep in mind when setting priorities in the workplace that your number one focus should be your customers (both internal and external) and the activities that support them.

POSITIVE GLOBAL SERVICE ACTION TIP

To get a better idea of how you spend time during a given day, keep a record of your activities in 15-minute increments for 1 week. Use a day planner or calendar, a PDA, a digital recorder, or an ordinary notebook to list your daily activities. As the week goes on, this process will become more familiar and easier.

Prioritization System

Creating a system to list and prioritize tasks and assignments is not all that difficult. Once you create a list of pending projects, it is a matter of looking at each item and objectively assigning it a level or priority. The following are suggested criteria for grouping tasks or assignments.

Priority A: Must-Do Items

Because of customer need or demand, management directives, local, state, or federal regulation, cultural expectations (e.g., religious requirement), or opportunities driven by personal desire to excel in your job or career field, these items on your to-do list might be listed higher. For example, if you promised a customer that you would return a call, take an action, or deliver a product or service on a given day, then that item might be designated as a high priority on your daily list. Additionally, if you are responsible for producing or filing applications, reports, or governmental or organizational forms that have specific deadlines or submission dates, these should be listed as a high priority.

Priority B: Should Do

Anything listed in this category falls into the midvalue category because it may increase customer satisfaction or enhance personal or organizational performance. Items in this category do not have specific deadlines or are not mandated or required. Examples include unsolicited mailings of new product samples or information to customers, a submission of a proposal to management on an idea you have for modifying an existing product line or adding a new service, or an e-mail to your supervisor sharing observations that you have made of another organization's efforts to gain new customers that are impacting your ability to compete effectively.

Priority C: Nice to Do

The final or lowest-priority category includes things that do not directly impact customer satisfaction. They might be tasks or projects that you would enjoy doing or that interest you personally and will not adversely impact service or your ability to do your job if they do not occur. These are basically the tasks that we often say, "One of these days, I want to . . . ," and they can be put off until you have free time on your schedule without impacting customers or your organization one way or the other. These "nice-to-do" tasks might include getting together team members to brainstorm ideas for a more efficient cubicle layout at the office, discarding old hard-copy files or deleting old e-mails, cleaning out a closet or your desk, or lining products neatly on display shelves before customers come into your store.

POSITIVE GLOBAL SERVICE ACTION TIP

As you periodically go through your e-mail and voice-mail messages at the times you have scheduled throughout the day, prioritize them and identify tasks to add to your list of things to do, as appropriate. This might mean that you have to reprioritize existing items on the list to insert a new one at a higher level.

SAVING TIME AS YOU SERVE

In addition to prioritizing, many strategies can save time and result in a better quality of customer service. A key to effective service is to allocate enough time to handle customer issues. With experience, you will get better at doing this and at estimating how much time you need for various situations. Until then, talk to other experienced service professionals, your supervisor or team leader, and your customers to find out how long a task should normally take. Also, be prepared to serve by being aware of company policies, procedures, products, and services. Make sure that you are familiar with any forms or paperwork used while serving customers and have what you need handy so that you do not inconvenience customers while you search for something.

The following are some specific strategies that might apply while serving customers in different situations. As you read through them, try to come up with more of your own.

Face-to-Face Situations

No matter whom you serve or where you serve them, time management can be an important element in your success. It does not matter whether you deal with complaints, counter service, sales, or on-site delivery; the amount of time expended and your level of efficiency will often determine customer satisfaction.

To effectively serve customers when they are present, *engage your customers* or otherwise get them involved. If multiple customers are present and you must serve others, think of strategies for occupying those waiting so that they are not as focused on how much time has elapsed since their arrival. You can accomplish this by getting them actively involved in a task or providing some type of distraction. Many organizations do this on the telephone by playing music or product and service announcements or by sharing helpful tips on various topics.

The following are some strategies for actively involving your customers in the service process in face-to-face situations:

- **Gather information.** If you need to gather information from customers in order to provide better service later, have them begin filling out an information form, as many medical or dentist offices do. Similarly, if people are returning a product, applying for a job or license, or registering for some type of service, have them write down pertinent information as they wait. This simple process occupies your customers while you handle others and gathers required information. Doing this increases your effectiveness by better managing time and saves your customers time once you get to them.

- **Provide reading materials.** Depending on the situation and the type of organization, you might give your customers brochures or promotional publications about new products and services or information about changes in laws or policies to read while they wait their turn for service. This occupies the customer's mind and provides information to questions that you will not have to answer later.

- **Use an electronic buzzer or number system.** Many organizations with high customer walk-up traffic like restaurants or sandwich shops use small electronic buzzer devices that vibrate and display rotating lights once activated by a host or hostess. This alerts customers that their table or food is ready.

  Other high-volume organizations such as delis, motor vehicle licensing offices, barbershops, or utility companies use tear-off number dispensers. Customers take a number, and an electronic light board displays one number at a time as each customer is served. This alerts customers when it is their turn to be served. Such systems are helpful during peak sales and service periods, such as during seasonal, back-to-school, going-out-of-business, or clearance sales. These systems were designed to let customers know where they are in the line for service, keep customers moving, and save service providers the unpleasant and time-consuming task of having to deal with angry customers who think that other customers have been served out of turn. Taking a number also gives customers some mental stimulation by giving them something to do as they watch the number board to determine their turn for service.

If your organization has such a system, be sure that you alert people to take a number as they enter. This will prevent confusion later over who is next for service. Also, with such a system, be careful not to fall into the practice of thinking of your customers only as numbers. Instead of shouting out "Number _____," a more appropriate approach would be to say something like, "May I help the customer with ticket number _____?" Then, as the person approaches, try to make eye contact, smile, and offer a greeting such as "Good morning. I apologize for your wait. How may I assist you?"

MOBILE TIME MANAGEMENT

If you travel for a living by visiting client sites or remote locations (e.g., branch offices), you may have heard or made statements like, "There just aren't enough hours in the day." Transit time can take a big chunk out of your day. Learning to make the best use of your time is crucial if you are in such a mobile service position. Here are a few mobile service tips. They might help you make the best of your situation.

- **Prepare in advance.** Take advantage of technology to make appointments in advance and be sure to confirm them the afternoon before the scheduled time to ensure that your customers have no change of plans. If you fail to do this, you might find yourself driving or flying to their location only to discover the meeting was canceled or postponed. As you have read already, even verifying may not always guarantee that the appointments will be kept when you are doing business in other cultures or with people who perceive time differently.

Additionally, make sure that you schedule your appointments far enough in advance to allow for emergencies, and gather the materials and information you will need well before the scheduled date and time. If you wait until the last minute to do this, you may run into challenges, especially if something is out of print or unavailable. You may also end up departing late as you scurry to obtain what you need. That can cause subsequent meetings or events to run late.

- **Plan travel during non–rush hour.** If you are going to catch public transportation or are driving to a client site, you should consider the normal flow of traffic at your scheduled appointment time; then build in a bit of extra time just in case of unforeseen events. When you drive to other locations in many areas of the world, something will likely slow you down (e.g., malfunctioning traffic lights, accidents, trains, or vehicle breakdowns). You can grumble and accept lost productivity time, or you can be prepared by adding extra time in your schedule, having alternative routes in mind, and making sure that your vehicle is well maintained so that it does not overheat or break down.

- **Group appointments or phone calls.** Depending on the cultural background of your customer, you may be able to set up multiple appointments in the same geographic area in order to save you and your customer time, effort, and frustration while reducing your travel miles. You can also use the "group" approach when customers or vendors come to your site for meetings. Just be sure to allow adequate time in case an appointment runs beyond its scheduled time; otherwise, subsequent customers will be disappointed and dissatisfied.

If contacting customers by telephone, consider scheduling or returning all such calls for one part of a day (e.g., the morning). This allows for more efficient use of your time during the remainder of the day without interruptions. For example, if you get all your phone calls taken care of in the morning, you can then focus on other customers and related activities during the rest of the day without having to stop or change pace.

- **Invest in a smart phone.** In today's changing world, cell phones have become an indispensable part of travel. The latest generation of smart phones allows calls, GPS directions and navigation, access to e-mail and the Internet, and many other functions. You can use your phone when you leave one client location for the next to verify an appointment and alert the next client that you are on the way. Do remember safety and do not drive while calling, texting, or searching the Internet.

SUMMARY

As you read through this chapter, you discovered differences in the way that people and cultures view and manage time as well as some specific strategies to better maximize your use of time when dealing with customers from around the world. Some of the key concepts that you investigated include:

- In different societies the view of time varies greatly from looking upon it as a necessary element for doing business to cherishing moments spent with others.
- Everyone has 24 hours each day. You get no more or less, and you cannot buy, trade, or sell it.
- The perspectives that many people have of time are often based on religious dogma or beliefs.
- The manner in which time is perceived and dealt with in the workplace often differs among cultures.
- A monochronic time system is one in which people take a linear view of time where events are typically present- or future-focused.
- Polychronic refers to a time system in which people perceive that time is reoccurring, with one season leading to the next and one year evolving into the next.

- Established guidelines for time allocation should provide acceptable ranges in which service is delivered and against which your performance is measured.
- No matter whether you are from a monochronic or polychronic society, you will still have to interact with customers with both cultural perspectives.
- Timing, personal judgment, and relativity are three prioritizing standards or guidelines that can help you in determining which tasks should be done first.
- Many people group tasks or assign a value through the use of labels like A, B, and C.
- A key to effective service is to allocate enough time to handle customer issues.
- Transit time can take a big chunk out of your day. Learning to make the best use of your time is crucial if you are in a mobile service position.

8

Reducing Stress on the Job

With all the stress in life, it makes no sense to create more through poor work habits.

KEY CONCEPTS

After reading this chapter and when applying concepts learned, you will be able to:

1. Define what stress is.
2. Identify common workplace stressors.
3. Explain how service providers might react to stress.
4. Discuss some of the causes of stress in a service environment.
5. Use strategies discussed to reduce personal stress levels.

Because of advancing technology, the world moves at a much faster pace than it did decades ago. People's values, beliefs, and expectations have caused much of this acceleration. Added pressure to succeed and remain competitive while trying to maintain some semblance of normality related to work-family life has come along with these changes. All these potentially cause stress in many workers.

Stress is a major contributor to loss of workplace efficiency. Each year, millions of dollars and countless worker-hours of productivity are lost because of stress-related illnesses. In all stress-related studies, customer service is often rated among the top most stressful occupations. In fact, many studies have consistently listed customer service in the top 10 most stressful occupations in the country. This is because the variety of people and situations service professionals face on any given day requires them to call on a multitude of skills and to think quickly. The results of pressures that people are facing in the workplace have been staggering, financially and from a health standpoint.

As you read through this chapter, you will discover a number of proven strategies that can assist in making your workday more productive and less stressful.

WHAT IS STRESS?

Stress is the feeling that factors in your personal and work life are so overwhelming that you cannot effectively deal with them. It is a major cause of lost productivity and increased health issues in the workplace today according to many studies. The term *stress* was used in 1950 by Hungarian doctor Hans Selye to relate to the strain or anxiety felt by humans.

Because of cultural variations and differing behavioral styles, people have different degrees of ability when it comes to coping with stressors or irritants on the job. What bothers one person might not affect another. Workers in more-developed countries have been dealing with stress as a factor of work for decades and often have more information and support to deal with it than those in less-developed countries, who are now starting to become aware of the issue and address it. In many instances stress might be related to how the culture approaches the concept of work and the role of workers.

According to the World Health Organization, "Due to globalization and changes in the nature of work, people in developing countries have to deal with increasing work-related stress. . . . Although some research has been conducted in developing countries, particularly in Latin America, there are still not enough in-depth studies to fully analyze both cultural differences and behaviors which vary from one country to another. Along with difficulties in controlling other well-known occupational risks, there is lack of awareness of work-related stress, and shortage of resources to deal with it."[1]

According to Dr. Selye, there are two types of stress—*distress* and *eustress*. Distress—or "bad" stress—can potentially cause problems when you are interacting with customers and other people, demotivate you, reduce your effectiveness, and lead to long-term mental and physical problems or death. While some of the negative stress that you encounter in the workplace can be avoided, some cannot; you simply have to learn to minimize as much of it as possible through the strategies you will read about in this chapter

Not all stress is bad. Dr. Selye coined the term *eustress* to describe "good" stress. You might experience eustress when you set and achieve a goal (e.g., graduating from high school or college, making a sale, getting a letter of appreciation from a customer for your excellent service, or delivering a successful presentation to clients). In such instances, you would likely feel good about your accomplishment. En route to achieving a goal, you might also experience some negative stress because of the tasks required to achieve your ultimate objective (e.g., staying up all night to study for an examination, learning effective sales techniques in a classroom, spending time calling or interacting with a customer, or researching and rehearsing your client presentation for hours). With eustress, you may go through the same physiological stages that you would for negative situations, but at the end, when you reach your goal, you have a sense of accomplishment and a feeling of exhilaration.

Each worker and workplace is unique, and yet there are similarities when it comes to factors that can lead to stress and the way someone copes with it. Some workers handle the pressures of their job better than others. An example of this might be seen in a high-pressure call center where productivity is measured by meeting established variables. Such a situation may prove daunting for some people, while others just learn to "deal with it." The gender, age, experience, personality, or cultural background of a person can determine how well he or she overcomes the stress of certain events and situations. For example, someone from a Westernized country, where demands of the job are high and people are used to being able to multitask, might readily cope with deadlines and quotas, whereas someone from a more relaxed culture, such as the Bahamas or other laid-back island nations, might not be as tolerant.

From a service provider perspective, you should also keep your customers' background in mind as you interact with them in order to provide quality global service in a relaxed, professional manner and avoid giving them undue stress. Numerous studies over years have substantiated that employees feel that stress is a major part of their lives (see Figure 8-1). In a world where people from all cultures and walks of life collide, stress is often an inevitable outcome for service providers. For example, on a typical day, you likely strive to professionally juggle what feels like a million different demands at once. While technology can assume some of these tasks, you and your coworkers often handle the brunt of the workload as stress mounts. Because of this, you should learn to identify signs of stress in yourself and others.

SIGNS OF STRESS

- Concentration problems
- Headaches or feelings of being tense
- Feelings of anxiousness, sadness, irritability, anxiety, or depression
- Lack of motivation or interest at work
- Autoimmune disease
- Fatigue
- General irritability
- Anger or short temper
- Withdrawal from others
- Trouble sleeping
- Stomach and bowel problems
- Loss of sex drive
- Increased or regular use of alcohol and drugs to cope

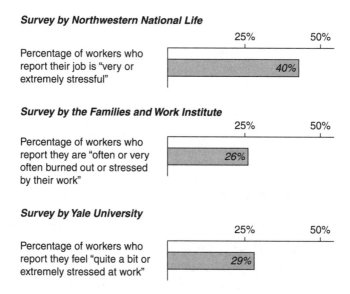

Survey by Northwestern National Life

Percentage of workers who
report their job is "very or
extremely stressful"

40%

Survey by the Families and Work Institute

Percentage of workers who
report they are "often or very
often burned out or stressed
by their work"

26%

Survey by Yale University

Percentage of workers who
report they feel "quite a bit or
extremely stressed at work"

29%

Source: NIOSH Publication No. 99-101, National Institute of
Occupational Safety & Health, www.cdc.gov/niosh/docs/99-101

Figure 8-1   Workplace Stress Survey Results

POSITIVE GLOBAL SERVICE ACTION TIP

When you accomplish a goal or difficult task or achieve some small
goal in the workplace, congratulate yourself, even if no one else
does. Reward yourself by taking a break and going for a soft drink
or snack in the break room or cafeteria.

FOCUS ON POSITIVE GLOBAL SERVICE: IDENTIFYING STRESSORS

Stress comes in many forms and impacts people in different ways. Take a
few minutes to think about what stresses you (e.g., tasks, types of people,
and life and workplace factors). Make a list of these along with the ways
that you normally deal with each. After you complete your list, finish reading this
chapter and then come back to see if there are some alternative ways you might
approach each item in the future.

Stressors	Strategies for Handling
_____	_____
_____	_____
_____	_____

WORKPLACE STRESSORS

It would be no surprise if the signs of stress mentioned previously sound familiar to you. Most service employees strive to come to work ready for their job activities; however, many arrive with an anticipation of dread over what the day will bring. Work is no longer fun for millions of employees around the world. Numerous factors contribute to stress in today's service environment. These *stressors* include anything that creates tension, anxiety, or frustration for you during a given workday. They might appear in the form of people, tasks, or elements of your job and environment. Some potential factors that may create pressure in your work environment include:

- The necessity to do more with fewer resources
- Inadequate supervisory guidance or poor management
- Job design where you have a heavy workload, get infrequent breaks, often do not have time for lunch, and have to deal with mundane tasks and rude people
- A feeling that you have little input or control over your daily activities
- Pressure to perform at higher levels without being adequately rewarded
- Regular friction or conflict with coworkers and customers
- Workplace turmoil or constant change that leads to high degrees of uncertainty related to expectations of you and your coworkers
- Unsafe or dangerous work conditions or job assignments
- Reduced levels of training to prepare you for job responsibilities
- Fewer opportunities for career advancement

- A constant barrage of negative news reports related to job security and cuts being made throughout many industries

The good news is that you can do some things to reduce some of your own anxiety and maintain a professional attitude while providing positive global service to your customers.

REACTIONS TO STRESS

Because people handle stress in various ways, you may witness a peer reacting to a customer situation in a manner that you feel inappropriate or that is different from the way you would handle it. For example, based on many personal factors that you read about earlier, you and your coworker might approach an angry or rude customer's response or a tight deadline in a different way. This is because the physical and psychological reactions to stress vary among people.

In addition, your job, workplace, and internal factors you encounter throughout your day can also have an impact on your mental and physical state and can affect how you react to stress that you encounter. This is partially because you are a product of evolution when it comes to your brain's reaction to stress. When your brain perceives danger (or stress), it triggers a chain reaction of events as part of a protection mechanism, starting with the release of chemicals (adrenaline) into the nervous system. In situations of danger, your heart starts beating faster, sending more blood throughout the body. Your breathing accelerates so that you take in more oxygen. This prepares you to face the situation (fight) or perhaps to escape (flight). This reaction is referred to as the *fight-or-flight response*. Typically, after such spurts of excessive adrenaline and activity, the body needs to take a break to recuperate. Think about times when you have worked very hard (studying all night for an exam or preparing for an interview or presentation) or had to deal with a verbally abusive customer. You were able to accomplish the task or handle the situation professionally but subsequently needed to take a break to recuperate or mentally process the event and get back to a normal state.

In a customer service environment, increased levels of adrenaline can be helpful in solving customer problems or can cause customer-provider relationship breakdowns if you lose control. On the positive side, getting excited about a project or helping a customer can work in your favor. This is especially true when deadlines are tight for extended periods or there is a sales contest where the representative with the most sales in a given period is rewarded. For example, assume that your organization just bought out a rival company and has taken over a call center site. A new computer-based communication system will be installed to better handle customer calls and contacts. You have an eight-week window during which you can move into the new facility, hire and train additional staff, and install the communication system before going online to take calls. You and other employees will have to work overtime for the entire period. Implementing the plans successfully and meeting the deadline will result in all employees receiving a bonus. If eight weeks was a realistic estimate of the time needed, you will probably meet your deadline, but then you and the others will need time to rest.

On the negative side of the fight-or-flight response in the customer environment, increased levels of adrenaline can create problems in maintaining the customer-provider relationship. For example, assume that you encounter a very disagreeable customer who has experienced a problem. No matter what positive communication and customer service skills you try, the customer will accept nothing less than what he is demanding. In addition, he is yelling and using profanity directed at you and the organization. In such a situation, the added adrenaline may lead you to react inappropriately (fight). In such instances you must remain professional and maintain control. You may need to excuse yourself and seek a supervisor or someone else to handle the situation (flight).

POSITIVE GLOBAL SERVICE ACTION TIP

If someone is doing something to cause you stress or is bothering you, speak up. Do not assume that he or she knows how you feel or what is going on in your head. Allowing something to fester not only will cause you suffering but can also negatively impact relationships long term. In a nonemotional manner, when you are no longer upset, share your thoughts or concerns with the other person.

CAUSES OF WORKPLACE STRESS

In a struggling economy, managers around the world realize the value of providing service on demand. With the competition for customers, many organizations are making ongoing advances in system efficiency to address customer needs. Tasks that used to take hours, days, and even weeks are now done almost instantaneously or certainly quicker than before. Because of evolving technology, transportation, and systems, customers are likely to demand speedier product and service delivery in the future. The idea of getting what you want now has so permeated consumer mentality that your failure to provide the quickest, most efficient delivery of products and services can be the kiss of death for your organization. As a result of this "get-it-now" mentality, each new generation has less memory of the long waiting times experienced by preceding generations. People are accustomed to getting what they want, when and where they want it, with little or no wait time. Today, if customers cannot get what they want from you and your organization when they want it, they go elsewhere; or in many cases, they just log onto a computer and surf the Internet to get it—often faster and cheaper. These continuing changes and expectations increase pressure and stress for you and your coworkers.

Some of the societal mechanisms that are fueling customer expectations that they can get what they want instantly include:

- ATM banking, where deposit slips are no longer required
- Smart phone and personal computer access to the Internet virtually anywhere
- E-mail, Twitter, instant messaging, and other means of contact
- Almost instantaneous access to telephone numbers via directory information over the telephone or on the Internet
- Supermarkets with bank services, florists, pharmacies, and delis
- Express delivery by the U.S. Postal Service and other carriers in less than 24 hours
- Book downloads to electronic readers
- Drive-up laundry and dry cleaning services

Personal Factors That Can Cause Stress

You cannot leave personal issues at the door when you enter your workplace. Many of the things that are on your mind continue to cause distractions and stress while you are at work. Habits, activities, and other aspects of your personal life can also create stress. Whenever possible, you should strive to resolve personal issues quickly to reduce your stress levels and allow you to better focus on your job. Failure to do so might cause a breakdown in effectiveness and efficiency or customer service.

Some more common personal issues that cause stress and potentially create challenges on the job include:

- **Relationships.** People are complex creatures when they are involved in a relationship. The challenge is that you may not be able to disassociate yourself from your spouse, significant other, or family members, especially when emotions are high or there are problems in the relationship. As a result, you bring emotional baggage with you to work some days. For example, recent arguments can stay with you when you report to work. In such situations, communication skills that you learned earlier in this book involving customers can also be a great help with your personal relationships.

   On a positive note, your relationships with others outside the workplace can also provide you with valuable tools for dealing with customers. In interacting with people outside the workplace, you build an interpersonal network of resources that might offer referrals or information when you need it. You also learn about behavioral styles, diversity, and human nature by interacting with others in a variety of situations.
- **Financial problems.** In today's economy, even many well-to-do people are struggling and stressing over how they will make ends meet and whether they will be financially ready to face the challenges of tomorrow. Many people are out of work, underemployed, or worried that they could lose their jobs. If you are like most people, you have financial problems from time to

time. Perhaps you don't have enough money in your checking or savings account to cover household expenses, to pay a bill, or to make a needed purchase. These problems can weigh heavily on your mind and lessen your effectiveness in dealing with customers. If you have financial problems, look for resources [e.g., books, classes, and employee assistance programs (EAPs)] that can help you get on a sound financial footing.

- **Chemical or substance use.** Using alcohol, prescription drugs, or chemical substances to help reduce stress not only potentially reduces your effectiveness on the job; it can affect brain functioning and be dangerous or deadly for you and those around you. Most health plans nowadays offer assistance in reducing substance dependency. If you use any of these substances, you may want to check with your human resources department or supervisor to find out whether programs to help you change your behavior are available through your EAP.

- **Nutrition and physical condition.** Peak performance and efficiency on the job require that you have good nutrition and be in good physical condition to be well and to feel good about yourself. Maintenance of proper weight and body conditioning helps enhance your mental capabilities and allows you to be more creative and focused at work while allowing you to better cope with stressful situations. Your energy levels and ability to perform in a variety of circumstances are also improved. Recent reports about the "fattening" of North Americans and other people throughout the world are alarming. After years of healthy eating and exercising, many people are reverting to a less active lifestyle. If you are not monitoring your food intake and exercising, you could be setting yourself up for health problems and lessening the chances that you will be ready to face the various customer service or workplace situations that surface. Your customers and organization also suffer when you are not working at full potential or are absent because of health-related issues.

- **Personal time.** We all need to take a "mental health day" or just
  some time to relax and do non-work-related things that we enjoy
  (e.g., gardening, reading a book, taking a walk, playing an electronic game, or watching a favorite television show) periodically
  in order to reduce stress levels. Taking some "alone time" occa-
  sionally is important for reducing stress and is crucial for overall
  good mental health. Sometimes the pressures of work and family
  responsibilities can build up and seem so extreme that you might
  feel helpless and simply shut down mentally. Physical agitation
  and crying are often reactions to this feeling. We all go through
  such moments; however, if these symptoms continue for more
  than a couple of hours, you should consider talking the situation
  over with someone. When such instances occur, you can resemble
  a bomb with a short fuse waiting to be lit. And if the match comes
  in the form of a difficult customer situation, problems for you,
  your organization, and your customer may be the result.
- **Overcommitting.** Does the term *workaholic* apply to you? Because
  of competition in the workplace, concerns about job security,
  overextension of credit by banks, downsizing or "rightsizing,"
  and numerous other factors, a lot of people spend more time at
  work than elsewhere. In North America, people have traditionally
  been reluctant to take vacation or other time off. Now with the
  concern of potential layoffs or job loss, the problem is even worse.
  Still, doing so is really important for your mental health and
  thus ultimately is important for your coworkers, customers, and
  organization.

  If you are a workaholic, you likely see the advantages as
  being able to accomplish more than others and gaining new skills
  and knowledge, while possibly moving up the career ladder. The
  downside is that other parts of your life may be suffering, and in
  time you may develop health or relationship problems. By taking
  a break or vacation, you can become reinvigorated and come back
  to work with new dedication and drive. The key to real long-term
  success is balance.

FOCUS ON POSITIVE GLOBAL SERVICE: WORK ATTITUDE SURVEY

Take a few minutes to honestly assess your attitude toward work and the workplace. These questions can help determine whether you fall into the workaholic category. If you answer yes to all or most of these questions, there is a good chance that you are a workaholic and your stress levels could be high and lead to future personal and medical problems.

- Do you find it difficult to "chill out" and be inactive or relax?
- Do you feel that no one else can complete a work task as well as you can?
- Do you arrive early for work, no matter how late you stayed up the night before?
- Do you take work home in the evenings, on weekends, and during holidays?
- Do you find it hard to take a vacation (and when you do, do you take work along)?
- Do you volunteer to take on new tasks, even if you already feel overcommitted?
- Do you skip lunch and breaks (and sometimes dinner) in order to work on job-related tasks?
- Do you regularly volunteer for overtime or work on weekends and holidays?
- Can you not envision yourself ever completely retiring?

Job Factors That Can Cause Stress

With everyone working harder with fewer resources in most workplaces, it is easy for situations to become very stressful. Many job-related factors can frustrate you and add tension to your day and that of your peers and customers. If you are finding that to be the case in your own workplace, take some time to work with others to reduce or remove some common stressors. For instance, suppose that your organization provides only one microwave oven in the lunchroom. During the 45-minute lunch period, 15 to 20 people need to use the microwave oven at the same time. People might get anxious and frustrated with the delay, and potential conflict could result. Such situations are sometimes not something you can control, but they are manageable if you think through them rationally and brainstorm them with others involved. Maybe something as simple as working out an alternating lunch schedule could help. Use the interpersonal communication skills you have read about in this book and do a bit of negotiating and planning and you will likely be able to professionally resolve such issues.

The following are some common *job factors affecting stress levels* that you might experience:

- **Poor job structuring.** When your job or supervisor requires that you work various shifts or overtime in order to complete assigned work, stress can result and lead to negative physical and mental side effects. Whether you work in a hierarchical or team-based environment can have an impact. Both organizational structures have advantages and disadvantages, based on how they are designed, managed, and allowed to function.

  To improve your chances for performance success, become aware of your job responsibilities quickly (especially when they change), try to focus on the positive side of change (e.g., new opportunities to learn, increased opportunity for promotion, and the possibility of streamlining job functions and becoming more effective and efficient), and take advantage of the changing situation. Service providers who act like victims rarely win in changing work environments. They perform poorly and let their service levels slip. Since many organizations are looking for ways to reduce overhead costs, increase efficiency, and enhance customer service, they are searching for service representatives who can support their goals. To better fit into this new paradigm, make yourself more marketable by continually gaining new knowledge and skills so that you will be better prepared for the inevitable change that will occur in your organization.

- **Job insecurity.** Whenever major shifts occur in organizations (e.g., downsizing, mergers, or acquisitions), workers typically go through a period of insecurity. Some of this can be attributed to the behavioral-style preferences that you read about earlier in the book; however, much of it is simply human nature. People typically resist change and often have adverse reactions to it or become stressed because it frequently brings about a learning curve for new knowledge and skills and requires that they do things differently. Such insecurity is often the result of a lack of adequate and effective communication from upper management. In today's fluctuating economy where technology is replacing numerous jobs, many people struggle to remain positive. If you find yourself in such a situation, use a proactive approach of gathering information, asking questions of your supervisor, reading materials given to you by your organization, taking the opportunity to get involved on committees or projects, and generally becoming a "player" rather than an "observer" as change occurs.

- **Unrealistic performance goals.** A normal part of most jobs is the performance appraisal period where your supervisor or others provide written feedback on how well you do your job and whether you meet established performance goals. There are typically personal and organizational goals. You will usually be held accountable for personal goals that can ultimately influence the attainment of the overall goals of the organization. Unfortunately, many supervisors and team leaders set goals with little or no input from their employees who have to meet them. The result is that service representatives are often held accountable for unrealistic production goals (e.g., telephone sales), and in some organizations their results are publicly displayed in reports or on boards in call centers. This practice can cause disillusionment for you and your peers, lower employee morale, and lead to stress, resentment, and frustration.

POSITIVE GLOBAL SERVICE ACTION TIP

You can help ensure that you get credit for performance by keeping track of personal and performance achievements throughout the year. In doing so, when the time for your performance review comes around, you will have documentation and can have some valid input in setting your goals for the next year based on your current results.

- **Conflicting demands.** A common stress factor in competitive environments is that most service providers have multiple, overlapping responsibilities. In many instances, the demands caused by these responsibilities may sometimes conflict. While you may successfully accomplish all your work, there are likely some instances where you do not achieve the degree of success that you prefer and desire or that is expected of you by supervisors, peers, or customers. This sometimes occurs because your efforts to provide quality service might be hampered by policies and procedures or other factors that are out of your control. In addition, personal demands can cause internal conflict while you are on the job. A good time management system is sometimes the answer. For other situations, you may have to use your interpersonal communication skills to negotiate a settlement or compromise. Remember that you cannot always eliminate sources of stress. Therefore, you must seek ways of dealing with them.

- **Repetitive or redundant tasks.** Many service positions involve repetitive or redundant tasks that provide little or no opportunity for initiation or change in routine. If you have such a job, you likely experience times when you feel lackadaisical toward dealing with customers. If you find yourself in such circumstances, consider volunteering for additional assignments, committees, or cross-training in order to break the monotony and better qualify yourself for other positions in the future while reinvigorating yourself.

- **Limited advancement opportunities.** Another job factor that could possibly reduce your effectiveness in dealing with customers is limited opportunity for professional development that could lead to job advancement. When such roadblocks exist, your desire to excel, be creative, and exercise initiative might be affected. You and others may be reluctant to abandon your position during poor economic times, but when times change, failure to provide opportunities could be an issue for your organization. If your organization offers educational assistance or cross-training, where you learn other job functions in different departments, take advantage of these avenues to prepare yourself when opportunities do arise.

STRESS REDUCTION STRATEGIES

The good news is that you can do some things to effectively reduce some of your own anxiety and maintain a professional attitude while providing positive global service to your customers. Unfortunately, many people adopt poor *stress reduction strategies* that can create more problems and ultimately increase stress levels. The sidebar "Unhealthy Stress Reduction Strategies" offers a list of some of these unwise practices.

UNHEALTHY STRESS REDUCTION STRATEGIES

The following behaviors will not reduce or eliminate stress if done to excess and can actually cause health issues that add more stress to your life:

- Overeating or undereating
- Procrastinating and letting things pile up
- Overcommitting and filling your schedule to avoid dealing with stressful issues or people
- Smoking
- Using alcohol, prescription drugs, or chemical substances to relax
- "Vegging out" in front of the computer or television for hours
- Becoming reclusive and avoiding friends and family
- Becoming sedentary and staying at home (often alone)
- Sleeping excessively
- Acting aggressively or taking your frustration out on friends, family, coworkers, or customers

Usually, good stress reduction comes down to learning to alter your behavior and the way that you react to stress. You are often the cause for some of your own stress because you behave in a manner that invites added pressures. Look at the following list of effective behavior changes and decide which ones will be helpful to adapt to reduce or eliminate stressors.

- **Regain control.** Sometimes, we just have to say "Enough!" and step back to analyze where we are with commitments and factors that are impacting our lives. If you regularly feel that you are "swimming upstream" and that all sorts of people or tasks are coming at you constantly, stop and take a deep breath; next look at what is causing you to feel this way and then develop a strategy for modifying or dealing with what is happening and how you are feeling. Don't be embarrassed or afraid to ask for help. Many times, when people become overwhelmed and start to get depressed about it, they are ashamed that they feel they cannot handle things themselves and they avoid seeking help. This only allows things to continue to build and overwhelm. If you get to such a point, it is crucial that you get help so that you can continue to perform professionally and help your customers.
- **Learn to say no.** Obviously, you are not likely to tell your boss or customers that you won't do something or help them, but when possible and feasible, decline to assist others when you have too much on your plate already. Take the approach that antidrug campaigns at schools have taught children for years in relation to drugs—"Just Say No." If you are overcommitted, seek assistance from others in the workplace. Speak to your supervisor or team leader about your workload and your time commitments. Often, people do not realize how much work they have given you if they routinely pass along assignments as tasks come up, especially in a high-pressure or chaotic work environment.
- **Avoid controversy.** If you find that certain topics or people irritate you or create a stressful situation, stay away from them. For example, if you are in the break room and a discussion comes up about which you have a strong opinion or feelings, excuse

yourself and leave the area. Similarly, if there is a coworker or other person whom you prefer to avoid for some reason, do so. When the person comes around, ask in a professional way to be excused and do not get drawn into a conversation that will raise your frustration level.

POSITIVE GLOBAL SERVICE ACTION TIP

Use humor to reduce the stress throughout your workday. Look for the humor in any situation that you confront and focus on that. For example, if you have an encounter with a particularly obnoxious or angry customer, serve the person professionally and later take some time to recuperate by sharing a joke or discuss the humor in the situation with a coworker in the break room. Just ensure that you are not near other customers when having such conversations.

SUMMARY

In this chapter, you have read about stress, the causes of stress, and some strategies for reducing or eliminating it. Some of the key concepts that you explored include:

- Stress is a major contributor to loss of workplace efficiency.
- Hungarian doctor Hans Selye coined the term *eustress* to describe "good" stress.
- Distress, or "bad" stress, can potentially cause problems when you are interacting with customers and other people, and it reduces your effectiveness.
- People handle stress in various ways; some peers may react to a customer situation in a manner that you feel inappropriate or that is different from the way you would handle it.
- When your brain perceives danger or stress, it triggers a chain reaction of events as part of a protection mechanism, referred to as the fight-or-flight response.

- With the competition for customers, many organizations are making ongoing advances in system efficiency to address customer needs.
- Today, if customers cannot get what they want from you and your organization when they want it, they go elsewhere; or in many cases they just log onto a computer.
- You should strive to resolve personal issues as quickly as possible to reduce your stress levels and allow you to better focus on your job.
- A healthy lifestyle helps enhance your mental capabilities and allows you to be more creative and focused at work while allowing you to better cope with stressful situations.
- We all need to take time for a "mental health day" or just relax and do non-work-related things that we enjoy periodically in order to reduce stress levels.
- With everyone working harder with fewer resources in most workplaces, it is easy for situations to become very stressful.
- One of the most frustrating situations for service providers and customers occurs when the provider does not have the authority to make decisions or assist customers.
- A common stress factor in competitive environments is that most service providers have multiple, overlapping responsibilities.
- Often, good stress reduction comes down to learning to alter your behavior and the way that you react to stress.

9

Addressing Service Breakdowns

*Customer complaints are the
schoolbooks from which we learn.*

KEY CONCEPTS

After reading this chapter and when applying concepts learned, you will
be able to:

1. Explain the concept of service breakdowns.
2. Describe some of the causes of service breakdowns.
3. Discuss the emotion-reducing model.
4. Identify some of the strategies for recovering from a service
   breakdown.
5. Use the six-step problem-solving model to resolve service
   breakdowns.

In a diverse world, communication and *service breakdowns* are common
in many organizations. These often occur because the intent of someone's

message is filtered by and received from another person's different values, beliefs, expectations, and experiences. In other instances, they occur because a service provider does not think about how to word and deliver a message or take the background of the customer into consideration.

The key to delivering positive global customer service is to remind yourself continually that not everyone views things as you do and to try to learn as much about your customers as possible in order to prevent misunderstandings or service breakdowns. If you consider the points discussed in this book and strive to get to know more about your customers, the success level that you and your organization will attain in serving customers can increase significantly. At the same time, your customers' expectations will more likely be met as you work toward delivering your organization's products and services as promised.

As you read through this chapter, you will learn some proven techniques for interacting with customers in a way that will help ensure more powerful and positive service delivery. You will also discover strategies for regaining customer trust and implementing effective *service recovery* strategies in situations when things do go wrong during customer-provider interactions.

FOCUS ON POSITIVE GLOBAL SERVICE: PERSONAL SERVICE BREAKDOWNS

Think of some times when you felt invisible or neglected by a service provider when you visited an organization or called on the telephone. Take a few minutes to list service provider behaviors that led to those feelings.

_____

_____

_____

_____

SERVICE BREAKDOWNS

Every organization experiences service breakdowns in some form on a regular basis. These incidents occur whenever the product or service delivered fails to meet customer needs, wants, or expectations. Because humans are complex and bring a variety of backgrounds to a customer-provider encounter, even though a product or service delivered may function exactly as it was designed, it may be perceived as defective if the customer expected it to perform in another manner. In such instances, a breakdown occurs. Furthermore, should a product or service fail to meet a customer's wants or needs or not meet advertised promises or standards, dissatisfaction and frustration can likely result.

Even though service breakdowns can be challenging and can damage or destroy a customer-provider relationship, there is hope. One study identified a *service recovery paradox* in which a customer might not necessarily view a service breakdown as a "deal or relationship killer" or too severe when "the customer has had no prior failure with the firm, the cause of the failure was viewed as unstable by the customer, and the customer perceived that the company had little control over the cause of the failure."[1] In effect, this study suggests that if an organization goes out of its way to correct service breakdowns and has a highly effective process in place, then service failures might even lead to overall higher customer satisfaction ratings than if a problem had never existed. In such instances, you and your peers might be able to turn a frustrated or unhappy customer into a loyal one through your positive global service efforts to recover and make the customer "whole" or feel compensated for loss or inconvenience.

CAUSES OF SERVICE BREAKDOWNS

There are so many potential reasons that something can go wrong when you are interacting with a customer or potential customer, that topic alone could be a chapter. The following are some of the more common reasons your customers might become irritated or dissatisfied with you. By considering each when you deal with a customer, you can potentially avoid situations in which your customers become angry, complain to management, defect to a competitor, or take some other negative action.

- **Being preoccupied when customers call or are present.** Have you have ever called an organization only to have the person answering disconnect you or put you on extended hold while he or she performed some task? Have you ever visited an organization where an employee failed to acknowledge your presence and serve you right away? If you answered yes to either of these questions, you know how your customers might feel under similar circumstances. If you must put someone on hold while on the phone, do so only if you are currently serving another customer or if you have no other option, but make sure that you explain why you are asking the customer to wait and how long it will take to get to him or her. You will read more about the proper manner for using various phone functions in Chapter 10.

  If a customer arrives and you are performing an administrative function, such as filing, calculating, or stocking, quickly get to a point where you can pause and serve the customer. In the meantime, take a moment to make eye contact, smile, and indicate either in words or nonverbally (by holding up a single index finger) that you will be with the customer as soon as possible. This is an especially important action when dealing with someone from a culture in which relationships are a significant aspect of business. Such efforts may not satisfy everyone, but they work with most customers, who understand that service providers are doing more with fewer employees these days.

- **Using slang, technical jargon, or local terminology.** As you read in Chapter 4, people outside your industry, organization, or culture may be confused or not understand what you mean if you use technical language or terminology. Keep your language simple, nontechnical, and to the point and watch for nonverbal reactions to what you say to help prevent potential communication breakdowns.

- **Taking the customer for granted.** Customers are your reason for existing as an employee. They are also the key element in your organization's success. For that reason, you must go out of your way to identify and anticipate their needs and then address those needs in an expedient and professional manner. Just because someone is a customer today does not mean that he or she will remain so in the future. Unfortunately, there has been a dramatic shift in *customer loyalty*. In the past, people often exhibited brand loyalty for products and services. New technology has provided easy access to alternative and comparable products and services, and it is no longer unusual for someone to move to a new product, service, or provider based strictly on factors such as price, service, or availability. The result is that many well-known major organizations and products have changed dramatically, evolved, or completely disappeared in past decades. Among those that suffered this last fate are Montgomery Ward, Pontiac and Plymouth automobiles, Eastern Airlines, and Steak and Ale and Bennigan's restaurants.

In order to help ensure customer loyalty, you must place your customers first and keep them happy. The simplest way of doing so is to know your products, services, policies, procedures, and competition well. You must also continually seek to enhance your knowledge and skills while staying attuned to current consumer behaviors and trends. Ultimately, you goal is to be the "go-to" person and organization for whatever products or services you offer.

- **Projecting an uncaring attitude.** You may experience instances in dealing with customers when service or communication is strained. This can occur if customers perceive that the products or services received did not meet their needs or expectations or were not delivered as promised. It could also happen if they think that you simply didn't care about them. To avoid this, strive to make sure that you are always prepared to focus on your present customers and their needs. Also, listen to and show interest in what your customers have to say. If a service breakdown occurs, use the problem-solving skills that you will read about later in this chapter in order to identify and resolve the issue quickly and professionally.

- **Failing to assume responsibility.** A big complaint that many customers have, especially when dealing with Web-based businesses, is that they cannot find a "real person" to talk to when they have a question or a problem arises. Many organizations intentionally make finding their contact information (if they even list it on their Web site) difficult to locate because they do not want people calling their representatives. They do this under the guise of making service delivery more efficient for customers through the technology they offer. When customers do finally locate the contact information, they often encounter an automated attendant system that requires numerous choice selections and often ends with a message saying something like, "You are important to us. All of our agents are currently helping other customers; your estimated wait time is ____."

To prevent being part of such problem situations, it's important to make yourself accessible to your customers and make recommendations to your supervisor for improving your system whenever you identify a glitch. When you are interacting with customers in person or via technology, make sure that you apologize when appropriate, assume responsibility for delays or service breakdowns, and offer to assist professionally. Avoid blaming the technology, your organizational system, or other people. Instead, work toward positive and immediate *service recovery* by telling your customers what you can do, not what you cannot. For example, "My sincere apologies for the inconvenience Mr./Ms. ____. However, I cannot get that information at the moment because our computer system is down. May I take your phone number or e-mail address and get that information to you as soon as it comes back up?" Be a problem solver and an information resource by taking responsibility and working to assist your customers, not an obstacle to good service and satisfaction.

- **Arguing with the customer.** There is nothing positive to gain when you engage in a verbal disagreement with a customer. You may feel better afterward if you think that you "won," but in reality, you are likely going to lose a customer, gain negative word-of-mouth publicity, and risk the possibility that the customer will complain to your supervisor and you may get reprimanded or worse. If customers become argumentative, allow them to vent

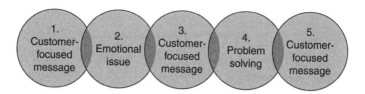

Figure 9-1   Emotion-Reducing Model

and try to discover the reason for their anger or frustration. Use the problem-solving strategies discussed later in this chapter to help identify and resolve the issue in a professional manner. Also, use the model for dealing with emotions that follows in the next section to help calm and interact with customers appropriately in order to recover the relationship while addressing the challenge.

- **Ignoring customer emotions.** You cannot effectively serve customers or recover from a service breakdown when they are upset or angry. In such instances, you must first recognize and address their emotional state. Often this begins by simply allowing them to vent their frustrations or explain what they believe to be the situation or cause of a service breakdown. Even if you disagree with what they are saying, do not interrupt them or offer your opinion. Doing so can only add fuel to their already growing emotional fire, and they could even become violent. Figure 9-1 shares a model for effectively dealing with emotionally charged situations.

EMOTION-REDUCING MODEL

When customers react in an emotional manner because of a breakdown in service—for example, by showing irritation in their tone of voice, raising their voice in anger, or even crying—it is important to remember that they are likely not upset with you (unless you did or said something to provoke them). Typically, they are stressed because of things that are out of their control, such as your organization's processes, policies, or procedures. In such situations, it is crucial that you remain calm and professional and that you handle the situation without exhibiting any emotion (e.g., without using sarcasm, raising your voice, or otherwise using potentially provoking words or actions). If you fail to heed this advice, you risk escalating the situation and becoming a part of the problem, not the solution.

To help customers calm down, take the time to listen calmly and acknowledge their emotions (e.g., Mr. Harris, I can appreciate that you are upset . . .). Once you deal with their emotional state, you can begin focusing on the issue and recovering the relationship. Only then will you be able to resolve the issue. This is true because until you can get the customers to regain composure, they will be unlikely and unable to listen openly and receive what you are saying objectively. They might even potentially perceive you as uncaring because you are focused only on business and do not acknowledge the degree to which they are upset.

The first step in calming an upset customer is to use customer-focused verbal and nonverbal messages that you read about in Chapters 4 to 6. For example, you might continue the dialogue earlier by saying something like, "Mr. Harris, I can appreciate that you are upset. Under the circumstances you have described, I'd likely be upset too. If you will permit me, I will speak to my supervisor and discuss ways that we can get this issue resolved quickly. Is that acceptable?" If the customers agree, thank them for their willingness to allow you to resolve the issue and assist them. Following their agreement or further comments, make sure that you follow up as promised on any agreement made; otherwise, they might escalate the situation further by complaining to your supervisor, CEO, or outside consumer advocacy organization. Remember to maintain a nondefensive body posture while interacting with your customer.

A key element in resolving service breakdowns is to use problem resolution strategies along with customer-focused messages. The *emotion-reducing model* works as follows. Assume that an irate customer calls you because of a problem with a product that he recently purchased on your organization's Web site.

- **Customer-focused message.** You answer the phone thusly: "Thanks for calling ABC Creative Toys, this is [your name]. How may I assist you?"

- **Emotional issue.** The customer is very upset because he ordered an item as a gift for his son's birthday, which is in three days, and it is missing a part.

- **Customer-focused message.** As you listen to the customer's story, you make comments such as "I can understand how you might feel because of this." Empathetic statements like that are intended to let the customer know that you are listening and that you understand the situation. As the conversation continues, show support and use positive reinforcement, assuring the customer that you will work with him to resolve the issue.

- **Problem solving.** Once the issue has been appropriately identified and you have a solution in mind, make sure your customer finds it agreeable. You might say, "Since your son's birthday makes time an issue, we will ship you a replacement part overnight so that you will have it by tomorrow. Would that be acceptable, Mr. Washington?"

- **Customer-focused message.** End the conversation on a positive note by reassuring the customer that you will handle the situation and thanking him for his business. For example, "Mr. Washington, I appreciate your giving me a chance to help resolve this issue, and I apologize for any inconvenience we caused. I assure you that we'll get the replacement part out in an overnight shipment this afternoon so that you'll have it in plenty of time for your son's birthday. Is there anything else I can do to assist you today?" And finally, "Thanks for having confidence in ABC Creative Toys, Mr. Washington. Have a great afternoon."

 ### POSITIVE GLOBAL SERVICE ACTION TIP

When dealing with an angry or irate customer, try the following strategies:

- Apologize.
- Move the customer away from others.
- Reassure the customer.
- Be firm but fair.

- Empathize.
- Don't give away the store (compensate fairly).
- Allow the customer to vent.
- Listen actively without interruption.
- Offer what you can do, not what you cannot do.

FOCUS ON POSITIVE GLOBAL SERVICE: AVOIDING HOT BUTTONS

Everyone reacts negatively to certain things. Related to service, these "hot buttons" might be a behavior someone exhibits, or an action someone takes, or something someone fails to do which really irritates a customer and can cause a service breakdown. Examples might be employees who chew gum while serving customers, or who call customers by pet names (e.g. *honey*, *sweetie*, or *darling*), or who fail to return voice messages in a timely manner (or at all).

Take a few minutes to think of examples of behaviors or actions that you have experienced from service providers and did not like. After you have a list, compare the items on it with those that fellow coworkers identified and discuss how these factors impact positive global customer service. Use the results of the activity as an action plan to ensure that you are not guilty of pushing your customers' hot buttons so that you can potentially avoid having to deal with service breakdowns.

SERVICE RECOVERY PROCESS

Service recovery efforts are made to salvage the customer-provider relationship and help ensure future customer loyalty when something goes wrong in the service process. While there is no one strategy that will ensure that you accomplish these things, the following strategies are proven ways to at least give you the opportunity to rectify a wrong and move forward with the relationship that you and your organization have with your customers:

- **Apologize, apologize, and apologize again.** By expressing your regret and taking ownership for the service breakdown during the recovery cycle, you improve the chances that your customers will see you as a compassionate professional and potentially forgive a mistake. As you are apologizing to your customers, pay attention to their verbal and nonverbal reactions. If they start to speak, quit talking, listen up, and show empathy as your customers share their perceptions of the situation. Be sure that you do not interrupt or make excuses. Your goal is to show that you are concerned about the situation and that your customers are important to you and your organization.

- **Show compassion.** Customers typically expect to see that you are truly remorseful when service breaks down and that you are going to be proactive in helping them resolve the situation. Empathizing with a statement such as "I can appreciate your frustration," "I understand how we have inconvenienced you," or "I can imagine how you must feel" will help ease a tense situation and can go a long way in winning customers over. As you read earlier, you must deal with your customers' emotions or feelings before you can really address their problems.

- **Take immediate action to correct a service breakdown.** Once you learn of a service breakdown, you should immediately try to determine the cause and identify potential solutions with your customers so that the matter can be resolved effectively and efficiently. As more time passes before resolution, your customers potentially become more disenchanted and angry about your efforts to resolve the problem. Part of the corrective process is to ensure that your customers are kept informed about what actions you are taking, whether there are potential delays, and when they can expect resolution. Even if you cannot rectify a situation immediately, you can reassure your customers that action is pending and give regular updates so that they do not feel left out of the process or become anxious. You must convince customers through your actions and words that you are doing your best to solve the problem in a timely manner. Do not forget that your customers want to hear what you can do for them, not what you cannot.

There may be instances in which there are prohibitions that prevent you from giving your customers exactly what they want, even though you would like to. For example, you might be in firearms sales and your underage customer wants to buy a hunting rifle. If you find yourself in such a situation, it is important to use all the interpersonal skills discussed throughout this book to let customers know that you are prohibited from fulfilling their needs. Explain why you cannot fulfill their needs or wants in such situations rather than just saying, "I'm sorry. The law won't let me do that." The latter response sounds as if you are not being truthful, do not want to assist, and are hiding behind an invisible barrier.

In any service interaction, you must remain positive and show a "can-do" attitude; otherwise, you risk the chance of sending your customers to a competitor and generating negative word-of-mouth publicity. As you can see from the examples in the sidebar "Handling Customer Requests," the willingness to assist customers and meet their requests even though you face obstacles can potentially lead to a positive outcome. By partnering with customers and offering alternatives when necessary, you keep the door open to possible business relationships.

There might be some situations in which your abilities, time constraints, resources, or the timing of a request may prevent fulfillment. When this occurs, look for ways to offer alternatives to your customers.

- **Provide compensation.** In order to demonstrate that you are concerned for a customer's loss in terms of money, time, or inconvenience, you should be prepared in advance to offer compensation when things go wrong. Show your customers that they are valuable to the organization and that you are trying to make up for their financial and personal loss and inconvenience.

Effective service recovery should involve compensation for a customer's original loss and add additional value. For example, if a customer had an oil change done on his or her car and oil was spilled on the carpet, an appropriate gesture might be to give the oil change free and have the carpet cleaned at your company's expense. This solution compensates for inconvenience and lost time while providing added value (saving the cost of the oil change).

By making the effort to show that you are sincerely sorry for a mistake, you can empower your customers and make them feel that they are back in control of a situation that may have made them feel like a victim. Any compensation should be significant enough that the customer feels not only that you and your organization have suffered a loss but that the loss is equal to your customer's loss in time, money, energy, or frustration. The key is to make the offer without the customer having to suggest or demand it by speaking to a manager.

HANDLING CUSTOMER REQUESTS

Here are some considerations that you should always take into account whenever you are called upon to handle customer requests, along with the proper response to such requests:

- **Your abilities:** You work in a grocery store, and a customer asks if you can move her car from the lot to the front door because an injury prevents her from walking long distances and her back is bothering her. You only have a learner's permit and cannot drive a vehicle alone.
  Your response: "Ms. Saunders, I'd love to be able to help you; however, I do not yet have a driver's license. I'd be happy to get one of the other baggers to move your vehicle for you. Is that okay?" *Note:* Before offering this, check with your supervisor.
- **Time constraints:** You work in a deli, and a customer comes in at 11:05 a.m. Apparently, she thought a coworker had ordered a sandwich platter for a noon office lunch meeting with a group of very important clients. She wants a tray of assorted sandwiches, side dishes, and condiments and says that she can wait. It normally takes about 45 minutes to prepare such a tray.
  Your response: "Ms. Norvell, I want to help make your meeting a success; however, one of my associates called in sick today so we are shorthanded, and sandwich trays normally take about 45 minutes to get together. What I can do is have a butcher slice up an assortment of

meats and cheeses and put them on a nice tray with salad items. We can also provide an assortment of sliced breads and condiments. That would take about 20 minutes. I'll even throw in some cookies for free. Would that be acceptable?"

- **Limited resources:** You work in a home supply store near the coastline in Florida. A customer comes in to buy plywood to board up his house a day before a major hurricane is predicted to hit the area. Since the announcement of the hurricane on the news, you have been overwhelmed with purchases of plywood and just sold out.

   Your response: "Mr. Patel, I can appreciate the urgency of your need. Unfortunately, it seems like everyone in town is buying plywood, and we do not have any more in stock. However, I do have a couple of options for you. I can call some of our stores in Orlando to find out whether they have any plywood in stock. They are only an hour away, and if they have it, I can ask them to hold some if you want to drive over to get it. The other option is that we have a shipment on the way that should arrive sometime around 8 p.m. tonight. I'll be here, and I can hold some for you if you want to come back at that time. Would either of those options work for you?"

- **Timing.** You are a wedding planner with a thriving business, and a potential referral client calls on February 16 to arrange for a June 1 wedding in a popular resort area. Normally such events are planned at least a year in advance. She explains that she just got engaged on Valentine's Day and wants to marry her fiancé before he ships overseas with the military.

   Your response: "Let me first congratulate you on your engagement. What a wonderful Valentine's Day present! I am not sure how much research you have done on planning for a wedding, but there is a lot of preparation that must be done. That does not mean a wedding is impossible by that date. The challenge is that from my experience in working with the resort you want, it is normally booked over a year in advance for weddings. I can check with my contact to verify the availability, but I suggest you and I discuss some alternatives just in case. What do you think of that idea?"

POSITIVE GLOBAL SERVICE ACTION TIP

Plan in advance for potential service breakdowns by discussing with your supervisor your level of authority in compensating customers for their loss whenever a problem arises. Also discuss the organization's policy for handling various types of service glitches. This will empower you and expedite your ability to handle service breakdowns when they occur.

FOCUS ON POSITIVE GLOBAL SERVICE

Service breakdowns are often created because of a company's return policy or approach to dealing with customers. Take a few minutes to research the following companies to see examples of some that get it right and some others that set customers up to complain.

Positive Service Policies

- *L. L. Bean* allows customers to return any item purchased at any time for any reason.
- *Southwest Airlines* permits two pieces of checked luggage at no charge, including sports bags (e.g., skis and golf clubs).
- *Costco Warehouse* allows returns of virtually everything in its warehouse within a 90-day period following purchase.
- *Orvis* provides an 800 toll-free number that connects with a "real person" along with e-mail support and live chat with a two-hour guaranteed response time.
- *Wal-Mart* permits returns without receipts for items under $25 or gives a gift card for purchases over $25 as long as no more than three returns occur within a 45-day period; otherwise, manager approval is required.

Negative Service Policies

- *Buy.com* does not accept returns of oversize televisions once a customer inspects and signs for receipt of the item.
- *CompUSA* charges a restocking fee of up to 25 percent of the item cost for returns that do not meet its criteria.
- *Spirit Airlines* charges a $30 fee for carry-on bags checked in online and $45 at the gate and does not refund fees for bags paid for if you ultimately do not have as many as originally planned. It also does not give refunds for canceled tickets, even if the ticket was purchased five minutes earlier online, though it does give a credit toward baggage fees or purchase of a future flight instead.

- *Verizon Wireless* charges a $350 early contract termination fee for customers who cancel a smart-phone contract after a 30-day grace period.
- *DirecTV* automatically extends a customer contract for 24 months when any new equipment is added. A customer who decides to cancel is assessed an early termination fee.

PROBLEM-SOLVING STRATEGIES

A major responsibility of any customer service representative is to keep customers happy. Part of that duty sometimes involves trying to figure out what they need and what to do when they do not receive what they expected. The following six-step problem-solving model (presented graphically in Figure 9-2) can assist in first identifying and resolving service challenges and then recovering the relationship with your customers afterward:

1. **Identify the problem.** Prior to resolving a service breakdown, you must first determine what happened or why your customer is not satisfied. This can sometimes take a bit of patience and understanding on your part, especially in situations where your customer speaks a primary language other than yours or has a disability. In such situations, you will need to take the time to identify the issue by using the positive communication skills you read about earlier in the book. You might even have to seek the

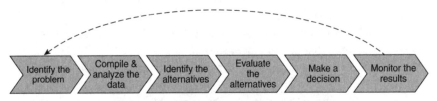

Source: R. W. Lucas, *Customer Service Skills for Success,* 5th ed., Burr Ridge, IL: McGraw-Hill Higher Education, 2011.

Figure 9-2   Problem-Solving Model

assistance of a coworker or nearby customer who speaks the customer's language and can translate. In the case of a person with a disability, perhaps he or she can write down the message or use electronic technology to explain the problem.

Typically, positive global customer service and service recovery can start with a sincere apology and acceptance of responsibility for the product or service breakdown. This might be appropriate even when you believe that you or your organization has done nothing wrong. That is because you want to maintain the relationship. By potentially defusing an angry or frustrated customer early, you might get the person to listen to reason or stay focused as you share what you are able to do. If the customer becomes emotional, your opportunities for problem resolution and recovery are reduced.

A simple "I'm sorry you were inconvenienced. How may I assist you?" coupled with some of the strategies that you read about earlier can help accomplish this. Keep in mind that you represent the organization to your customers. Since you are representing the company, you are "chosen" to be responsible. Don't point fingers at other employees, policies, procedures, or other factors. Let your customer know that you are sincerely remorseful (on behalf of the organization) and that you will do whatever possible to quickly and effectively resolve the issue. The sidebar "Problem Identification Questions" offers some sample questions that you might use to identify a problem and its cause.

PROBLEM IDENTIFICATION QUESTIONS

To learn as much about the issue as you can, start by speaking directly to the customers, when possible. Collect any documentation or other background information available. Ask questions of your customers similar to the following:

- When and where did you buy the item?
- Do you have a receipt?
- What exactly is the problem or issue?
- When did you first notice the problem or issue?

- Depending on the item: What model is it?
- If appropriate: Did you review the owner's manual?
- What have you done to try to resolve the issue to this point?
- Have you contacted anyone from our organization about this previously? If so, who, and what was the result?

2. **Compile and analyze the data.** For you to effectively analyze, diagnose, and resolve a problem, you must first gather as much information about the situation as possible. Questions that start with *who, what, when, how,* and *why* generally get you the information that you will need. After asking the questions, be sure to listen actively to your customer's response. As you gather information, do a quick assessment of the severity of the problem by listening to your customer's words and tone and determine if the problem is similar to other problems or complaints from others. If so, there may be a product defect issue or a systemic breakdown that may require getting your supervisor or other appropriate party involved in the resolution (e.g., the manufacturer or a consumer agency).

   After you have gathered adequate information, spend time analyzing it, if necessary. If your customer is not present (i.e., if the person complained by telephone or in writing), seek the advice or guidance of technical experts, peers, team leaders, or supervisors, if you think that is appropriate. Your ultimate goal is to weigh all alternatives and come to a decision on the best course of action for your customer and the organization.

3. **Identify alternatives.** Part of any successful problem-solving effort in a service environment is to partner with customers to identify and resolve issues. When you are using this process, make sure to share that you are willing to collaborate with your customers in order to find a solution that is acceptable to them. This is known as trying to achieve a *win-win outcome* in which both the customers and your organization get what they need from the transaction. Let your customers know what you can do, get their agreement, and then take action to resolve the issue.

Many service providers find a lot of satisfaction in being able to successfully assist their customers in resolving problems and finding solutions that meet their needs. When you are working with your customers, you have an opportunity to bring an objective perspective to a situation and then use this problem-solving model to improve it. You may be able to suggest potential solutions or point out things that the customer had not considered. For example, if you have ever contacted a computer technical help desk, you may have noticed that the person starts by asking very basic questions like, "Is the power cord connected?" or "Have you turned the computer off and restarted it after a brief wait period?" While these may seem almost insulting to some people, it is surprising how such questions have actually helped customers resolve what they believed to be a computer problem. In your role as problem solver, you must "get back to the basics" and think from your customer's perspective.

Ask questions and listen to the responses in order to gather the information needed and then consider alternatives available for resolving the issue. When you are thinking of potential resolutions, make sure that you consider the needs and expectations of your customers and that you also keep the interests of your organization in mind. To do this, you might ask the customers for what they believe is needed to resolve the issue before making your own suggestions. As part of this negotiation, do not opt for the cheapest, fastest resolution at the cost of customer satisfaction. Remember that some people from different parts of the world may not outright reject an idea you propose because of wanting you to save face. At the same time, they may go away unsatisfied and spread the word about their experience and how they were treated.

4. **Evaluate the alternatives.** The fourth step in the problem-solving process is to consider all identified options in an effort to find the most effective one to resolve the issue and meet the needs of your customer. It is prudent not to use the same solution for every situation that is similar since what works for one person

does not always work for all. Even though some options may be more expensive and time consuming, they may be worth the investment if they enhance customer satisfaction and loyalty. When considering possible solutions, ask yourself the following questions:

- What has worked in similar situations, and will it work in this one?
- What options are most effective for resolving this issue?
- What is the most expedient manner to use to resolve this issue?
- What is the most cost-effective means of resolving this issue?
- What is most likely to satisfy this customer?
- Will the options available create additional problems or issues with this customer or for the organization?

5. **Make a decision.** After you have weighed all available options, it is time to decide on a course of action. One simple way to put the customers in a position of power and better ensure their satisfaction is to present the top two options you can think of and let the customers decide which they prefer. For example, "Mrs. Wang, I know that you wanted a navy blue bedspread; however, since you need it right away and that color is not available, we have light blue, green, and yellow ones. Which one of those colors works for you?" Notice that an assumptive question (that one of the colors *will* work) is used rather than a closed-ended question like, "Would one of those colors work for you?" This type of question encourages the customer to choose an item that meets her needs. She can still say, "None of them," but you are psychologically encouraging a positive response and she is still getting to make a choice. A question like this puts your customer in a decision-making position, and she likely will feel self-empowered.

By allowing customer involvement in the decision-making process, customers will likely take ownership of the solution and will be less likely to regret it later since it is their choice. Should they offer an alternative solution to your suggestions, consider it and resolve the issue.

6. **Monitor the results.** You should follow up on problem resolution rather than assuming everything went well. Just as buyers
   sometimes have remorse, your customers may feel that they made
   a bad decision in accepting the solution offered. By being a proactive service professional, you can avoid making assumptions
   that satisfaction resulted and instead contact your customers via
   e-mail or telephone or ask them face-to-face if they are regular
   in-house customers. You might also send along a written thank-
   you via e-mail or regular mail and provide a customer satisfaction survey. Many organizations have contracted companies
   to do customer satisfaction follow-ups with all customers or send
   out satisfaction surveys via e-mail. Simply tell the customers that
   you appreciate their bringing the problem to your attention and
   working with you to resolve it and ask them if they are happy
   with the outcome. Listen to their response and react appropriately. Should you determine that a customer is not satisfied or
   that additional issues need to be resolved, go back to step one of
   the problem-solving process and start over.

POSITIVE GLOBAL SERVICE ACTION TIP

Do not make assumptions that customers are satisfied following a
service breakdown and resolution. Ask them, and make sure of it.

SUMMARY

Part of any successful business venture is the ability to predict, plan for, and
deal with unforeseen breakdowns in service. In this chapter, you have read
about service breakdowns, their causes, and some strategies for potentially
preventing and dealing with them. Some of the ideas that you explored
include:

- Because humans are complex and bring a variety of backgrounds
  to a customer-provider encounter, even though a product or

service delivered may function exactly as it was designed, it may be perceived as defective if the customer expected it to perform in another manner. This can lead to service breakdowns

- There are so many potential reasons that something can go wrong when you are interacting with a customer or potential customer. By considering each when you deal with a customer, you can potentially avoid situations in which your customers become angry, complain to management, defect to a competitor, or take some other negative action.
- To help reduce emotion when dealing with a stressful customer situation, "sandwich" the emotional issue between two customer-focused messages.
- Service recovery efforts are made to salvage the customer-provider relationship and help ensure future customer loyalty when something goes wrong in the service process.
- Using the six-step problem solving model is one strategy for figuring out what customers need and what to do when they do not receive what they expected.

CHAPTER

10

The Role of Technology in Closing the Global Service Gap

Customers are still setting the technology agenda.
—Carly Fiorina, former CEO, Hewlett-Packard

KEY CONCEPTS

After reading this chapter and when applying concepts learned, you will be able to:

1. Explain how various forms of technology are impacting the way that customers access and receive service.
2. Describe the benefits of using different types of technology to provide positive global customer service.
3. Discuss strategies for delivering service via technology.
4. Apply basic technology etiquette when using the telephone, fax, and e-mail.

Virtually every aspect of our lives is impacted by some form of technology. People around the world are now part of a *24/7/365* culture, meaning that many have access to technology 24 hours a day, 7 days a week, 365 days a year, and can communicate at any time and virtually from any place. According to the Web site Internet World Stats, there are over 6.8 billion people, of which more than 1.9 billion now use the *Internet*, and nearly 518 million people are using *Facebook*.[1] Furthermore, the UN International Telecommunication Union reports, in an Associated Press article from February 2010, that there are now over 4.6 billion cell phone users throughout the world.[2] In the United States alone, there are nearly 277 million *wireless phone* service subscribers.[3]

Through all this technology, consumers spend billions of dollars each year. For example, on Cyber Monday, the day that follows Thanksgiving weekend's Black Friday shopping day in the United States, online sales in 2010 rose more than 19 percent over those of the previous day, making that Monday the biggest online shopping day of the year, according to an article from Bloomberg.[4] Some analysts had predicted record Internet sales of close to $1 billion. These numbers do not take into consideration sales of online retailers from other countries.

As well, many people turn to the Internet to research products and services. A study from the Pew Research Center found that "Nearly six-in-ten adults (58%) have done research online about the products and services they buy, and about a quarter (24%) have posted comments or reviews online about the things they buy. On a typical day, 21% of adults search for product information online. This is an increase from 15% in 2007 and 9% in 2004."[5]

Only people in remote and underdeveloped countries have avoided the full impact of modern electronic communication devices. Even in some of those cases, technology is creeping in, as recently evidenced when this author made a trip to the jungles of Panama to visit an Emberá Indian village. Living nearly two hours from Panama City by car and boat, the village chief uses his cell phone by climbing a tall palm tree to receive a signal. The villagers use their cell phone for emergencies and also for coordinating tour groups coming to the village from Panama City.

Most people want to connect on an interpersonal level, and the world seems awash with social networking Web sites that allow millions of people to connect not only on a personal level but also on a business level through

LinkedIn, Facebook, Together We Served, Bebo, Twitter, and dozens of similar technologies. In addition, service professionals use various systems, such as e-mail, telephone, fax, text messaging, the Internet, and the intranet, to connect, inform, and exchange information with customers daily. Another Web site that is being used more frequently to gain recognition and build relationships with existing and potential customers is YouTube (a social media–sharing Web site where members can upload and download video segments on various topics). Organizations and professionals are posting all types of videos, including advertisements, training, company information, personal biographical information, and entertainment segments. For people in remote locations, technology may be one of the few connections they have with the outside world to gather information and learn about trends, opinions, fashions, products, and services.

You can capitalize on this primal need that many customers have by utilizing existing and future technology to gain access to and share information with your customers. Many successful service providers and organizations have created Web pages that allow customers to connect directly to them in order to share product and service updates. The key to effectively using technology to communicate with your customers is to recognize the ways people can misinterpret your message when they cannot see you face-to-face. More than one service professional has damaged a customer-provider relationship by using an inappropriate word or action or by not following technology protocol or etiquette.

As you read through this chapter, pay attention to specific strategies for interacting with your customers via technology.

EFFECT OF TECHNOLOGY ON SERVICE

In years past, *service-based technology* consisted of the telephone and the fax machine. Now, many new developing technologies are becoming available each year as organizations strive to gain and hold the edge over local and international competition. Billions of dollars are being spent worldwide to create systems through which customers can access products and services to satisfy their ever-changing needs and whims. This is occurring because the quality of service received or perceived by customers can either enhance or diminish an organization's brand and reputation. As organizations strive to hang onto market share and customers while eking out some degree of profit in a sluggish economy, they are seeking viable alternatives to be responsive to customer needs, requests, problems, suggestions, and complaints. Technology-based service delivery systems are an option.

As you've already read, many organizations now assign customer service professionals to staff their telephones and communicate with customers via the Internet, blogs, and e-mail and through other technological means. Some organizations also outsource and offshore their service functions to call centers and marketing and similar companies in order to remove direct, ongoing staff expenses from their budgets and receive tax breaks. This less expensive strategy does not always work since many consumers have begun to rebel against having to talk to people located in other countries, whom they sometimes feel do not understand them or their needs.

Organizations of all sizes in different parts of the world are struggling to harness the power of service technology. The wonderful thing about technology is that through the use of such innovations, even small organizations can create an image equal to that of their larger counterparts, since someone visiting their Web site or contacting them would have no idea how many employees or assets they have. The key is that once a customer does contact an organization, service providers must project a positive and professional image during interactions.

Larger organizations continue to add and upgrade hardware and software capable of contacting, tracking, and serving customers while adding human resources and training to meet customer needs. In smaller organizations and in those that have yet to use alternative servicing strategies to maximum potential, the responsibility for answering the telephone and providing service through other means often falls on any staff member who hears the telephone ring, receives a message, or is available when a customer visits. No matter the size of your organization, everyone must accept ownership for service delivery in order to provide positive global service and ensure that customers are satisfied and maintain some degree of loyalty.

No one can doubt the influence and power of the Internet. Introduced in the early 1990s, this "information superhighway," as former vice

	2008	2009	2010	2011	2012	2013	2014
Non-Hispanic							
White alone	72.0%	74.0%	76.1%	77.5%	79.0%	80.1%	81.2%
Black alone	58.2%	60.5%	63.8%	66.9%	69.6%	71.7%	72.3%
Asian alone	70.0%	71.2%	73.4%	75.5%	77.5%	79.5%	81.0%
Other*	46.4%	50.0%	52.5%	55.0%	58.0%	62.0%	65.5%
Hispanic†	**53.5%**	**56.5%**	**59.5%**	**62.9%**	**65.0%**	**67.6%**	70.0%

*Includes Native Americans, Alaska Natives, Hawaiian and Pacific Islanders, and biracial and multiracial individuals.
†Could be of any race.

Source: eMarketer, March 2010

Figure 10-1   U.S. Internet Penetration by Race and Ethnicity, 2008-2014 (% of population in each group)

president of the United States, Al Gore, famously called it, has opened the world to billions of people from all backgrounds. For example, Figure 10-1 shows the percentage of U.S. population groups by race and ethnicity that use or will use the Internet.

BENEFITS OF TECHNOLOGY

With the fast pace of today's world, customers have come to expect that an organization will invest in service-based technology. When organizations employ various technology initiatives, customers and service providers benefit from such applications. The following are some standard service benefits:

- **Convenience.** By providing a vehicle for customers to access information and service representatives through technology 24/7/365, your organization can often differentiate itself from competitors while providing positive global service.
- **Cost savings.** When customers have the option of accessing products and services from the comfort of their home or automobile via the Internet or even their cell phone, they can save

time and reduce the need to physically go to an organization. If they do have to go to meet with a service representative, they can gather information and directions in advance to prevent getting lost or having to wait while they complete forms upon arriving. Instead, they can go directly to the appropriate person or location to pick up, drop off, or discuss something.

By using technology as a backup or replacement for service representatives, the organization can continue to identify and address customer needs. Once the initial investment costs for the technology have been offset, these systems begin to produce a return on investment by providing information in a consistent manner while allowing an organization to reduce the ongoing costs, salaries, benefits, and associated overhead costs for employees. As long as managers do not try to totally eliminate the human factor in the service environment, they can be successful at providing positive global service through a blended approach of human and technological means.

- **Efficiency.** One of the quickest things that many customers note when they contact an organization utilizing technology effectively is that their wait time is reduced. This can occur in many ways. For example, when they contact a customer care center via a toll-free telephone number, e-mail, or online chat (electronic dialogue), they can connect with a customer service representative to get information, place an order, or address a need. Through the use of an *interactive voice response (IVR) system* or a *voice response unit (VRU)*, customers can call in 24 hours a day, 7 days a week, even when customer service representatives are not available. Such systems use a text-to-speech conversion to present database information audibly to a caller (e.g., telephone extensions, account information, hours of operation, and virtually anything a customer might need). By simply pressing telephone keypad numbers or verbally responding to audible prompts from the system, customers can be directed to the information or person they seek. This is a significant improvement over the days, decades ago, when people had to visit an organization's customer service or complaint department, wait in line, and then talk to a live person.

- **Enhanced Information flow.** There are many means of providing information to customers via technology. Through *computer-telephone integration (CTI)*, a customer service representative's computer, telephone, fax, and e-mail can be integrated to allow the electronic retrieval of a customer's name, telephone, e-mail address, customer or membership or loyalty number, and other contact information along with pertinent historic files of previous orders, issues, and contacts. This kind of system allows a more personalized touch when someone calls or e-mails because the system identifies and matches incoming e-mail and telephone numbers and automatically populates the service provider's computer screen so that the service representative can refer to and reference the information during a contact.

  Other systems allow access to information and education and training that can be conducted via technology-based systems. For example, customers can access a telephone system that provides a prerecorded training module or information about the organization, products, services, and hours of operation or whatever else might be useful. They might also log onto a Web site and access a "frequently asked questions" section to obtain desired information. Some organizations and educational institutions use *Webinars, podcasts, teleseminars,* and other means to provide information, training, and other useful information to internal and external customers and students.

POSITIVE GLOBAL SERVICE ACTION TIP

To better prepare for your role in using technology to serve your customers, you can research organizations similar to yours, join professional networking groups such as the International Customer Service Association, and become a member of LinkedIn and similar social networking groups through which you can share best practices and learn from other service professionals. Compare notes to learn positive ways to utilize automation and increase efficiency and effectiveness.

TECHNOLOGY-BASED SERVICE STRATEGIES

Integration of technology components and training of employees on effective usage and etiquette are key elements of any successful organizational marketing and service strategy. Poorly planned or implemented technology can quickly lead to frustrated customers and employees and result in lost business and productivity. As a service provider, you must be vigilant in approaching each customer situation as unique and putting forth effort to show ownership and professionalism when interacting with your customers. Your goal in providing positive global service should be to be proficient with any technology that you will be using with customers.

Since you never know who the next customer will be to contact you face-to-face or via technology in the workplace, you must prepare for all the different scenarios that you read about in earlier chapters related to gender, culture, age, abilities, and other diversity factors. For example, a common mistake that many service providers make is to assume that because they deal with various electronic devices and communicate through them regularly, their customers are equally adept and knowledgeable. Such an assumption can lead to service breakdowns, especially if jargon or technical terminology is used when interacting with a customer.

In many cases, people choose not to use technology, do not have a lot of proficiency with equipment, or do not have access to technology, especially the latest updates. This does not make them stupid, incapable, or incompetent; it simply may mean that they approach communication and deal with service situations in a way that is different from yours, or it may mean that they do not have access to such devices. They do not have to adapt to what you and your organization have decided is the "best" way to handle orders or service. You and your organization need to be flexible and adapt to them. Never forget that your customers are the reason that you have a job and that without them you are not needed.

Like computers, cell phones, and other technology, service systems are evolving at an extremely rapid pace. Tasks previously handled by people are now often completely automated. The key to implementing a service technology strategy is to recognize the extent to which it should be used. Because newer types of systems are constantly being introduced, organizations must remind employees that they are still dealing with live customers who may not want or like to interact strictly with technology. For example, many Generation X and Y customers may be more accepting of technology because they have been around it their entire lives and are more comfortable interacting with it. Some customers from other generations or people from countries, cultures, or subcultures that do not embrace technology to the same degree as your organization may avoid or even shun technology. Instead, they may want to do business with a person.

The following are some typical technology-based systems being used by many organizations or service providers:

- **Online chats.** Increasingly, many organizations are providing the option for customers to log onto a Web site and interact through a written live electronic dialogue with a customer service representative. Unfortunately, many service representatives are not receiving adequate product, service, and technology training and often disappoint their customers. According to a report by Forrester Research, an independent research organization that provides advice to business and technology leaders, "Of the 18% of consumers who have used chat, most are initiating the interactions themselves, rather than accepting pop-up chat invitations. But only slightly more than half of consumers who chatted with a representative said that they were satisfied with the experience. And the consumers who said that they didn't get the information they needed via chat were more dissatisfied than those who did."[6]
- **Text messaging.** There are numerous occasions when a company might need to quickly send out bits of information or a brief update to customers. *Text messaging* to someone's cell phone is an easy way to accomplish this. For example, if a meeting or wedding planner, travel agent, or doctor's office receptionist wanted to alert a client, customer, or patient of changes to a conference or event agenda, a fare increase, or an appointment, he or she could easily do this through a text message. On-call maintenance, law enforcement, engineers, medical staff members, or others could quickly be recalled as well.

- **Twitter.** Although some experts think that Twitter will eventually go away because of limitations on message size, it currently offers a means for sending short messages (140 characters or less) via a number of communication networks and electronic devices. Originally designed to give people a way to stay socially connected, many service providers have harnessed its capabilities to send customers brief messages in which they ask or answer questions and share alerts regarding new products and services.

- **Podcasts.** Podcasts are an easy-to-use and expedient form of social media that allow service providers to send information to individual current and potential customers or those linked in a "community." Product and information updates, training program content, video segments, advertisements, or virtually anything else can be provided free, or by paying per view or event, or through a subscription service. Many businesses and consultants use this type of media to educate or train employees and customers and to provide consistent information to franchisees or others needing products, services, and policy information in remote or geographically dispersed locations. This is a great cost-savings mechanism since travel time and expenses are reduced or eliminated.

- **Media-sharing Web sites.** With the progression and power of today's smart phones, the idea of using media sharing to get active messages about products and services out to current and potential customers has really caught on with many businesses. YouTube and DIGG are two of the most recognizable Web sites where people easily upload and download video information and provide an avenue for social and business connections. Commercial software is also available for any service providers or organizations to use to start their own media-sharing Web site. Everything from video advertisements and images to training programs can be found.

POSITIVE GLOBAL SERVICE ACTION TIP

To get an idea of the potential for using media sharing to promote your own products and services, visit www.youtube.com and search the phrase "customer service."

- **Smart phones.** Cell phones have progressed way beyond the standard ability to call someone and now include touch screen and voice recognition capability along with the standard features of many computers. Today's generation of cell phone truly harnesses the capability of many devices (e.g., telephone, Internet, PDA, e-mail, text messaging, entertainment and gaming systems, and movie players). As such, with certain regulatory restrictions, service providers can access customers virtually anywhere and anytime to deliver information and content to them.
- **Blogs.** Weblogs (blogs) offer organizations another venue for providing ongoing material and information to anyone who logs onto a company's Web site to view its blog. These modern-day diaries allow individuals and organizations to produce a steady stream of updates about products (including product recalls), services, policies, and procedures; commentary and advice to customers; and various other information and video and graphic material. Often they contain *hot links,* or connections, to Web site pages or other electronic information sources. In addition to reading information, customers are able to ask questions or leave comments for others to read later. An important aspect of any successful blog is to have a dedicated person to add and monitor dialogue and updates regularly so that the information is fresh and customers have a reason to return regularly. This also prevents erroneous or potentially offensive information from being added by a prankster or disgruntled person.

FOCUS ON POSITIVE GLOBAL SERVICE: IDENTIFYING SERVICE LEVELS

Contact your own organization and several other large companies or government agencies via the telephone or through one of the electronic means identified in this chapter to see how they address customer service. As you make contact, evaluate them on the following:

If you call the organization

- How many times does the telephone ring before you are routed to another person or voice mail?
- If you get an automated attendant and choose the "O" (operator) option, does the call go to a live person at another number, do you get an automated message, or does the system just "kick you out" or hang up?
- If you choose the voice mail option, is the person's outgoing message:
  - Upbeat and friendly?
  - Concise?
  - In compliance with suggested guidelines in this chapter for voice messages?

If you e-mail the organization

- Does the message go through without a problem?
- Do you get an "out of office" message that is automatically sent when people are away from their office for a defined period of time? If so, does the message share basic information needed to determine when they will return? For example, a response might be generated that tells correspondents that "I'll be out of the office from [date] until [date], but I will be checking my e-mail during that period and will respond as soon as possible."
- Does the service representative return your message in what you consider to be a timely manner?

COMMUNICATIONS TECHNOLOGY ETIQUETTE

Just like any other area of human interaction, in dealing with your customers, there are some basic rules of etiquette that you should consider when communicating through technology. If you fail to adhere to some fairly standard practices, you risk a breakdown in the service-provider relationship. While some people may already be aware of the following suggested strategies and view them as logical or common sense, others may not be familiar with them. No matter which group you are in, they may help build and maintain stronger customer experiences.

Telephone

The manner in which you answer your telephone can help determine the outcome of a call. Think of times when you called an organization and all you got was a lackadaisical "Hello" when the phone was answered. What was your immediate mental reaction? If you are like many people, you likely responded with "Who is this?" and then started mentally thinking about how unprofessional the person on the other end must be. Since customers will quickly form an opinion of you and your organization based on your words and tone of voice; always strive to sound upbeat and professional, even if you are having a bad day. Their perception of your message can often determine how they react to you during the conversation and in your future relationship with them. Since many telephone calls are short, you only have limited opportunity to make a positive impression. Make it count.

If you have a positive self-image and feel good about yourself and the job that you do, you are likely to project a naturally confident and pleasant image. Here are some suggestions to help serve your customers effectively and leave them thinking well of you and your organization:

- **Answer promptly.** Answer ringing telephones within three to four rings and use a standard greeting. This sends a nonverbal message that you are available and ready to serve customers. Because many phone systems automatically transfer to a recorded message after four rings, many people often hang up after the third ring. They are conditioned for service "when and where they want it" and may not be willing to leave a message and wait for a callback, especially since many service providers do not return voice messages. And if they do, it is often not in a timely manner.

- **Use a professional greeting.** Typically, business phone responses should contain four elements:

  1. A greeting
  2. Your organization's name
  3. Your name
  4. An offer to assist

  For example, "Good morning. This is ABC Corporation, Sanjay Prasad speaking. How may I assist you today?"

- **Speak naturally.** Whether you are calling someone or providing information to a caller, speak in a conversational voice and try to sound upbeat and confident. Avoid sounding "canned" or mechanical in your message delivery and do not read from a prepared script, unless you are required to do so by your company. If you must read from a script, *practice, practice, practice.* Before you connect with a customer, become very comfortable with your presentation so that you can deliver it in a fluid, warm, and sincere manner. Nothing sends a more negative message than a service representative who stumbles through opening comments, seems disorganized, or later mispronounces a customer's name after the customer has shared it.

- **Continually evaluate yourself.** To ensure that you always come across professionally to your customers, become a critic and regularly evaluate your message delivery. If your organization records customer interactions for training purposes, periodically ask your supervisor or team leader to allow you to listen to recordings. Evaluate them from the standpoint of what went well, what did not go well, and what could be improved and then immediately incorporate necessary changes into your greetings or conversations.

- **Watch your body posture.** As you read in the chapters on communication, your posture sends powerful messages nonverbally. It can also impact the way your voice sounds on the telephone. The following actions can negatively affect the sound and quality of your voice:

- Looking down, with your chin on your chest, as you read something or search through drawers
- Resting the telephone handset between your cheek and shoulder as you do other work (e.g., type data into a computer, look for something, write, or doodle)
- Slouching in your chair or sitting with your feet on the desk

Strive to sit or stand upright and speak clearly into the mouthpiece whether you are using a headset or handheld receiver. If you are using a handheld receiver, make sure that the earpiece is placed firmly against your ear and the mouthpiece is directly in front of your mouth.

- **Conclude calls professionally.** A positive closing—ending a call on an upbeat note, using the caller's name, and summarizing key actions to be taken by both parties—is just as important as a positive opening. For example, you might say, "Ms. McCormick, I have enjoyed serving you. I'd like to confirm what we've discussed to ensure I did not get anything wrong, would that be all right?" Once permission is granted, continue with, "I will contact our manufacturer and have _____ sent out to you before the seventh so that you will have it by your anniversary on the twentieth. I will also send you an e-mail at the e-mail address that you provided to give you the package tracking number. Is that correct?"

Once agreement has been reached, thank your customer for calling, ask what other questions she has or what other assistance you can provide, and then allow her to hang up first. This last point is important because many people often think of one last question, and before they have time to ask it, the service provider has already disconnected and gone on to the next customer. This small gesture helps prevent that and also sends a nonverbal message to customers that they are in control, which is important in some cases, depending on someone's behavioral style.

By taking the approach described previously for dealing with customers on the telephone, you can provide positive global customer service and help strengthen your customer-provider relationship. On the other hand, failing to bring the conversation to a formal close or hanging up abruptly may cause your customer to feel you are in a hurry to finish serving her (regardless of the fact that you have just spent 15 minutes talking!). Think of this final step as wrapping a gift: it looks fine wrapped in paper; however, by adding a nice ribbon and bow, you make it look even better. The thank-you and polite sign-off are your ribbon and bow.

Transferring Calls Effectively

To deliver positive service to all your customers via the telephone, you need to ensure that you understand what all the equipment features are and how to properly use them. Nothing is more frustrating for many callers than getting shuffled from one telephone extension to another or being placed on what seems to be endless hold as they listen to promotional announcements or outdated or poor-quality recordings of music they may not enjoy because a service representative did not effectively use the equipment. To help prevent this from occurring and the possibility of creating a tense exchange once someone does answer, get to know the features of your phone system well and practice positive telephone customer service.

- **Always request permission before transferring callers.** Doing so shows respect for the callers and puts them in a position of power where they can say either yes or no. If you assume that it is okay to transfer someone and then do so, you potentially irritate the caller and put the person receiving the transferred call in a position of possibly having to deal with an emotional customer.

    If you are not the correct person to handle a customer's request or needs, you can offer the caller two options:
    1. To allow you to transfer the call to the correct person
    2. To have you take a message and give it to the correct person when he or she is available

    These options are useful when the customers are already irritated, have stated they are on a tight schedule, or have a problem for which they need a timely solution. Before transferring any call, explain why you need to do so. For example, you might say, "The person who handles technical questions is Deshawn Williams at extension 291. May I transfer you to him, or would you rather I take a message and pass it along to him?" This saves you and the caller time and effort, and you have provided professional, courteous service. If the caller says, "Yes, please transfer me," follow by saying something like, "I will be happy to connect you now. Again, Deshawn's extension is 291, in case you are accidentally disconnected."

- **Announce the customer.** Once you successfully connect the customer with the intended party, let that person know what you are doing by saying something like, "Deshawn, this is [your name] from [your department]. I have [customer's name] on the phone, and she has a [question, concern] about _____. Are you the right person to handle this?" If Deshawn says yes, connect the customer and announce, "[Customer's name], I have Deshawn Williams on the line. He will be happy to assist you. Thanks for calling." You can now disconnect, and they can converse.

  Should Deshawn not have been the correct person to assist the caller in the previous example or is not available, reconnect with the customer and explain the situation. Then offer to take a message rather than trying to transfer to different people while keeping the customer on hold. You would make an exception if the call taker informed you of the appropriate person to whom you should transfer or if the customer insisted on staying on the line while you tried to transfer to the right person.

- **Avoid making blind transfers.** A *blind transfer* occurs when you transfer a caller without permission, and then once the intended transfer party answers, you simply hang up and the caller is now connected to somebody else. This approach is ineffective, unprofessional, rude, and not customer-focused. Always announce your customer so the person you've transferred to knows the customer's name.

- **Use holds professionally.** Whenever you need to place a customer on *hold*, where he or she is electronically "parked" or paused and cannot hear you on the other end of the line, do so professionally. Only use this feature to serve that customer or another and not to take care of administrative or other non-customer-focused functions.

Before putting a customer on hold, always ask permission, wait for an affirmative response, and then come back every 30 seconds or so to let the person know how long the wait time will be and to reassure him or her that you have not forgotten the call. This action becomes more important if the phone system you are using does not offer information or music that the customer hears during the holding time. Do not forget to thank the customer for waiting once you do return to the call.

- **Use speakerphones with caution.** Speakerphones make sense for people who have certain disabilities and in some environments— for example, when you need free hands or are doing something else while you are on hold or are waiting for a phone to be answered. From a customer service standpoint, speakerphones can send a cold or impersonal message, and so use them sparingly. Many customers do not like the devices and even think that speakerphone users are rude or unprofessional. Also, depending on the equipment used and your distance from the telephone, the message received by your customer could be distorted, or it might seem as though you are in an echo chamber. Before using a speakerphone, ask yourself whether there is a valid reason for not using a headset or handheld phone.

  When you are using a speakerphone, make sure that your conversation will not be overheard if you are discussing personal, proprietary, or confidential information. Also, if someone is listening in on the customer's conversation, make sure that you inform the customer of that fact and explain who the listener is and why he or she is listening.

Fax Machine

As with any other form of communication, there are certain things to abide by when you use a fax machine to transmit messages. If you fail to adhere to these simple guidelines, you may anger or frustrate your customers and weaken the relationship. Following these tips can also help maintain good relationships with coworkers who may depend on the fax machine to conduct business with their customers.

- **Be considerate of your receiver.** Before you transmit a large number of pages, telephone your customer to ensure that is a good time to do so. If a customer only has one fax machine and depends on it to get a lot of documents each day, your lengthy dispatch that will tie up the machine and deplete paper and ink supplies may irritate the customer. It might be better to wait until the end of the workday or the beginning of the next before you send the transmission. Also, keep in mind geographic time differences.
- **Limit graphics.** Graphic images that are not needed to clarify written text (e.g., extravagant logos or large images) waste the receiver's printer cartridge ink, tie up the machine unduly, and can irritate your receiver. To avoid this, delete any unnecessary graphics (or solid-colored areas), including your corporate logo on a cover sheet. If appropriate, create a special outline image of your logo for your fax cover sheets.
- **Limit correspondence recipients.** As with e-mail and memo-randums, limit the recipients of your messages. If they do not have a need to know, do not fax them messages. Check your mailing list (a list of people who will receive all messages, often programmed into a computer) to ensure that it is limited to people who "have a need to know." This is also important from the standpoint of confidentiality. If the information you are faxing is proprietary or sensitive in any way, think about who will receive it. Do not forget that unless the document is going directly to someone's computer fax modem, it may be lying in a stack of other incoming messages and accessible by people other than your intended recipient.

E-Mail

This form of technology provides a rapid and inexpensive way to share information with your customers via your computer or portable devices (e.g., cell phones). *Electronic mail*—*e-mail*—was not originally intended to replace formal written correspondence sent through the postal service, although many organizations now use it instead. They use e-mail for notifying customers of an order status, gathering additional information needed to serve a customer, and achieving numerous other business-related purposes. One significant advantage of e-mail over traditional letters is that you can write a single message and have it delivered to people all around the world in seconds (and without incurring the cost of postage stamps). Unfortunately, it is this feature that has generated much negative publicity and bad feelings from consumers. This is because many unscrupulous businesspeople frequently send out *spam*, or unsolicited e-mail. As a result, many people have negative views of e-mail when organizations use it.

If you are going to use e-mail to conduct business with your customers, you can reduce some negativity by following some basic guidelines:

- **Watch document length.** Because of differing reading abilities, language differences, disabilities, behavioral styles, and many other diversity factors that you have read about, some people do not like to receive long e-mail messages. If you do not remember this point, you may well lose their attention and thus fail to have them read your message. Keep messages short, concise, and to the point. Give only brief background information and tell your customers what they need to know or your reason for writing early in the message. If you need to provide more detail, consider attaching other documents to your message and refer your customers to the information. They can then decide whether to read the extra material or not.
- **Be thoughtful in your use of abbreviations and acronyms.** Since many people view e-mail as an informal way to communicate, you can often use short forms of words, such as abbreviations or acronyms, as long as your customer has a point of reference and will know what you mean. If in doubt, write out the full word or explain a term the first time you use it in the message. If you are writing to someone who speaks a language other than

your native language, you may want to skip the shortened versions of words.

- **Use both uppercase and lowercase letters.** Using all capital letters in e-mail messages is typically viewed as "shouting" and might offend your recipients or cause relationship problems. Further, using all capital letters makes reading difficult (imagine what it would be like to read this book if it were set only in capital letters) and thus slows comprehension.

- **Punctuate correctly.** Just as with the issue of all capital letters, you should use caution with punctuation marks, especially exclamation points, since they project strong feelings or emotion and might be misinterpreted or cause offense.

- **Proofread and spell-check before sending.** Most people can share multiple examples of messages that they have received from a service provider who failed to review the message before hitting the send button. Often, the customers got a good laugh or were confused because the message was not clear. If you fail to read over your message and don't use the electronic spelling, grammar, and syntax checkers on your computer, you risk the appearance of being unprofessional or uneducated. Depending on what you are sending and to whom it will be going, you may also ask someone else to read over the document and provide feedback before sending it. Remember that you are representing your organization and that poor grammar, spelling, and syntax can lead to a bad impression about you and your company.

- **Communicate rationally.** In other words, think before you send off an e-mail to a customer. If you are angry, upset, or emotional because of something that a customer said or did, hold off on answering until you have time to calm down and reflect on the situation and an appropriate response. If necessary, ask a peer, team leader, or supervisor what you should do or say. Once you put words to a screen and hit the send button, you cannot recall your message or hide it. Do not put anything in writing to a customer (or anyone else) that you might be embarrassed or sorry about later. It is very easy for the recipient to forward or cut and paste your message elsewhere on the Internet, and as a result, your reputation could be tarnished.

Similarly, never forward negative, racist, or discriminatory comments, jokes, articles, images, or other materials about a person, a group, or an organization that you receive from others. Remember that your e-mail address (along with your company name) remains attached to that forwarded message as it travels around the globe. To prevent such occurrences, many organizations have policies preventing the use of their e-mail system for personal use. Violations often lead to disciplinary actions or termination.

- **Use blind courtesy copies sparingly.** Most e-mail systems allow you to send a copy to someone without the original addressee knowing it (a blind courtesy copy, or bcc). If the recipient becomes aware of the bcc, your actions might be viewed as suspicious and your motives brought into question. A customer might view your actions as an attempt to hide something from him or her. Thus, a relationship breakdown could occur if the original recipient discovers the existence of the bcc or if the recipient of the bcc misuses the information.
- **Copy only necessary people.** With the volume of e-mail that most people receive these days, they welcome fewer messages to review. If people do not need to take action or know about something, do not include them in your e-mail. They will likely appreciate your efforts. Related to this is avoiding the use of "Reply to All." When you use that feature, all recipients on the "To" and "Courtesy Copy" (cc) lines get a copy of the message.
- **Get permission to send advertisements or promotional materials.** In order to protect consumers against the avalanche of spam mail being sent via electronic media, the U.S. government and most organizations prohibit sending unsolicited material, such as advertisements and promotional material, to people who did not request it. U.S. companies must offer an "opt-out" option where recipients can notify the sender that they do not wish to receive future messages. Violations are submitted to the

U.S. Federal Trade Commission Bureau of Consumer Protection, which often takes legal action against companies and individuals that intentionally violate the law. Other countries have similar restrictions in place.

- **Complete the "To" line last.** As a protection against inadvertently sending an e-mail before you complete the text portion, wait until you have read over and thought about your message before you fill in the addressee information. Without that, the message cannot be transmitted and you will have one last chance to make changes.

POSITIVE GLOBAL SERVICE ACTION TIP

Whenever you are given new technology to aid in better serving your customer, take the time to read any equipment and operational manuals and to ask any questions that you have before attempting to use the devices with your customers. It is unfair and unprofessional for you to "practice" or get used to your equipment at the expense of your customers. They value their time and will not likely appreciate your lack of preparation.

SUMMARY

In this chapter, you have read about the manner in which technology is affecting positive global customer service and some ways in which service providers are using a variety of technology formats to meet the needs of their customers. Some of the key concepts that you explored include:

- Billions of dollars are being spent worldwide to create systems through which customers can access products and services to satisfy their ever-changing needs and whims.
- The wonderful thing about technology is that through the use of such innovations, even small organizations can create an image equal to that of their larger counterparts, since someone visiting their Web site or contacting them would have no idea how many employees or assets they have.
- With the fast pace of today's world, customers have come to expect that an organization will invest in service-based

technology. When organizations employ various technology initiatives, customers and service providers benefit from such applications.

- Convenience, cost-savings, efficiency and enhanced information flow are some of the benefits of information technology use when delivering service.
- Integration of technology components and training of employees on effective usage and etiquette are key elements of any successful organizational marketing and service strategy.
- Like computers, cell phones, and other technology, service systems are evolving at an extremely rapid pace. Tasks previously handled by people are now often completely automated. The key to implementing a service technology strategy is to recognize the extent to which it should be used.
- Just as with any other area of human interaction, in dealing with your customers, there are some basic rules of etiquette that you should consider when communicating through technology. If you fail to adhere to some fairly standard practices, you risk a breakdown in the service-provider relationship.

Endnotes

Chapter 1

1. *CIA—The World Factbook*, January 6, 2010, Central Intelligence Agency, https://www.cia.gov/library/publications/the-world-factbook/geos/countrytemplate_xx.html, retrieved July 28, 2010.
2. *Forrest Gump*, Paramount Studios, 1994.
3. U.S. Census, Current Population Reports: Population Projections of the United States by Age, Sex, Race, and Hispanic Origin: 1995 to 2050, www.census.gov/prod/1/pop/p25-1130.pdf, retrieved July 17, 2010.
4. Konstantinos Giannakouris, "Population and Social Conditions," *Statistics in Focus, 2008*, Eurostat, European Commission, epp.eurostat.ec.europa.eu/cache/ITY_OFFPUB/KS-SF-08-072/EN/KS-SF-08-072-EN.PDF, retrieved August 1, 2010.

5. T., Alessandra and Michael J. O'Connor, *The Platinum Rule: Discover the Four Basic Business Personalities and How They Can Lead You to Success*, New York: Warner Business Books, 1998.

Chapter 2

1. J. M. Humphreys, The Multicultural Economy 2008, Selig Center for Economic Growth, Terry College of Business, University of Georgia, www. terry.uga.edu/selig/docs/buying_power_2008.pdf, retrieved August 14, 2010.
2. *The Gay and Lesbian Market in the U.S.: Trends and Opportunities in the LGBT Community*, 6th ed., Witeck-Combs and Packaged Facts, 2010, www.marketresearch.com/browse.asp?categoryid=1695&g=1.
3. Kit Yarrow and Jayne O'Donnell, *Gen Buy: How Tweens, Teens and Twenty-Somethings Are Revolutionizing Retail*, San Francisco: Jossey-Bass, 2009.
4. H. Manning, Customer Experience, September 12, 2007, Forrester Research, www.forrester.com/rb/Research/topic_overview _customer_ experience/q/id/43140/t/2.
5. Karl Albrecht, *Service America*, Homewood, IL: Dow Jones-Irwin, 1985, p. 27.
6. Jim Collins, *Good to Great: Why Some Companies Make the Leap . . . and Others Don't*, New York: HarperCollins, 2001.
7. Internet World Stats: Usage and Population Statistics, www.internetworldstats.com/stats.htm.
8. Whois Source, http://www.whois.sc.

Chapter 3

1. "Consumers See Customer Service as a Dying Quality," *Impact Today*, www.getmaximpact.com/Impact_Today/IT-Customer_Service.html, retrieved August 8–31, 2010.
2. J. Willis and A. Todorov, "First Impressions: Making Up Your Mind after a 100-Ms Exposure to a Face," *Psychological Science*, Princeton

University, http://www.princeton.edu/~atodorov/Publications/Willis& Todorov-PsychScience.pdf, retrieved August 29, 2010.

3. Cheryl Riana Reitan, "UMD's Sunnafrank Says It Takes Only Minutes to Decide if a Relationship Will Last," *First Impressions*, University of Minnesota Duluth, February 4. 2005, www.d.umn.edu/unirel/home page/05/firstimpressions.html, retrieved August 29, 2010.

4. Karl Albrecht, *Service America*, Homewood, IL: Dow Jones-Irwin, 1985, p. 27.

5. Dale Carnegie, *How to Win Friends and Influence People*, New York: Simon & Schuster, 2009.

6. Terri Morrison and Wayne A. Conaway, *Kiss, Bow, or Shake Hands: The Bestselling Guide to Doing Business in More Than 60 Countries*, 2nd ed., Avon, MA: Adams Media, 2006.

Chapter 4

1. M. P. Lewis (ed.), *Ethnologue: Languages of the World*, 16th ed., Dallas, TX: SIL International, 2009.

2. Most Widely Spoken Languages in the World, http://www.infoplease. com/ipa/A0775272.html#axzz0xWr1xOxp, retrieved August 24, 2010.

3. Edward T. Hall, *The Hidden Dimension*, New York: Anchor Books, 1990.

4. Matthew W. Brault, Americans with Disabilities 2005: Household Economic Studies, issued December 2008, www.census.gov/prod/2008 pubs/p70-117.pdf.

Chapter 5

1. Julius Fast, *Body Language*, New York: Pocket Books, 1970.

2. J. Hargrave, *Let Me See Your Body Talk*, Dubuque, IA: Kendall/Hunt, 1995, p. 3

3. John Gray, *Men Are from Mars, Women Are from Venus: The Classic Guide to Understanding the Opposite Sex*, New York: Harper Publications, 2004.

4. Deborah Tannen, *Talking from 9 to 5: Women and Men in the Workplace—Language, Sex and Power*, New York: Avon Books, 1994.

Chapter 6

1. Randolph T. Barker, C. Glenn Pearce, and Iris W. Johnson, "An Investigation of Perceived Managerial Listening Ability," *Journal of Business and Technical Communication,* vol. 6, no. 4, October 1992, pp. 438–457.
2. Ralph G. Nichols, "Listening Is a 10-Part Skill," *Nation's Business,* 45, 1957, p. 56.
3. Back from Vacation? How to Get Over Jet Lag, National Sleep Foundation, www.sleepfoundation.org/alert/back-vacation-how-get-over-jet-lag, retrieved September 18, 2010.
4. Excessive Daytime Sleepiness, Health and Safety, National Sleep Foundation, www.sleepfoundation.org/alert/excessive-sleepiness-public-health-and-safety-concern, retrieved September 18, 2010.

Chapter 7

1. H. M. Robert, *Robert's Rules of Order Newly Revised,* Cambridge, MA: Perseus, 2000.
2. Edward T. Hall, *The Silent Language,* New York: Doubleday, 1959, 1981, p. 7.

Chapter 8

1. I. Houtman and K. Jettinghoff, "Raising Awareness of Stress at Work in Developing Countries," Protecting Workers' Health Series, no. 6, Geneva, Switzerland: World Health Organization, 2007, whqlibdoc.who.int/publications/2007/924159165X_eng.pdf, retrieved October 23, 2010.

Chapter 9

1. Vincent P. Magnini, John B. Ford, Edward P. Markowski, and Earl D. Honeycutt, Jr., "The Service Recovery Paradox: Justifiable Theory or Smoldering Myth?" *Journal of Services Marketing,* vol. 21, no. 3, 2007, pp. 213–225.

Chapter 10

1. Internet World Stats, www.internetworldstats.com/stats.htm, retrieved November 27, 2010.
2. Number of Cell Phones Worldwide Hits 4.6B. February 15, 2010, CBSNews Business, www.cbsnews.com/stories/2010/02/15/business/main6209772.shtml, retrieved November 27, 2010.
3. Annualized Wireless Industry Survey Results–December 1985 to June 2009, Cellular Telecommunications Industry Association, files.ctia.org/pdf/CTIA_Survey_Midyear_2009_Graphics.pdf, retrieved September 18, 2010.
4. Joseph Galante and Kelly Riddell, U.S. Online Sales on "Cyber Monday" Increase 19.4%, IBM's Coremetrics Says, www.bloomberg.com/news/2010-11-30/cyber-monday-2010-online-sales-increased-19-according-to-coremetrics.html, retrieved November 30, 2010.
5. Jim Jansen, Attention Shoppers: Online Product Research, Pew Research Center Publications, September 29, 2010, pewresearch.org/pubs/1747/e-shopping-researched-product-service-online, retrieved December 1, 2010.
6. A. Sage, How Satisfied Are US Consumers with Online Chat? Forrester Research, August 3, 2010, www.forrester.com/rb/Research/how_satisfied_are_us_consumers_with_online/q/id/55955/t/2?src=Alert%20RSS_CustomFeed&cm_mmc=Research_Alert-_-email-_-08_04_10-_-55955, retrieved December 10, 2010.

Index

About the Author

Bob Lucas is a founding managing partner for *Global Performance Strategies*, LLC, an organization specializing in workplace performance-based training and consulting services. He has over three decades of experience in human resources development, management, and customer service in a variety of organizational environments. He is also the 2011 president of the Central Florida chapter of the American Society for Training and Development (ASTD), a position he held in 1995. Bob has lived, traveled, and worked in 19 countries, and his experience gives him a real-world perspective on the application of the theory he has studied and used.

In addition to having the top-selling customer service textbook in the United States, Bob has written and contributed to 28 other books. For the past 17 years, through the Webster University Master of Arts program in Orlando, Florida, he has shared his knowledge with workplace professionals from organizations such as Walt Disney World, SeaWorld, Universal Studios, Martin Marietta, and Wachovia Bank. In addition, he has provided consulting and training services to numerous major organizations on a variety of workplace learning topics, such as customer service, presentation skills, creative training and management program development, train-the-trainer, interpersonal communication, adult learning, diversity, team building, and employee and organizational development. Bob regularly gives regular presentations to various local and national groups and organizations, such as the ASTD and the International Alliance for Learning.

Additionally, since 1992, Bob has been a contributing author for the *Annual: Developing Human Resources* series by Pfeiffer & Company and for several compilation works by other publishers.

Bob has earned a BA in law enforcement from the University of Maryland; an MA with a focus in human resources development from George Mason University in Fairfax, Virginia; and a second MA in management and leadership from Webster University in Orlando, Florida.

Contact Information:
Bob Lucas
407-695-5535
blucas@globalperformancestrategies.com
http://www.globalperformancestrategies.com